Children's Literature

Volume 10

Volume 10

Annual of
The Modern Language Association
Division on Children's Literature
and The Children's Literature
Association

New Haven and London
Yale University Press
1982

Children's Literature

Editor-in-Chief: Francelia Butler
Co-Editors: Samuel Pickering, Jr., Compton Rees, and Glenn Edward Sadler
Book Review Editor: David L. Greene
Editorial Correspondents: Federica Colavita (Argentina), Barbara Rosen (England), Milla Riggio (Italy)
Advisory Board: Robert Coles, M.D., Elizabeth A. Francis, Martin Gardner, Alison Lurie, William T. Moynihan, Albert J. Solnit, M.D.
Editorial Assistants: Lisa Degnan, Lisa Liegeot
Board of Directors: The Children's Literature Foundation: Francelia Butler, Rachel Fordyce, John C. Wandell

Editorial Correspondence should be addressed to:
The Editors, *Children's Literature*
Department of English
University of Connecticut
Storrs, Connecticut 06268

Manuscripts submitted should conform to the *MLA Handbook.* An original on non-erasable bond and a copy are requested. Manuscripts must be accompanied by a self-addressed envelope and return postage.

Volumes 1–7 of Children's Literature can be obtained directly from the Children's Literature Foundation, Box 370, Windham Center, Connecticut 06280.

Set in Baskerville type by United Printing Services, Inc., New Haven, Conn.
Printed in the United States of America by Vail-Ballou Press, Binghamton, N.Y.

10   9   8   7   6   5   4   3   2   1

Contents

Robin Hood and the Invention of Children's Literature

Bennett A. Brockman

Literary historians usually regard English children's literature as an invention of the 1740s, when Thomas Boreman and John Newbery, independently moved by John Locke's *Some Thoughts Concerning Education* (1693) as well as by the prospect of tidy profits, published the *Gigantick Histories* and *A Little Pretty Pocket-Book*. Given the definition of children's literature as imaginative literature marketed to children and designed for their amusement as well as their edification, scholars have not seriously questioned that date of origin, even though they have shown that chapbook fiction probably designed for children appeared in the later seventeenth century.[1] We have left unexplored, however, a conceptual problem which may be of greater interest than determining the date of the first book of children's fiction: how did it become possible for entrepreneurs like Boreman and Newbery to perceive a distinct market for children's books? What led to the emergence of the genre that we today call children's literature? The extant evidence does not permit absolute answers to these questions. If my speculations are valid, however, the consequences of the way in which the genre was invented are serious and have been largely detrimental to the content as well as to the study of children's literature.

Befitting a study of children's literature, this essay has its heroes and its villains. The heroes are the authors of medieval romance, whose works maintained popularity well into the sixteenth century. The villains are a well-intended and familiar lot: those implacable enemies of medieval romance, the sixteenth-century humanists—whom C. S. Lewis charitably berated in the *Oxford History of English Literature*—and their puritanical contemporaries. I propose to lay one more sin to their charge by arguing that their hostility to things medieval, particularly romance, created a conception of children's literature which implied that it was second-class (or third-class) literature, and that their mistrust of fiction, especially romance fiction, separated children's literature from other literature and implied that the former was intrinsically inferior. With the aid of the religious reformers, their unsuspecting allies, the new humanists became the unwitting parents of children's literature; an illegitimate child, it still bears, at least in academia, the stigma of its conception.[2]

Robin Hood enters this story as neither hero nor villain but merely as an illustration taken from the larger world of popular literature that the Renaissance inherited from the Middle Ages and bequeathed in chapbook form to the seventeenth and eighteenth centuries. Most of us share, I suspect, a more or less vivid impression of Robin Hood carried over from our childhood reading. We can scarcely think of him as anything other than a hero of children's books. The process by which he in fact became the property of children provides evidence for my thesis.

The key to the evolution of this new genre lies in the pervasive Renaissance mistrust of fiction and in the new humanists' devoted hostility toward romance inherited from the Middle Ages.[3] To be sure the Middle Ages no less than the Renaissance had difficulties with the idea of fiction: if it is by definition untrue, then it must be a form of lying, and hence morally suspect. But medieval theorists seem to have lived more comfortably with their misgivings than did their successors. As Professor Nelson summarized, the Middle Ages characteristically sought "an accommodation of two conflicting attitudes: on the one hand, the insistence of the Judeo-Christian tradition on veritable report, testified to as by witnesses in a courtroom; on the other, a sense that in tales of the past truth mattered little in comparison with edification or even entertainment" (p. 27). The outrage which Renaissance purists reserved for fiction was not typical of the Middle Ages. Far more characteristic was the intent to use fiction to convey truth, to entice readers' interest, and to veil high mysteries from those unwilling to make an effort to comprehend.[4]

Medieval theorists likewise made distinctions in *kinds* of fiction —distinctions their humanistic successors were to echo with more practical effect. A third-century account, for example, reports that

Menippus preferred the verisimilitude of poetic fiction, which invents plausible human action, to the outright impossibility of Aesop's fables, in which beasts debate one another. With prophetic insight, Menippus declared that beast fables "are nonsense only fit to be swallowed by old women and children."[5] Likewise Macrobius, while tolerating Platonic allegory, assigned fiction which only amuses —Menander, Petronius, Apuleius—to the nursery, as did Boccaccio at the end of the era.[6]

But the Middle Ages, especially the later Middle Ages, did not enforce the separation which Menippus, Macrobius, and Boccaccio envisioned. Indeed, the medieval audience seems more likely to have been divided along class lines than age lines; children seem not to have been purposefully excluded from what we would regard as adult literary occasions. A manuscript illumination of Ovid reading the *Metamorphoses* includes in the outdoor audience, discreetly to one side, a pair of children.[7] And the audience of the Middle English romance, which most closely concerns us here, typically heard the reading or recitation in the hall of a great house, in a domestic setting where both adults and children would have been present, as Marc Girouard and Lawrence Stone have recently reminded us. Medieval and early modern children, recent research shows, both read and listened to the same romances as did their elders.[8] At the end of the Middle Ages, when a market for printed books developed, English publishers aimed similarly at a broad spectrum of readers, including youthful ones, as Pearsall, Bennett, and Wright demonstrate in passing.[9]

Ironically, the very popularity of romance in the fifteenth century, at least in England, is associated with a redefinition of the purposes of the genre—a redefinition that finally became the weapon the humanists turned most effectively against romance. By the latter part of the fifteenth century, the fashion turned toward prose romance in the Burgundian mode: romance was designed to chronicle historical events efficiently and comprehensively.[10] But the proclaimed historicity associated with the revitalized romance merely provided a more compelling rationale for the humanists of the next century to demolish the historical pretense and to categorize the romances as worse than lies. The fabulous romances, with their wildly improbable heroes and villains, were manifestly contemptible to the humanists; and even when the romancers tried to recount testamentary truth, in their stories of Alexander, Caesar, Charlemagne, or Richard I, they appeared equally dangerous to the humanists because they celebrated the wrong heroic attributes. In the famous phrase of Roger Ascham's *Scholemaster* (1570), they encouraged "bold bawdry and open manslaughter" and thus were particularly dangerous as models for the development of the juvenile character. Romance was not only fiction; it was dangerous fiction.[11]

The scope of the antipathy of Renaissance humanists, educators, Puritans, academicians, philosophers, and belletrists toward medieval romance has been thoroughly documented.[12] We need now to see how their more or less thoughtful execrations caused the evolution of a new literary genre and how Robin Hood illustrates that evolution.

Renaissance attacks on romance shows that children (broadly defined) continued reading romances. That children might thus remain in their childishness indeed gave Renaissance polemicists much concern. The strident attack of the religious reformer Tyndale in 1528 is notable because it explicitly denounces the Robin Hood stories as indicative of "a thousand histories and fables of love and wantonness, and of ribaldry, as filthy as heart can think," which serve only "to corrupt the minds of youth withal."[13] Tyndale's alarum echoes throughout the age. Erasmus, Juan Luis Vives, Hugh Rhodes, Francis Meres, John Florio, and Robert Ashley variously testify to children's attachment to romance and to the corruption its foolishness engenders in them.[14] Well into the eighteenth century, pious educators like Isaac Watts and his imitator Thomas Foxton intended to supplant vicious chapbook romances with virtuous "Divine Songs" and "Moral Songs" in children's affections.[15] Parents and educators were convinced that children found the romances appealing indeed.

Clearly there was a very real association of romance with children and childishness. Those associations in fact gave literary theorists pause when it came to justifying fiction generally. If the most popular medieval English romance, *Guy of Warwick*, was "childish follye" to the typical critic,[16] fiction in any of its guises was for the severest critics reserved for those whose circumstances—or character deficiencies—deterred them from productive labor: the sick, the elderly, frivolous wastrels, children, and noble ladies.[17] Even Sidney felt compelled, in justifying poetic fiction, to dignify its puerile reputation by turning the criticism to a moral advantage: men, who the moralists insist should confront the naked truth, do better to approach truth through the enticing veil of fiction, since most men are "childish in the best things, till they be cradled in their graves."[18]

Further, the Renaissance critics found equally disturbing the association of the romance audience (especially after the 1560s) with the lower classes and the uneducated. The Elizabethan dramatists, for example, considered the taste for the old romances hopelessly plebian and uncultivated, characteristic of "old women, servants, country squires, the sons and daughters of citizens, and children."[19]

By the 1580s romance was inextricably associated with children and other groups lacking social and intellectual status and was laden with critical scorn. To refined, academic critics, the old romances were contemptibly childish, and they believed that children who continued to read them did so at the peril of their minds and souls. Serious writers and readers who wanted to persevere with romance had accordingly to come to terms with its disrepute; they seem to have done so essentially by reacting to "the vocabulary of denunciation" with which the critics had attacked romance and other poetic diversions.[20] As Sidney and his successors made clear, poetry—and romance—could be vigorously defended against charges of falsehood, immorality, and triviality. Indeed, the new romance of the 1580s exemplified the utility, truthfulness, substantiality, and wholesomeness of poetic fiction; and, of greater interest at the moment, romance during the last two decades of the century became courtly and academic, demonstrating thereby its distance from the plebeian audience of the older popular romance. As we shall see, the Robin Hood stories clearly evince this progressive alteration of an old form; and it was in this way, and at this moment, prompted by artistic reaction to humanistic and moral criticism, that children's literature silently emerged, as the sinister twin to the fair new romance: for as the new romance flourished, the old romance was left to its audience of country people, apprentices, and bourgeois children—ultimately to the children alone.

The new romance vogue, which attracted Lyly, Lodge, Greene, Spenser, Sidney, and finally the dramatists, was characterized by tales like *Amadis of Gaul*, imported from the continent. Their style most concerns us: they were tales in "high style very close to the elaborate diction Sidney favored," marked at the extreme, during the eighties and mid-nineties, by the fashionable Euphuism of Lyly.[21] Since style is the barrier denying the relatively uneducated access to sophisticated literature, it is instructive to remind ourselves how explicitly the Elizabethan and Jacobean writers were aware of the equation between style and social and intellectual standing; as Wright (pp. 91ff.) and Smith (I, xxxii–xxxiii) have shown, writers went to astonishing lengths to dignify their style and thus avoid appearing common. Chapman, for example, never tires of assuring us that he, like Jonson, refuses to write for "ev'rie vulgar, and adult'rate braine."[22] He speaks thus for a substantial company of Renaissance writers who seem to have taken literally Sidney's suggestion in the *Apology* "that there are many mysteries contained in poetry, which of purpose were written darkly, lest by profane wits it should be abused" (p. 88). Sidney of course is echoing familiar medieval doctrine, that poetry properly veils high truths from the unworthy. But he appears to speak far more accurately of the practice of his fellow Renaissance intellectuals, who indeed echo the *Apology* countless times, than of his medieval forebears' practice.

Complexity of style, therefore, even when taken to outrageous extremes, served to distinguish the new fiction of the eighties and nineties, particularly the romances following *Euphues*, as poetic fiction designed for an audience of social standing and intellectual attainment. The audience exclusivity thus attained did away in a stroke with the objections of childishness and immorality attached to the old stories. Youth can not be led astray by romances if youth is unable to read them; nor can romances be labeled as childish amusement without a child audience.[23] To be sure, market realities lowered standards,[24] particularly during the nineties when the popular journalistic mode of Greene's *Cony-Catching* pamphlets caught on. There may have been writers who, in Ben Jonson's words, "would taste nothing that was popular" (Prologue to *The Silent Woman,* 1609). They, however, were independently wealthy or, as time went on, they starved, like Chapman, in splendidly confident isolation.

The antipodes, nevertheless, had been established. At one extreme was the new romance, typified by *Arcadia* and *Euphues*; the values it displayed were the academic, aristocratic values that Ascham found in *Euphues,* which he called one of the seven true notes for child-rearing in *The Scholemaster* (1570). In sharp contrast, the other extreme, as Crane showed, was associated with peasants, apprentices, old people, and homely children. Its defining works were the old romances inherited from the Middle Ages and reprinted in progressively pedestrian redactions.[25] The Robin Hood stories illuminate this evolution by protracting it and by trying to make the yeoman hero into an Arcadian gentleman; they demonstrate very efficiently how the medieval literature which the humanists attacked finally evolved into a literature worthy of their contempt. Clearly this decadent medieval literature, closely associated throughout the Renaissance with children and with childishness, was in academic minds—and quite possibly in publishers' minds—the paradigm for literature written expressly for children.

Robin Hood is evidently a latecomer to the pantheon of medieval heroes, and his origins at least in literature (whatever may have been his historical roots) seem to have been humble. We first hear of Robin Hood when Sloth, in the B-version of *Piers Plowman* (c. 1378), confesses that he knows rimes of Robin Hood and Randolf Earl of Chester even though he can't perfectly say his paternoster (B. V. 401f). Robin Hood evolves during the course of the next three centuries from yeoman to earl and back again to yeoman. And even though the late Middle Ages seemed to want him to be more than a yeoman bandit, it is significant that his elevation to the peerage did not occur until the second half of the sixteenth century, when the dying vogue of medieval romance was being replaced by the new romance of courtly refinement and academic style. It is clear that Renaissance writers interested in Robin Hood hoped by magnifying his aristocratic connections to make him a proper subject for refined audiences, or at least audiences who thought of themselves as refined. They were anxious to remove him from his degraded associations with the provincial, the powerless, the uncultured, and the juvenile—the audience of the old romance.

Robin Hood was current by the last quarter of the fourteenth century. During the next century he figured in hybrid poetic accounts—*The Gest of Robin Hood* (early fifteenth century; printed c. 1500), "Robin Hood and the Monk" (c. 1450), and "Robin Hood and the Potter" (c. 1500)—which share attributes of romance, ballad, and the fashionable chronicle.[26] At approximately the same time, attempts were made to incorporate the newcomer into comprehensive chronicles. As J. B. Bessinger, Jr., has shown, these chronicles not only recorded (or invented) and transmitted the substance of the Robin Hood legend, but they also shaped that material away from a fairly clear original conception of Robin Hood as a rather brutal sort of yeoman outlaw—the kind we would expect from our knowledge of actual medieval brigands—into a prince of thieves and a courtly gentleman.[27]

The first of these chronicles, Andrew of Wyntoun's in 1420, does little more than establish Robin Hood's historicity. The second, Walter Bower's continuation of Fordun's *Scotichronicon* (c. 1445), establishes Robin Hood as a follower of the Baron Simon de Montfort in 1266; but in the same breath Bower speaks disdainfully of popular dramatic celebrations of the greenwood hero.[28] How popular such celebrations were may well be indicated by the earliest surviving dramatic Robin Hood fragment, apparently performed for the Paston family in the 1470s. The fragment shows emphatic interest in open manslaughter; it is, alas, too abridged to judge the interest in bold bawdry, but it likely owes something to the May games of the folk.[29] Thus it appears that before 1500 Robin Hood was the hero of romance narratives implying his historicity as a yeoman bandit; that he was the focus of broadly popular dramatic entertainment; and that, in the serious chronicles, he was at least the companion of gentlemen.

Nobler things were in store for Robin, however. John Major (c. 1500) makes Robin Hood "the kindest of all robbers and their prince," and John Leland (c. 1540) refers to him as "that noble outlaw." Edward Hall's famous *Union of Lancastre and York* (1548) informs us that a Robin Hood figure participated in the May games of Henry VIII in 1510 and 1515.[30] By mid-century our hero was moving in lofty social circles.

Still, no yeoman's quest for gentility is without setbacks. Around 1560, when William Copland published his edition of the *Gest of Robin Hood,* he attached to it two Robin Hood plays which are distinctly popular (see Dobson and Taylor, pp. 208–19). And it is the *Gest of Robin Hood,* which presents the medieval yeoman hero and not the Tudor courtier, that supplies the substance of many of the seventeenth-century ballads in which Robin Hood reasserts himself as the yeoman hero. As late as 1592–93, Robin appears along with a lusty Marian in a distinctly popular *George a Greene, Pinner of Wakefield,* attributed to Robert Greene.

Meanwhile, however, Robin's waxing gentility made him a perfect subject for the vogue of the new, refined romance. Richard Grafton's *Chronicle at Large* (1569) considers Robin Hood a disinherited earl. That note is taken up by William Warner's *Albion's England* (1586) and is reflected in Shakespeare's allusions to Robin Hood in *Two Gentlemen of Verona* (1593?) and *As You Like It* (1599).[31] *Two Gentlemen* sets the impeccably genteel tone. The banished Valentine, gentleman, takes up with a band of refined outlaws who, swearing "by the bare scalp of Robin Hood's fat friar," proclaim him their "king," "general," "captain," and "commander." These outlaws abhor "vile base practices" and assure Valentine that "some of us are gentlemen" (IV.i). *As You Like It* presents an even more genteel world in the Forest of Arden, the golden world where the banished Duke plays Robin Hood; "many young gentlemen flock to him every day," we are told (I.i). Robin Hood's baser parts are left completely behind when in 1597–98 Anthony Munday produced a two-part tragedy on Robin Hood, whom he styled, with a partisan allusion to a stalwart in the Puritan cause, Robert, Earl of Huntingdon (or Huntington).[32] We know from Henslowe's diary that these plays were revised for court performance and evidently were produced there.[33] Maid Marian here becomes Matilda, daughter of Lord Fitzwater. Both parts of the tragedy are marked by suitably high-flown rhetoric and relentlessly moral sentiment.[34] Triumphantly acknowledged a member of courtly society, Robin is confirmed in his standing by the "pleasant comedy" *Looke About You* (1600), in which he is not simply Earl of Huntingdon but a "nice choyse faire Earle" (M. A. Nelson, p. 161), and by his appearance in the courtly, Arcadian *Famouus Hystory of George a Greene* (c. 1600), which is based on Munday's plays (M. A. Nelson, pp. 98–106).

The apex of his courtly ascendancy comes in 1641, in Ben Jonson's posthumously published, unfinished *The Sad Shepherd, or A Tale of Robin-Hood*. Here the mode is pastoral, Theocritan; the style elegant, allusive, lyrical. Robin Hood is not titled here, but he is presumably modeled on the Earl of Rutland, near whose seat at Belvoir Castle the action takes place, and the play was probably intended for court performance.[35]

Perhaps one reason Jonson did not finish *The Sad Shepherd* was that he recognized the inherent contradiction in a genteel Robin Hood. That contradiction is indeed much more evident in some of the works inspired by Munday's *Downfall* and *The Death of Robert, Earl of Huntingdon*. While *Looke About You* makes Robin an earl, it also makes him cavort in female disguise among a bevy of lords and ladies, an entertainment which seems to owe more to the ancient May revels than to decorous masques (see M. A. Nelson, p. 167). In the *Famouus Hystory* Robin plays earl while George, the Pinner of Wakefield, assumes the courteous yeoman's role originally belonging to Robin Hood. Even when Robin appears as the Earl of Huntingdon, he seems but in disguise: most preposterously so in Anthony Munday's second Robin Hood assay, *Metropolis Coronata*, staged for the installation of Sir John Jolles, a draper and stapler, as Lord Mayor of London in 1615 (see M. A. Nelson, pp. 169–71). This time, as befits the setting in the court of Richard I, our hero's name is normanized; the yeoman has become an earl, and the earl is called Robert de la Hude. Much more sensibly, Michael Drayton, in a sixty-line passage in Song XXVI of *Poly-Olbion* (1622), looks back to an earlier Robin Hood tradition. Drayton's Robin is innately courteous, though not a peer; Mistris Marian, "soveraigne of the Woods, chiefe Lady of the Game" (line 354), evidently claims no loftier style. But Drayton's Robin Hood is not characteristic of the era.

Indeed, looking further into the surviving Robin Hood material of the seventeenth century makes it clear that the contradiction between the courtly and the popular traditions was resolved emphatically in favor of the latter. Munday had once and for all established in the popular mind Robin's identity as Lord Robert, Earl of Huntingdon; but his courtliness extended no further than his title in the broadside ballads of the seventeenth century. The *True Tale of Robin Hood*, which the celebrated ballad-monger Martin Parker published in 1632, is unrewarding enough; yet it adheres to higher standards of poetic technique and plot elaboration than do the typical anonymously produced ballads finally collected in the *Robin Hood's Garlands*. Parker's second stanza may stand for the whole piece:

> It is a tale of Robin Hood,
> That I to you will tell,
> Which being rightly understood,
> I know will please you well.
> [Dobson & Taylor, p. 188]

The earliest extant *Garland* (1663) contained seventeen ballads which multiplied during the course of the next century to twenty-seven, some of which bear only the most tenuous connections to earlier tradition.[36] The seventeenth-century ballads preserved in the *Garlands* typically appeal to the crassest tastes: "the single

combat type . . . is carried to absurd and odious lengths . . . as
Robin Hood is bested by tinkers, pedlars, rangers, keepers, and
shepherds. 'Robin Hood and the Beggar' (Child 134) . . . shows
its debasement most clearly when Robin Hood is made to order the murder of the beggar who thrashed him" (M. A. Nelson,
p. 22). The *Garlands* were "of outstanding importance in perpetuat-
ing the ballads current in the 1660s and the 1670s into the next
century and beyond," as Dobson and Taylor rightly emphasize
(p. 52); but that tradition unfortunately was distinctly inferior
to that of the late medieval narrative poems like the *Gest, Robin
Hood and the Potter,* and *Robin Hood and Guy of Gisborne,* which
share properties of romance, ballad, and chronicle.

Robin Hood's sojourn among the aristocracy casts into sharper
relief the disparities between popular and sophisticated versions
of his adventures. Regrettably, only the most popular tradition
remained when the polite strand failed under the contradictions
inherent in it, and the popular strand progressively became, along
with the other chapbook versions of medieval tales, a matter typically for children's attention. Had there been a more proximate
tradition of Robin Hood stories in a middle style resembling the
mode of medieval romance narration, Drayton's brief excursus
might have become an influential paradigm rather than a lonely
voice in the desert of seventeenth-century Robin Hood ballads.
Unfortunately, the Robin Hood ballads of the seventeenth century and after are pretty much of a kind with the contemporary
chapbook versions of the medieval romances: they are crude in
feeling, style, and thought; action and description incline to absurdity and are either compressed to the minimum required for
intelligibility or padded to the limit of the reader's forebearance.
In the late, seemingly endless "Pedigree, Marriage, and Education
of Robin Hood," for example, Robin is declared the protégé of one
Squire Gamewell, the grand-nephew of Sir Guy of Warwick, and
the suitor to Clorinda, Queen of Titbury feast.

So it is that throughout the eighteenth century, at the time children's literature was being conceived as a marketable commodity,
the chapbook ballads, Robin Hood's characteristically among them,

were finally identified with the juvenile readers who had always been prominent in the chapbook audience. At the beginning of the century Steele reports in *The Tatler* (1709) that his young godson was an authority on chapbook heroes like Guy of Warwick and Bevis of Hampton. James Boswell confessed that "I have always retained a kind of affection for them, as they recall my early days." Later in the century, Cowper regards the chapbooks as nursery tales (*Conversation*, 1782), and the romantic poets typically recall them fondly, in Lamb's phrase, as "the old classics of the nursery" that were the companions of their youth. Samuel Bamford (b. 1788) acknowledged lavishing on them every farthing he could lay hands on as a child (Neuburg, p. 1). By then it was no wonder that children sought out the chapbooks, for the alternative was the moral-laden books Lamb called "Mrs. Barbauld's stuff"; indeed the chapbook publishers were meeting the new competition by advertising their wares as both entertaining and instructive. The attitude of the academic world toward the chapbooks, apart from the antiquarian interest encouraged by Bishop Percy's *Reliques of Ancient English Poetry* (1765), is perhaps indicated by a contributor to the January 1792 *Critical Review*: the Robin Hood ballads were to him simply "the refuse of a stall," where presumably the stableboy read them (see Dobson and Taylor, p. 54). Until their discovery by the antiquarians, the popular ballads were to the neoclassical "man of taste . . . verses . . . worthy of the attention of children only."[37]

What has happened, our evidence suggests, is that at the time Boreman, Newbery, and their successors were producing books that can accurately be called children's literature, a vague but powerful preexisting academic conception of children's literature as the chapbook derivatives of medieval romance at once determined the nature of, and colored henceforth the academic reaction toward, the new literature expressly for children. Given the academicians' hostility toward any fiction, and given the increasingly pedestrian chapbook romances with which juvenile readers had become progressively identified, it was inevitable that Locke's great stimulus to education should produce a stridently didactic body

of children's fiction implicitly aiming to counter the frivolous and
vicious qualities perceived in the chapbooks. Abandoning the un-
relieved austere didacticism of Bunyan and the religious writers
for children, Newbery understandably felt compelled to dedicate
Little Goody Two-Shoes "to all Young Gentlemen and Ladies who
are good or intend to be good." But it was perhaps also inevitable
that the academicians associated the new body of children's fiction
with childishness, just as their humanist forebears had done, and
continued to dignify their own fiction through stylistic and philo-
sophic rigor. Newbery's contemporary Richardson published *Pamela* "in order to cultivate the Principles of Virtue and Religion
in the Minds of the Youth of Both Sexes," and Newbery in fact
published a shilling abridgement of it in 1769; but by its language, plot, and sheer volume, *Pamela* remains respectable within
the academic tradition of the humanists, whereas *Little Goody
Two-Shoes* emphatically does not. That regrettable, and in recent
decades increasingly unjustified, association of children's literature
with childishness likewise remains. It is perhaps the inescapable
consequence of the separation of the two categories, fiction and
children's fiction, in the post-Renaissance world.

Notes

A version of this essay was presented at the Fourteenth International Conference
on Medieval Studies at Kalamazoo, Michigan, in 1979.
   1. See Victor E. Neuburg, *The Penny Histories: A Study of Chapbooks for
Young Readers Over Two Centuries* (Oxford: Oxford University Press, 1968),
p. 28ff., and F. J. Harvey, Darton, *Children's Books in England*, 2nd edition (Cambridge: Cambridge University Press, 1958), pp. 33–43, 70–78.
   2. In "Children's Literature: Theory and Practice, "*ELH*, 45 (1978), 542–
61, Felicity A. Hughes shows how Henry James's attempt to dissociate the novel
from child and female readers had similar motives and a similar adverse impact
on the development of, and attitudes toward, literature for children in the twentieth century. James's assault is conducted from grounds much the same as
those of the Renaissance theorists and reinforces the old prejudices.
   3. William Nelson, *Fact or Fiction: The Dilemma of the Renaissance Storyteller* (Cambridge: Harvard University Press, 1973), and Russell A. Fraser, *The
War Against Poetry* (Princeton: Princeton University Press, 1970) closely examine Renaissance attitudes toward fiction, and what follows is very much indebted to their findings. Arthur Kinney follows a complementary line of inquiry
in "Rhetoric as Poetic: Humanist Fiction in the Renaissance," *ELH*, 43 (1976),

413–33. He shows that the humanists were vividly aware of the uses and abuses of fiction and ultimately of the treachery and potential of language itself.

4. Boccaccio's discussion of fiction and poetry in *Genealogia Deorum Gentilium* summarizes these medieval attitudes. See *Boccaccio on Poetry*, trans. Charles G. Osgood (Princeton: Princeton University Press, 1930), Books 14 and 15. See also W. Nelson, pp. 23–37.

5. W. Nelson, p. 15, quoting Philostratus' *Life of Apollonius of Tyana*, v. 14, trans. F. C. Conybeare (London: Heinemann, 1912), I, 493–95.

6. W. Nelson, p. 13, citing Macrobius, *In Somnium Scipionis*, II, 3–17, in *Commentary on the Dream of Scipio*, trans. W. H. Stahl, Records of Civilization, Sources and Studies, No. 48 (New York: Columbia University Press, 1952); Boccaccio, Book 14. Cf. Richard de Bury, in D. W. Robertson, Jr., ed., *The Literature of Medieval England* (New York: McGraw-Hill, 1970), p. 284.

7. Holkham Hall Library, MS. 324, fol. 159v; Flemish, c. 1497. I am indebted to Prof. Elizabeth Salter for calling this illumination to my attention.

8. Marc Girouard, *Life in the English Country House: A Social and Architectural History* (New Haven: Yale University Press, 1978), pp. 10–11, 14–80; Lawrence Stone, *The Family, Sex and Marriage in England, 1500–1800* (New York: Harper & Row, 1977), pp. 6–8, 253. See further, on the romance as entertainment for the household, Derek Pearsall, "The English Romance in the Fifteenth Century," *Essays and Studies*, n.s. 29 (1976), 64; A. C. Baugh, "The Middle English Romance: Some Questions of Creation, Presentation, and Preservation," *Speculum*, 42 (1967), 1–31; Dieter Mehl, *The Middle English Romances of the Thirteenth and Fourteenth Centuries* (New York: Barnes and Noble, 1969), pp. 1–13; Derek Pearsall, "The Development of Middle English Romance," *Medieval Studies*, 27 (1965), 91–116; Bennett A. Brockman, "Children and Literature in Late Medieval England," *Children's Literature*, 4 (1975), 58–63; and Karl Brunner, "Middle English Metrical Romances and their Audience," *Studies in Medieval Literature in Honor of Prof. A. C. Baugh*, ed. MacEdward Leach (Philadelphia: University of Pennsylvania Press, 1962), pp. 219–27 Cf. Marc Soriano, "From Tales of Warning to Formulettes: The Oral Tradition in Children's Literature," *YFS*, 43 (1969), 24–25.

9. Pearsall, "Fifteenth Century," pp. 64, 81, and 83 n. 1; H. S. Bennett, *English Books and Readers, 1475–1557*, 2nd ed. (Cambridge: Cambridge University Press, 1969), ch. 2, and Louis B. Wright, *Middle Class Culture in Elizabethan England* (1935; rpt. Ithaca: Cornell University Press for Folger Shakespeare Library, 1958), ch. 3 and 4. The Middle Ages and early modern era vaguely placed childhood along the continuum of seven to twenty-one years of age; see Stone, pp. 405–79, and Philippe Ariès, *Centuries of Childhood*, trans. anon. (Harmondsworth, Middlesex, England: Penguin, 1969), pp. 90–95.

10. Pearsall, "Fifteenth Century," p. 73.

11. See Robert P. Adams, "Bold Bawdry and Open Manslaughter: The English New Humanist Attack Upon Medieval Romances," *HLQ*, 23 (1959–60), 33–48.

12. See especially Adams, ibid.; R. S. Crane, "The Vogue of *Guy of Warwick* from the Close of the Middle Ages to the Romantic Revival," *PMLA*, 30 (1915), 125–94, and Crane's *Vogue of Medieval Chivalric Romance During the English Renaissance. An Abstract of a Thesis* (Menasha, WI: Banta, 1915), pp. 1–29;

C. S. Lewis, *English Literature in the Sixteenth Century* (Oxford: Oxford University Press, 1954), pp. 28–30; and Velma Bourgeois Richmond, *The Popularity of the Middle English Romance* (Bowling Green, OH: Bowling Green University, Popular Press, 1975), pp. 1–24.

13.   Cited from *The Obedience of a Christian Man* (1528) by Crane, *Chivalric Romance*, p. 12.

14.   Erasmus, *Christian Prince*, trans. Lester K. Born, (New York: Columbia University Press, 1936), p. 200; Vives, *Christen Woman*, trans. Richard Hyrde (London, 1541), sigs. Div–Diir; Rhodes, *Book of Nurture*, ed. F. J. Furnivall (London: Roxburghe Club, 1867), p. 6; Meres, *Palladis Tamia*, in *Elizabethan Critical Essays*, ed. G. Gregory Smith (London: Oxford University Press, 1904), II, 308; *Essays*, Everyman edn. (London: Dent, 1910), I, 187; Ashley as quoted by Crane, "*Guy*," p. 131.

15.   See the introduction and facsimile edition of Watts's *Divine Songs* (1715) and Foxton's *Moral Songs* (1728), ed. B. A. Brockman (New York: Garland Press, 1978), esp. Watts's commendation prefacing Foxton (p. [xi]) and his own preface to the *Songs*. See also Peter Burke, *Popular Culture in Early Modern Europe* (New York: New York University Press, 1978), pp. 223–43.

16.   The phrase is Edward Dering's, in *The Bryfe and Necessary Catechisme* (London, 1572), as quoted by Crane, Vogue, p. 13.

17.   See W. Nelson, p. 56, and Fraser, ch. 3 and 4 on the age's scorn for the inutility of "idle tales."

18.   *An Apology for Poetry*, ed. Forrest G. Robinson (New York: Bobbs-Merrill, 1970), p. 38.

19.   Crane, "*Guy*," p. 167 n.7.

20.   G. Gregory Smith, I, xxxii. The bewildering complexity of the humanists' own fiction has been emphasized recently by Arthur Kinney (above, n. 3). In a sense, fiction is used by the humanists to demonstrate the paradoxical ambiguities of truth and the slipperiness of language as a vehicle for expressing truth. The admiration of complexity leads of course in the seventeenth century to the elaboration of metaphysical conceits.

21.   John J. O'Connor, *Amadis de Gaule and Its Influence on Elizabethan Literature* (New Brunswick: Rutgers University Press, 1970), p. 200.

22.   Quoted from the *Commentarius* to *Chapman's Homer*, ed. Allardyce Nicoll, Bollingen Ser. 41 (New York: Pantheon, 1956), I, 295, by Millar MacLure, *George Chapman: A Critical Study* (Toronto: University of Toronto Press, 1966), p. 183.

23.   To say that children could not read the new fiction of scholar-poets is not, of course, to say that they could not read at all; Wright and Bennett show conclusively the breadth of literacy and its desirability in Renaissance England (note 9 above); see also Burke, pp. 56–57, 250–59.

24.   See H. S. Bennett, *English Books and Readers, 1558–1603* (Cambridge: Cambridge University Press, 1965), pp. 82–85.

25.   By century's end we may perhaps include the new fiction of Thomas Deloney, Emmanuel Forde, and Anthony Munday in the children's literature category. Their narratives, extremely popular—in two senses of the word—signaled "a strong revulsion in taste from the fantastic aristocracy of Lyly and Greene" (Tucker Brooke, "The Renaissance [1500–1660]," in *A Literary History*

of England, ed. A. C. Baugh, 2nd ed. (London: Routledge, 1967), p. 432).

26. The *Gest* especially shares the three-fold traits of romance, chronicle, and ballad, as its title implies; see Paul Strohm, "*Storie, Spelle, Geste, Romaunce, Tragedie*: Generic Distinctions in the Middle English Troy Narratives," *Speculum*, 46 (1971), 348–59.

27. See "Robin Hood: Folklore and Historiography, 1377–1500," *TSL*, 11 (1966), 61–69; Maurice Keen, *The Outlaws of Medieval Legend*, rev. ed. (Toronto: University of Toronto Press, 1978), passim; and John Bellamy, *Crime and Public Order in England in the Later Middle Ages* (London: Routledge, and Toronto: University of Toronto Press, 1973); passim.

28. Andrew of Wyntoun, *Orygynale Cronykil of Scotland*, ed. F. J. Amours (Edinburgh: Scottish Text Soc. 1907), V, 136ff.; *Scotichronicon*, ed. Thomas Hearne (Oxford, 1722), V, 744; both are cited by Bessinger, "Folklore," p. 65 and nn. 18, 20. I am particularly indebted to Malcolm Anthony Nellson's discussion of the sixteenth-century Robin Hood material in *The Robin Hood Tradition in the English Renaissance*, Salzburgh University Sts. in Eng. Lit., Elizabethan Sts., No. 14 (1973).

29. See M. A. Nelson, ch. 2, and R. B. Dobson and J. Taylor, *Rymes of Robin Hood* (Pittsburgh: University of Pittsburgh Press, 1976), pp. 203–07. I am much indebted to Dobson and Taylor's authoritative discussions of the Robin Hood literature.

30. Major, *Historia* (Paris, 1521), fol. LXV; Leland, *Collectanea*, ed. Thomas Hearne (Oxford, 1715), p. 54; both are cited by Bessinger, "Folklore," p. 65ff. and nn. 21ff. For Hall, see Dobson and Taylor, pp. 40–43 and p. 43 n.1.

31. See M. A. Nelson, pp. 32–83, and his general analysis of Robin Hood's evolution from commoner to earl in ch. 3.

32. See David Bevington, *Tudor Drama and Politics* (Cambridge: Harvard University Press, 1968), p. 295ff.

33. *Henslowe's Diary*, ed. R. A. Foakes and R. T. Rickert (Cambridge: Cambridge University Press, 1961), pp. 86, 88, 101ff.; and see M. A. Nelson, p. 124.

34. *The Death of Robert, Earl of Huntingdon*, prepared by John C. Meagher for Malone Soc. Reprints, 106 (London, 1965). The companion play, *The Downfall of Robert, Earl of Huntingdon*, is volume 102 of the same series.

35. See *Ben Jonson*, ed. C. H. Herford and Percy and Evelyn Simpson (Oxford: Clarendon, 1925–52) II, 217, VII, 1–50; and Dobson and Taylor, p. 231.

36. See the facsimile of the 1787 edn., ed. B. A. Brockman (New York: Garland, 1978).

37. Burke, p. 5, quoting V. Knox, *Essays Moral and Literary*, 2nd ed. London, 1779), essay 47. See further Neuburg's discussion of the displacement of romance into chapbook and of chapbook from adult to child readers, pp. 1–10, especially the 1764 advertisement for wholesale purchase of chapbooks for children; see also Darton, pp. 33–43, 70–79; and Dobson and Taylor, pp. 8ff., 72, 79. Ariès notes the analogous displacement of French popular literature in "Point of Origin, *YFS*, 43 (1969), p. 16, and *Childhood*, pp. 92–95. See further Wright, p. 103; Crane, "*Guy*," pp. 165–67, 193, and Burke, pp. 58–63, 270–77.

"The Mansion of Bliss," or the Place of Play in Victorian Life and Literature

Ira Bruce Nadel

In nineteenth-century historical sources we find numerous discussions of children at work but rarely of children at play.[1] Social histories of the period between the passage of the first Reform Bill (1832) and the death of Queen Victoria (1901) emphasize labor and toil for the young as well as the old. Carlyle vividly described the situation in *Past and Present* (1843):

> Life was never a May-game for men: in all times the lot of the dumb millions born to toil was defaced with manifold sufferings, injustices, heavy burdens, avoidable and unavoidable; not play at all, but hard work that made the sinews sore, and the heart sore.[2]

Ruskin denigrated the usefulness of play and stressed its immoral character some twenty years after Carlyle: "Men will be taught that an existence of play, sustained by the blood of other creatures, is a good existence for gnats and jellyfish; but not for men."[3] Edmund Gosse in *Father and Son* (1907) illustrated the partial accuracy of the common presumption that Victorian children neglected play when he admitted that he "had not the faintest idea how to 'play'" with his first playmate. "I had never learned, had never heard of any 'games,'" he confessed.[4] Nathaniel Hawthorne summarized the frame of mind that seemed to dominate Victorian attitudes toward play when he wrote in his *English Notebooks* that "the English do not appear to have a turn for amusing themselves."[5]

But despite these published opinions, Victorians created a thriving industry out of play activities and popular entertainments. Madame Tussaud's waxworks, for example, which opened in 1835, received extraordinary coverage in the press and drew immense crowds. Panoramas depicting unobstructed views of London from atop St. Paul's, cycloramas recreating the 1755 Lisbon earthquake, and dioramas producing movement and perspective in scenes like the "Burning of York Minster" were remarkably successful attractions for children and adults alike.

On a larger scale, the pleasure gardens, beginning with Vauxhall and Ranelagh and culminating in the notorious Cremorne Gardens in Chelsea, flourished as centers of entertainment and extravaganza, providing elaborate spectacles such as a depiction of the Battle of Waterloo or a view of Venice from the Grand Canal amidst fireworks and acrobatics. The circus, music hall, zoological garden, and cricket match all attracted massive followings. The railway excursion, guided tour, and vacation became institutions.

It is on a smaller scale that concern for the educational and moral aspects of leisure activities becomes apparent, in the numerous children's games and amusements designed to release play from its stigma as a frivolous pastime. Through the use of games as an educational device, one fundamental principle of Victorian life clearly emerged: the importance of competition. Learning to compete became a justification, whereas play as a trifling pastime has been condemned.

Play for the Victorians became the means to teach the very qualities that best characterized Victorian behavior, or at least its ideal: industry, competitiveness, probity, determination, and judgment. Herbert Spencer, the Victorian sociologist and psychologist, explicitly described one major element of the Victorian sense of play in *Principles of Psychology* when he explained the contribution of play to the moral character of the age:

> No matter what the game, the satisfaction is in achieving victory—in getting the better of an antagonist. This love of conquest, so dominant in all creatures because it is the correlative of success in the struggle for existence, gets gratification from a victory at chess in the absence of ruder victories.[6]

Play taught the Victorians, individually and collectively, the importance or rules, the basic code that defines and establishes every

game. In an increasingly complex world, the Victorians felt the
need to create an existence that was manageable, self-contained,
and regulated.[7] The existence of rules thus gave instantaneous
meaning. The irony, however—an irony the Victorians soon realized—was that rules were not absolutes, as Alice learned when
she stumbled down the rabbit hole.

The literature and games of the period trace an evolution in
the concept of play. In reaction against the rule-making and rationalist appropriation of play came an insistence on the value
of imagination and creativity, most forcefully presented in *Hard
Times* (1854) by Charles Dickens. In his critique of the limitations
of fact and the dangers of the Utilitarian perspective, Dickens
exposes the inadequacies and inhumanity of life based solely on
rules. Quite simply, such a life means the destruction of feelings
and of love as well as of play. In the novel, Sissy Jupe, Sleary, and
the circus people circumvent the regulations and facts of Gradgrind
and Bounderby to show that play, associated with performance,
provides people with a necessary element of amusement: "People
mutht be amuthed," Sleary announces at the end of the book, expressing a view the Victorians gradually, if grudgingly, accepted.[8]
At a time of enormous social change, there developed both the
recognition of the artificiality of rules and a new approach to the
nature and practice of education.

Lewis Carroll most clearly advanced the revised attitude toward play through his inversion of rules and logic. In his various
mathematical and language games, he created what Dickens called
a "region where rules, and figures, and definitions were not quite
absolute."[9] Rules for Carroll subvert reason, as shown when Alice
plays croquet. In frustration she tells the Cheshire cat that the
game "doesn't seem to have any rules in particular: at least, if
there are, nobody attends to them." To add to the confusion,
everything in the game is alive: croquet mallets are flamingoes;
the balls are live hedgehogs and the arches are doubled-over soldiers.[10] The anger and threats of the queen are further signs of
the absurdity of the game and its rulers, showing that they cannot regulate experience or, at the very least, are immensely un-
reliable controls. In the Alice books the world becomes a game in

which we try to figure out the rules as we play. Inventing, creating, imagining—these are the real values that result from play. When unsure how to act or to deal with reality, create your own rules, as Carroll urges, establish your own reality which can then be incorporated into your own experience. In this way, play becomes self-discovery; it remains instructive but in personal rather than public terms.

The translation of creative play into educational practice in Victorian England, however, was not the accomplishment of English educators. It was the work of the German, Frederick Froebel, as interpreted by Johannes and Bertha Ronge, that presented to the Victorians a plan to unite play and learning through a unique play space, the kindergarten. By coincidence, Dickens was linked to this development. The earliest kindergarten modeled on Froebel's principles was established at Number 32 Tavistock Place by the Ronges; Dickens lived around the corner at Number 1 Tavistock Square, and it is possible that his large garden partially adjoined the kindergarten area of the Ronges.

In 1855 *Household Words,* the weekly journal edited by Dickens, featured an article entitled "Infant Gardens," by Henry Morley. It describes the Ronges' establishment, and its theme was the need for English acceptance of the ideas of Froebel. Morley argued that we should study the play of children: "They fall into a fatal error," he wrote, "who despise all that a child does, as frivolous. Nothing is trifling that forms part of a child's life."[11] What impressed Morley was that instruction in the "infant garden" was always by means of play and that the garden was meant "to assure more perfectly the association of wholesome bodily exercise with mental activity."[12] Through the use of simple toys such as balls, cubes, and sticks, the child was to develop naturally:

> Up to the age of seven there is to be no book work and no ink work; but only at school a free and brisk but systematic strengthening of the body, of the sense, of the intellect, and of the affections managed in such a way as to leave the child prompt for subsequent instruction, already comprehending the elements of a good deal of knowledge.[13]

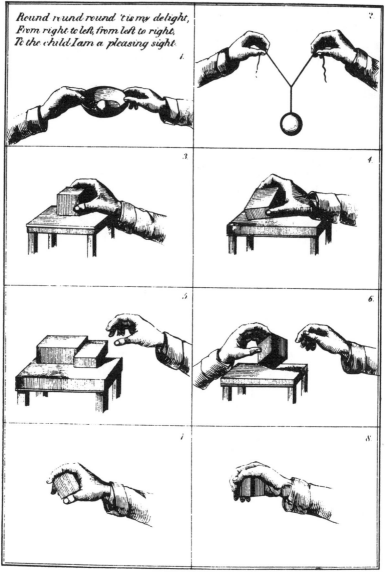

Round round round 'tis my delight,
From right to left, from left to right,
To the child I am a pleasing sight.

"Second Gift," from J. and B. Ronge, *A Practical Guide to the English Kinder-Garten*, 3rd ed. (London: A. N. Myers & Co., 1865).

In *A Practical Guide to the English Kinder-Garten,* published in 1855, the Ronges attempted to show in meticulous detail the operation of Froebel's system based on "instructive and amusing games, and industrial and gymnastic exercises." The book proved popular, reaching a third edition by 1865. The majority of the volume consisted of drawings of the games and toys Froebel invented for children, and their applications. The crucial concept, however, was that "the child produces for itself . . . learns everything itself."[14] The two rooms of the kindergarten are clearly defined in purpose: one is for games, the other, attached to a garden, for exercise.

Although the Ronges stressed the creativity of play, for their Victorian readers they took pains to emphasize the moral and utilitarian quality of activity, as in this comment on the benefits of folding, cutting, and plaiting paper:

> In this occupation, not only the eyes and hands of the children are educated, but the taste for beauty is developed; order, neatness, and industrial habits are promoted; they exercise their inventive powers, and prepare themselves for useful occupations. . . . This occupation has a moral effect, because when children know that they can do something useful, their self-reliance increases.[15]

Most significant for the Ronges is that "the children are to be . . . the masters or free workers, not the slaves of the material; they are led to produce and to compose, not to copy. The dignity of man—the germ of which is also in every child—is thus the moral ground-work for the teacher," they conclude.[16]

The appearance of *Hard Times* in 1854 and Dickens's publication of Morley's article "Infant Gardens" in *Household Words* in 1855 may have contributed to the popularity of the Ronges' book; but the entrenched practices of the Gradgrinds and the M'Choakum-childs prevented widespread or systematic implementation of Froebel's kindergarten program in England. The practical impact of the Ronges' concepts was negligible. Nonetheless, the attitudes toward play were shifting and the change was notable in the lit-

erature of the period, especially the novel. Increasingly, play became important not only as an aspect of social life but as an
element in the contests and themes of Victorian fiction.

II

The Victorian novel is a remarkable register of the kinds of play
permitted in Victorian homes, as well as of the significance and
influence of play on the moral and social life of the time. As early
as 1814 distinctions regarding play were appearing in the nineteenth-century novel. In *Mansfield Park* by Jane Austen, for example, the performance of a play at the home of Sir Thomas
Bertram is considered (in the circumstances in which it takes
place) to be an affront to the moral reputation of the family, but
the playing of whist, speculation, or even billiards is acceptable.
These activities were considered amusingly educational and in
their playing reveal for the reader significant elements of character
and story. Dickens extends the idea of play in a work like *Great
Expectations* (1861), where it becomes a metaphor for relationships, desires, and actions. Young Pip is sent to the macabre home
of Miss Havisham precisely in order to play. He and the beautiful
Estella play "Beggar-my-neighbor," a simple high-card contest used
by Dickens not only to emphasize Pip's social ineptitude but to
display the scornful beauty of the aggressive and vengeful Estella.
The very name of the game evokes the nature of their relationship. Play becomes a source of fear in the novel, a metaphor for
Estella's power and Miss Havisham's control. "Play the game out,"
orders Miss Havisham, who admits that she has "a sick fancy . . .
to see some play."[17] Other forms of play exist in the novel, such
as the activities at the chaotic home of Mr. and Mrs. Pocket, whose
children alternate between "tumbling up and lying down," but
the essential notion of play in the novel is negative—it is forced
and performed, not spontaneous and pleasurable.

The Heir of Redclyffe, a once popular novel by Charlotte Yonge
published in 1853, provides an example of the importance of play
in the Victorian family. Using inheritance and love as its themes,

George Cruikshank, "At Home in the Nursery," from *Cruikshank Prints for Hand Colouring* (New York: Dover Publishing).

the novel also displays a representative survey of the diversions, games, and amusements that were dominant in the mid-Victorian period. The opening paragraph introduces us to two young characters involved with traditional Victorian pursuits—drawing and reading. And within the first seventy pages the book refers to the following domestic forms of play: chess, singing, walking, word games, battledore, shuttlecock, and billiards. The last is the most interesting, because one would expect that its connection with games of chance and, certainly, with gambling would have rendered it unacceptable. Yet Browning, Trollope, and Gilbert and Sullivan, among other Victorian writers, also refer to billiards, indicating its attraction and acceptability as a Victorian pleasure. Ida Frange, the mother of Maisie in Henry James's *What Maisie Knew* (1897), is in fact an international billiards champion.

III

In both fiction and reality the Victorians displayed incredible energy and ingenuity in creating new games and methods of play. By the 1840s games expressly for children developed; until then, there were few divisions between games for children and those for adults or adolescents. Specialized journals devoted to games rapidly appeared, with titles such as *The Puzzler's Manual, a monthly journal of enigmatical amusements; The Play-hour, a paper for children; Games, Toys and Amusements;* and one simply titled *Fun.* Publishers and manufacturers of games began to use original methods of packaging and presentation to attract children and their parents. A few families, however, dominated the toy and game market in the nineteenth-century: John Harris continued the Newbery family's tradition as a publisher of children's books; Edward Wallis created dissections (jigsaw puzzles) and board games; William Darton published a large variety of puzzle games; while William Spooner concentrated on witty and humorous games.

Henry Mayhew, Victorian journalist and reformer, left a vivid account of the work of Victorian toy manufacturing devoted to wheeled, mechanical, and papier-mâché toys. Bristol toys, so called

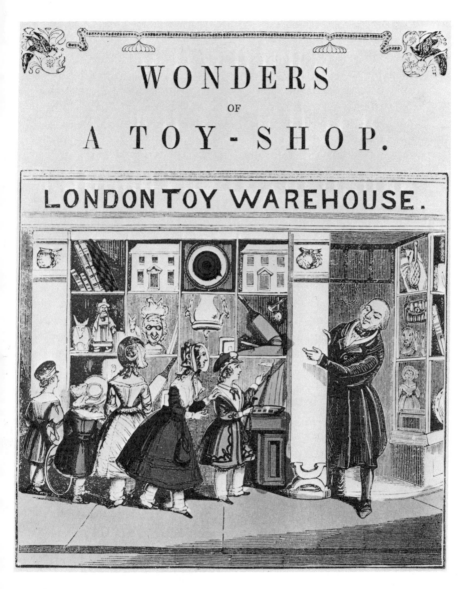

"Wonders of a London Toy Shop," from *Little Wide Awake, An Anthology from Victorian Children's Books and Periodicals*, selected by Leonard De Vries (London: Arthur Barker Ltd., 1967).

because they were fashioned out of green or "Bristol" wood, were very popular, he tells us, especially in the form of cats, omnibuses, steamers, and carriages. The most fascinating toy manufacturer he describes is a French papier-mâché worker who not only clothes his make-believe animals in real skins but has invented a barking papier-mâché dog.[18] The factual accounts by Mayhew find their way into fiction through such characters as Jenny Wren from Charles Dickens's *Our Mutual Friend.* She is a crippled dwarf who survives as a dolls' dressmaker and reveals her occupation only in "a game of forfeits."[19]

Inventing games oneself was a popular Victorian pastime. Elizabeth Hitchner, a friend and correspondent of Shelley, published "Enigmas, historical and geographical by a clergyman's daughter" in 1834. Henry Mayhew, with his brother Augustus, created "Acting Charades or Deeds not Words. A Christmas game to make a long evening short" in 1850. Edward Lear originated a variety of illustrated children's games, but the most prolific inventor was Lewis Carroll. Carroll created such games as "Court Circular," "Croquet Castles," "Natural Selection," "Circular Billiards," and "Curiosa Mathematica, Part II: Pillow Problems Thought Out during Sleepless Nights." Carroll also treasured unusual toys and kept a mechanical bat in his rooms at Oxford, which one afternoon unexpectedly flew out the window across the quadrangle only to land unassumingly on a tea-tray carried by a startled servant.

Among the most vivid examples of the Victorian forms of play were the varied board games for children, each providing a lesson in geography, history, or society. "The Mansion of Bliss," invented by T. Newton in 1810, involved a journey from a world of corruption to a house of purity (see the accompanying illustration). Its didactic moral purpose made the game acceptable to the Regency, but the connotations of its title stretch beyond that age. "The Mansion of Bliss" may be seen as a metaphor which describes the Victorian middle-class home where children found delight and instruction through play.[20]

Another example of a single game successfully produced, clear in its intent, and readily accepted by Victorian families for the

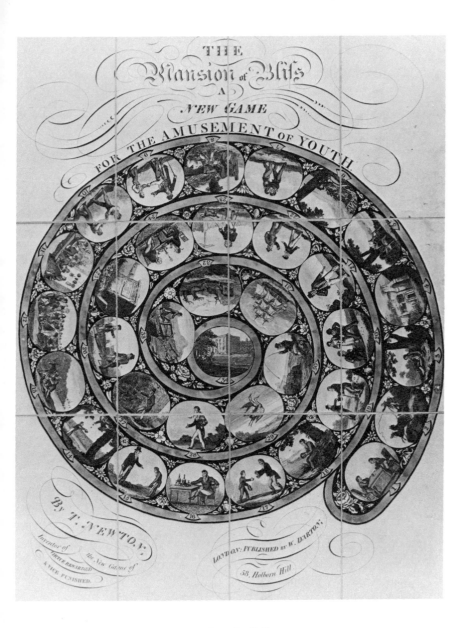

"The Mansion of Bliss"

edification of their children was "Wallis' picturesque round game of the produce and manufactures, of the counties of England and Wales." This board game, with one sheet mounted on canvas but folded to fit into a traveling case with a twenty-page instruction and information booklet, is a geographical race game. Each player attempts to get to London but along the way must study a short description of each town he lands in; if there is a wonderful view he might have to skip a turn to admire it; if there is a new railway station he might be able to travel ahead to the nearest large city. Published in 1840, this game not only taught the young player the details of England and its countryside, but presented a compilation of British industrial and civic achievements in the guise of a race to London. It united Victorian accomplishment with nineteenth-century ambition.

Two additional forms of educational Victorian play that appeared to be frivolous but were clearly instructive were dolls and optical toys. The purpose of these "toys" was to teach social rank, tasteful dress, and the occupations of various classes. Dolls were male and female, and the "protean figure and metamorphic costumes," consisting of a male paper-doll with twelve different outfits ranging from an officer's uniform to a monk's habit, was not unusual. Edmund Gosse, in chapter 2 of his autobiography *Father and Son* (1907), speaks about his three dolls, two female and the other a soldier. Telescopic peepshows that introduced geography, history, or nature to children were equally appealing. Many were constructed of folded illustrated papers joined together and viewed from a peephole to establish perspective and dimension. Views of Regent's Park or London improvements were typical subjects. The "Fantascope" produced in 1833 was an advance in optical toys as aquatint-painted disks spun about, giving the illusion of movement. Peepshows recorded such historical events as the construction of the Thames Tunnel (1824-43) or the opening of the Great Exhibition by Queen Victoria on May 1, 1851.

Card games, thought to be idle pursuits, were again transformed into educational activities and often involved magic tricks. "Sybilline leaves or Detector of the Thoughts," or "The Magic Swans, or Feather'd conjurers who will discover any secret number, or age of any person in company" are two examples. In Chapter 3 of *David Copperfield,* Dickens comically describes the hero trying to learn "all fours" and fortune telling. Cards were, naturally, used to instruct, often in the form of the rebus, in which words or phrases were presented in pictures. "Battalion," for example, is represented on a card as a bat flying over a playfully fierce lion with the caption stating "a body of soldiers"; "Ramsgate" is represented by two rams standing before a farm gate with the caption "a town in Kent"; "deriding" is indicated by a large letter *D* resting upon a horse with the phrase "a term for scoffing."

The rebus led to illustrated alphabets, the most famous being those of Edward Lear, author of the *Nonsense Books.* Commissioned by various families to aid their children's learning, Lear's illustrated alphabets soon grew in popularity. An instance of his talent is the letter *A* with an ape pictured underneath with this rhyme:

> A was an ape
> Who stole some white tape
> And tied up his toes
> In four beautiful bows
> a!
> Funny old Ape!

Lear also created geographical nonsense limericks to teach place names and countries. Some examples:

> There was a Young Lady of Tyre,
> Who swept the loud chords of a lyre;
> At the sound of each sweep, she enraptured the deep,
> And enchanted the city of Tyre.

> There was an Old Man of Coblenz,
> The length of whose legs was immense;
> He went with one prance, from Turkey to France,
> That surprising Old Man of Coblenz.

There was an Old Man of Vesuvius
Who studied the works of Vitruvius;
When the flames burnt his book, to drinking he took,
That morbid Old Man of Vesuvius.[21]

Other forms of indoor play popular with Victorian children but also promoting educational values were dissections, lead figures, and theatrical toys. The first—better known as jigsaw puzzles, a phrase that became current in 1873—originated as geographical maps, such as the 1811 "England and Wales dissected upon the Best principle to teach Youth Geography." Later puzzles deal with genealogical charts, board games (such as the Wallis round game of 1840, simultaneously published as a dissection), and general illustrations. Lead figures could be assembled against backdrops to depict miniature scenes of daily city life; theatrical toys allowed for imaginative "stagings" involving actual dramatic scripts. Generally categorized as "juvenile theater," these toys consisted of cut-outs and mounted scenes against a backdrop. Special prints at a "penny plain, two pence colored" could be bought for use with the various backgrounds.

IV

The changing attitude toward play in the late Victorian and early Edwardian period can be measured in a variety of ways. In the 1880s and 1890s recreation and amusement together held a strong attraction for the public, as a series of published articles justified the shift from a qualified acceptance to an enthusiastic celebration of play. "The Philosophy of Amusement," "The Gospel of Recreation," "The Amusements of the People," and "An Apology for Idlers" are representative titles suggesting the new awareness of leisuretime activities and the importance of play.[22] This change from a restricted, educationally focused view of play to sheer enjoyment of it paralleled a shift in administrative policies. More precisely, the concept of playgrounds became a metaphor for the new social attitude toward play and its relation to children, while reflecting the social need for playing spaces.

Earlier in the century David Copperfield, about to meet the schoolmaster of Salem House, Mr. Creakle, in chapter 6 of the novel, compares a new "snug bit of garden" to the area he formerly played in. David recalls this area as a "dusty playground, which was such a desert in miniature, that I thought no one but a camel, or dromedary, could have felt at home in it."[23] The playground in Yarmouth illustrates in comic form the quality of Victorian playgrounds, a subject of some importance to Dickens. The parks of London were open by law only to the select or, at the very most, to the middle class; playgrounds were nonexistent. *London: A Pilgrimage,* the important visual and verbal record of the city in the 1870s by Gustave Doré and Blanchard Jerrold, contains no mention of playgrounds, although it has a chapter devoted to "London at Play." Beatrice Webb, the late Victorian reformer-sociologist, describes a Sunday in the 1880s in Victoria Park, London, in her autobiography but reports on the social and political activities, not the recreational.[24]

In contrast to these views, numerous social critics and politicians were becoming aware of the need for adequate areas of public recreation and for playing spaces for children. One of the most vocal spokesmen was the earl of Meath, who founded the Metropolitan Public Gardens Association and was the first chairman of the Parks Committee of the London County Council. In an 1893 article entitled "Public Playgrounds for Children," Meath cited the advances in creating more "public open spaces, gardens and playgrounds in the metropolis" but complained of the lack of playgrounds in areas other than those of the upper middle class. He was specific about the size, character, and location of the playgrounds to be built, although his detailed descriptions betrayed certain Victorian prejudices that contradicted the ideas of Froebel. The playgrounds Meath proposed were to be divided into sections for girls and boys with the girls' area screened off from view and partly roofed over in case of poor weather; adequately trained supervisors should always be present. The goal was a series of small playgrounds scattered throughout the city where it would be convenient for children to play. Meath stressed the moral virtue of play and playgrounds, noting also that truant schoolchildren could be located easily when playgrounds were in the neighborhood.[25]

The essay by Meath exemplifies the planning that gradually came to organize play in public spaces. His article also marks the shift from private play at home, either indoors or on the grounds of the house, to public play in large, open areas, purposely designed for that activity. Consequently, the nature of the play changed as more group games replaced solitary or limited children's games. Of course, working-class children still made their neighborhoods their playgrounds, a practice D. H. Lawrence described in chapter 4 of *Sons and Lovers* (1913). And institutionalized educational facilities still failed to respond to the challenge and need for play. A report on a district boarding school in the Forest Gate section of London, written the year after Meath's article, records that "the hours out of school were not play hours. The girls scrubbed the vast area of boarded rooms . . . the boys quarrelled or shivered in the yard." But the boys could play if they wanted; the girls could not. Collectively, however, the children had "no toys, no library . . . no playing fields . . . no pets . . . no pleasures in music. Life for them was surrounded with limitations."[26]

In 1879 Lewis Carroll asked a child friend,

> Do you ever play at games? Or is your idea of life 'breakfast, lessons, dinner, lessons, tea, lessons, bed, lessons, breakfast, lessons' and so on? It is a very neat plan of life, and almost as interesting as being a sewing-machine or a coffee grinder.[27]

How to reject "the neat plan of life" or break free from the "limitations" that restricted the boarders at the Forest Gate school became an acute problem for the Victorians, which often manifested itself in the conflict between repression and indulgence. Victorian children felt it first and their response was measured by the inventive amusements that became so meaningful to them. Succeeding the Victorians, the Edwardians—literally grown-up Victorian children—played passionately. And until the shock of the First World War, the place of play was supreme.

Notes

1. See, for example, E. P. Thompson, *The Making of the English Working Class* (1963; Harmondsworth, Middlesex: Penguin, 1970), pp. 366–84; Geoffrey Best, *Mid-Victorian Britain, 1851–75*, rev. ed. (1971; London: Panther, 1973), pp. 129–36.

2. Thomas Carlyle, *Past and Present*, ed. Richard Altick (Boston: Houghton Mifflin, 1955), pp. 209–10.

3. John Ruskin, "Work," *The Crown of Wild Olive: Works of John Ruskin*, ed. E. T. Cook and Alexander Wedderburn (London: George Allen, 1905), 18, 409.

4. Edmund Gosse, *Father and Son* (1907; Harmondsworth, Middlesex: Penguin, 1973), p. 110.

5. Nathaniel Hawthorne, *The English Notebooks*, ed. Randall Stewart (New York: Modern Language Association, 1941), 13 September 1854, p. 41.

6. Herbert Spencer, "Aesthetic Sentiments," *Principles of Psychology*, 2nd ed. (London: Williams and Norgate, 1872), 2, 631.

7. That the Victorian period was an age of rules, regulations and discipline, particularly in sport, can be seen in the establishment of the Cambridge Rules for football in 1863, the Queensbury rules for boxing in 1867, and the English Rugby rules in 1871. The first manual on golf appeared in 1857, although the St. Andrews rules for playing were set up in 1754.

8. Charles Dickens, *Hard Times*, ed. George Ford and Sylvere Monod (1854; New York: Norton, 1966), p. 222.

9. Ibid. p. 165.

10. Lewis Carroll, *Alice's Adventures in Wonderland*, in *The Annotated Alice*, introd. Martin Gardner (1865; New York: Clarkson N. Potter, 1960), pp. 113, 111.

11. Henry Morley, "Infant Gardens," *Household Words*, 11, No. 278 (21 July 1855), p. 578. On Tavistock House, see E. Muirhead Little, "Historical Notes on the Site of the Associations New House," *The British Medical Journal*, 18 July 1925, 111–14.

12. Morley, p. 580.

13. Ibid.

14. J. and B. Ronge, *A Practical Guide to the English Kinder-Garten (Children's Garden), for the use of Mothers, Nursery Governnesses and Infant Teachers*, 3rd ed. (1855; London: A. N. Myers, 1865), pp. v–vi.

15. Ibid., p. 46.

16. Ibid., p. 49.

17. Charles Dickens, *Great Expectations*, ed. R. D. McMaster (1861; Toronto: Macmillan, 1965), pp. 57–59.

18. Henry Mayhew, "Toy Makers," *Voices of the Poor: Selections from the Morning Chronicle*, ed. Anne Humphreys (London: Frank Cass and Co., 1971), pp. 157–78. The material was gathered in January and February 1850.

19. Charles Dickens, *Our Mutual Friend* (1865; New York: Modern Library, 1960), p. 231.

20. An excellent facsimile of "The Mansion of Bliss" was reproduced in color in 1972 for the Friends of the Osborne and Lillian H. Smith Collections, Toronto Public Library, Toronto, Canada. On seeing it, one is reminded of

the structure of some morality plays. The mansion, looking like a substantial English Victorian country house, is at the center of the spiraling diagram. The facsimile is accompanied by a brief survey of Victorian games by Margaret Maloney.

21. Edward Lear, *The Nonsense Books of Edward Lear,* ed. Howard Moss (New York: Signet, 1964), pp. 161, 62, 57, 50.

22. The articles respectively appeared in *Meliora,* 6 (1864), 193–210; *Popular Science Monthly,* 20 (1882), written by Herbert Spencer; *Contemporary Review,* 45 (March 1884), 342–453, written by Walter Besant; *The Cornhill Magazine,* July 1877, written by Robert Louis Stevenson, reprinted in his *Virginibus Puerisque* (1881).

23. Charles Dickens, *David Copperfield,* ed. George H. Ford (Boston: Houghton Mifflin, 1958), pp. 69–70. Cf. Johan Huizinga, *Homo Ludens* (1938; London: Temple Smith, 1970), pp. 28–29, on the special nature of playing grounds.

24. Gustave Doré and Blanchard Jerrold, *London: A Pilgrimage* (1872; New York: Dover, 1970), pp. 161–78; Beatrice Webb, *My Apprenticeship* (1926; Harmondsworth: Penguin, 1971), pp. 304–05. For an earlier discussion of Sunday activities see Charles Dickens, *Sunday under Three Heads* (London: Bradbury and Evans, 1836).

25. Reginald Brabazon, Earl of Meath, "Public Playgrounds for Children," *Nineteenth Century,* 34 (1893), 267–71. Meath is best remembered, perhaps, as the originator of "Empire Day," celebrated on 24 May, the birthday of Queen Victoria.

26. Dame Henrietta Barnett in *The Victorians,* ed. Joan Evans (Cambridge: Cambridge Univ. Press, 1966), p. 141.

27. Lewis Carroll to May Forshall, 6 March 1879, in *The Letters of Lewis Carroll,* ed. Morton N. Cohen with the assistance of Roger Lancelyn Green (London: Macmillan, 1979), 1, 333.

The Neverland of Id: Barrie, Peter Pan, and Freud

Michael Egan

The serious study of children's literature may be said to have begun with Freud, who found in folk and fairy tales evidence supporting his theory of the unconscious. More recently Bruno Bettelheim, taking his cue from *The Interpretation of Dreams* and other texts, has argued persuasively that the enduring appeal of many of the ancient classics of children's literature derives from their ability to resolve satisfactorily the symbolized confusions in their audiences' psyche.[1] The great tales, he says, depict sibling rivalry, as in *Cinderella* and *Goldilocks;* they touch on incestuous love-feelings between children, as in *Brother and Sister;* they deal with separation anxieties, for instance in *Hansel and Gretel;* many of them, such as *Snow White* and *Rapunzel,* explore the sexual rivalry between mothers and daughters or, as in *Jack and the Beanstalk,* between fathers and sons; and still others dramatize, in rich, symbolic images, the theme of adolescent sexual awakening. The most striking examples of this latter type are *Sleeping Beauty, The Frog Prince,* and, although Bettelheim does not discuss it, *Beauty and the Beast.*

The reading of *Peter Pan* undertaken here accepts the broad outlines of Bettelheim's Freudian approach. I shall argue, first, that in his story Barrie unconsciously created a vast, symbolic metaphor—the Neverland—of the child's id; and that, secondly, he populated it with figures of an almost archetypal resonance. For example, the confrontation between Peter and his rival, Captain Hook, is, as we shall see, sharply Oedipal both in its nature and its resolution. Finally, I shall suggest that a Freudian analysis not only is the key to the fundamental meaning of Barrie's greatest work but is also indispensable in understanding its enormous popular success. Like the classics of the genre, *Peter Pan* successfully works through some of the important psychic tensions struggling for resolution in the child's developing mind, and this is the basis of its captivating charm.

Andrew Birkin's *J. M. Barrie and the Lost Boys* is a recent study which has updated and brought together in a masterly way the biographical and literary evidence bearing on the genesis of *Peter Pan*.[2] What Birkin suggests is that in his work Barrie dramatized, to an unusual degree, the most distressing conflicts at war in his unconscious mind. Further, it appears that Barrie himself was only partially aware of the profound nexus between his inner psychic tensions and his art, and even then only towards the end of his creative life. Not until 1922, for example, when he was in his sixties, was he able to record in his literary notebooks following a particularly upsetting personal dream: "It is as if long after writing 'P.Pan' its true meaning came to me—Desperate attempt to grow up but can't."[3]

Birkin's conclusions, while by far the best-supported in terms of evidence and scholarship, are nevertheless—as he would be the first to agree—neither original nor unique. Cynthia Asquith, among others, made a similar point in her *Portrait of Barrie* (1955):

> Besides, I know that, whatever his views about reticence, once Barrrie took a pen into his hand something unpremeditated nearly always ran out of it. His subconscious was more than a collaborator. It could, too often did, take control. He might make a myriad notes before he began to write, but he never quite knew what would emerge.[4]

Asquith's observations are more than merely ancedotal; they are borne out in every way by Barrie's own revelations about his mode of composition. In 1928, for instance, he wrote a prefatory dedication to the playscript of *Peter Pan*, some twenty-four years after the first production. In it he remarked how "suspicious" it was that, despite his customary ability to "haul back to mind the writing of every other essay of mine, however forgotten by the pretty public," he had no recollection of having composed his most famous work.[5] There seems to have been nothing tongue-in-cheek about this remark. It suggests either that he repressed what was in his thoughts at the time of composition, or that he wrote *Peter Pan* directly from his preconscious. As we shall see, a close reading supports both possibilities.

It is also relevant to recall that Barrie often spoke of himself as a divided personality, identifying what he called his "writing half" with an uncontrollable, "unruly" self. His sense of psychic fracture seems to have run deep. In December 1915, for instance, he had a nightmare which he subsequently drew on for a play, *The Fight for Mr. Lapraik,* the story of a schizophrenic. According to Cynthia Asquith the dream recurred—a significant emphasis. It was of "some vaguely apprehended interloper who was, and yet somehow was not, himself," attempting to thrust him from his bed. In Barrie's own words the struggle came to this terrifying climax:

> At last I rushed from darkness to my mother's room (she has been dead many years) & cried to her abt my degenerate self —thing I have evolved into was trying to push me out of bed and take my place. Till that moment of telling I had no idea what the thing was.[6]

The unpublished play Barrie based on this experience described the struggle between two personalities, one good and one evil, for the possession of an ordinary man. Asquith later spoke of the "unforgettably eerie" experience of listening to Barrie read scenes from it, so persuasively was he able to enter into both roles. "I can't describe the disquieting tricks he played with face and voice," she wrote, "now how visibly and audibly he split himself into the two Mr. Lapraiks."[7]

We may note additionally that in 1920, when Barrie was working on *Mary Rose,* a play about a dead mother who returns as a ghost to search for her son, he developed what appears to have been a psychologically determined cramp in his right hand and was forced for the rest of his life to continue writing with his left. (Barrie was naturally left-handed but had been compelled as a child to learn to use his right.) Again the schizoid note is struck: his left side, he said, directly recalling the odd disclaimer pub-

lished in the Preface to *Peter Pan*, "doesn't even know the names
of my works." It seemed, he continued, to have "a darker and
more sinister outlook on life," and was at that time "trying to
egg me on" to make a woman knife her son. He warned his friends
that "anything curious or uncomfortable" in his plays of this
period should be attributed to the fact that they were "the prod-
ucts of my left hand."[8] Later, again in that curiously revealing
Preface, he noted his own preoccupation with islands as settings
for his dramas and observed that over the years they had grown
significantly "more sinister." The reason, he said, was that he
had now begun to write "with the left hand, the right having
given out; evidently one thinks more darkly down the left arm"
(Play, p. xv). He might have added, "and more clearly, too,"
for his notoriously illegible scrawl had suddenly become sharper
and more readable.

The evidence then supports the view that as a writer Barrie
had unusual access to his own unconscious. An analysis of *Peter
Pan* will bear this out. For in both versions of the story—play and
novel—he appears to have successfully developed a complex set
of metaphors and images which, as we shall see, agrees remarkably with Freud's tripartite theory of the human personality (id,
ego, superego). And since Barrie cannot have been familiar with
psychoanalytic thinking, given the exigencies of place and time,
we must conclude that he achieved all this by scooping unwitting-
ly, as it were, into the bubbling turmoil of his own half-formu-
lated wishes and ambitions.

II

Peter Pan is evidently a childish dream, a psychodrama of the
unconscious. We are plunged at the outset without warning into
the surreal universe of a child's uncertain psyche as Nana, a St.
Bernard, is shown turning down the beds, tidying the nursery,
and preparing Michael's bath. Yet these opening sequences, together with the story's almost equally Beckett-like conclusion (a
man lives and works in a dog kennel) are nevertheless the most

daylit of the play. What transpires on the island is the real dream, the fulfillment of a range of childish wishes, including Oedipal sex, lust, flight, murder, and the capacity to transcend both Death and Time. The primitive nature of these gratifications and their resolution are among the reasons *Peter Pan* is a children's book.

The movement of the story, then, is from the recognizably everyday world of a middle-class household in Victorian London to the unconscious universe of the Neverland, and then back again to the waking reality of the closing scenes. By the time we and the Darling children return safely to the nursery, all the conflicting psychic tensions presented on the island have been pleasantly resolved—at least for now. Like Freud, however, Barrie emphasizes that each new generation of children must undertake the pilgrimage afresh, an essential condition for maturity. He looks ahead four generations and comments: "and thus it will go on, as long as children are gay and innocent and heartless."[9]

The bathetic climax of this verbal sequence—it is also the conclusion of the novel—sends us back in search of Barrie's meaning. What he seems to have in mind is something close to Freud's notion of the selfishly amoral child, a human whose superego is still in formation and thus whose conscience is still relatively weak. To be heartless, he says, is to be "entirely selfish." It is to be what children are, "the most heartless things in the world," creatures who abuse love and who take emotional security for granted. On the other hand—it is the paradox of the child—this heartless selfishness is the essential quality (after fairy dust) making flight to the Neverland possible. Adults may be more considerate, but they can neither fly nor venture into the child's unconscious. In other words, the world of *Peter Pan* is open to us only so long as we are free from the constraints of conscience (Novel, pp. 138, 213).

Near the beginning of the novel there is a nodal passage (given in the play as an extended stage direction) in which Barrie both clarifies and dramatizes his notion of the fully developed superego. Naturally, he does not call it this, nor does he deploy the metaphors of censorship or guardianship we find in psychoanalytic

theory. Instead he allows the concept to gather around a senti-
mentalized vision of the role and function of the mother, principally in the character of Mrs. Darling but also in certain important secondary images to which she is explicitly related. Of
course, as we would anticipate if our wider hypothesis about the
story is correct, Mrs. Darling and all her subsidiaries have to be
evaded or weakened before the dream itself may commence.

Barrie begins by observing that it is the custom of Mrs. Darling
and every good mother to "rummage" in her children's minds
"after they are asleep." The process, whose purpose is to "put
things straight" for the next day, is "quite like tidying up draw-
ers." This is an analogy perfectly consistent with Freud's theory
of repression. What the mother does as her children sleep is "re-
pack into their proper places" those thoughts that have either
"wandered" or, even more disturbing, have inexplicably found
their way in from the outside. Thus Mrs. Darling one night finds
Peter lurking in her children's minds.

Barrie goes on to remark that as the busy mother continues
her mental cleaning she makes other "discoveries." These may be
of matters either "sweet" or "not so sweet." The nicer thoughts
she fondles, like a kitten; the others she "hurriedly . . . stows out
of sight," wondering nervously "where on earth" her children
can have "picked up" these things. Barrie then concludes, addressing his reader directly:

> When you wake up in the morning, the naughtiness and evil
> passions with which you went to bed have been folded up
> and placed at the bottom of your mind; and on the top,
> beautifully aired, are spread out your prettier thoughts, ready
> for you to put on. [Novel, p. 18]

The parallels with Freud's depiction of the censoring purpose
and activity of the superego are striking. Note too the accuracy
of Barrie's intuition that the repressing mechanism is capable only
of concealing from the child its "naughtiness and evil passions";
they cannot be thrown out. Instead these unsettling impulses are

merely hidden at the bottom of the mind, ready to surface again as soon as mother's back is turned.

Barrie later supplements his image of the maternal superego with two associated figures. The first is the nursemaid, Nana, a character whose nurturing role establishes her both sociologically and psychologically as a surrogate for the mother. The second is the group of nightlights, earlier identified by Mrs. Darling precisely as an extension of herself—"the eyes a mother leaves behind her to guard her children" (Novel, p. 36). All three—Mrs. Darling, Nana, and the nightlights—are united in a tight, protective alliance which the unconscious must contrive to overcome before Peter, as Barrie neatly puts it, can "break through." Again, the language is strikingly Freudian.

The disabling of the superego is achieved elegantly and persuasively. Mrs. Darling goes out for the evening. Nana is literally chained up. And as for the nightlights: "Wendy's blinked and gave such a yawn that the other two yawned also, and before they could close their mouths all three went out" (Novel, p. 37). We gather that some mysterious agency wants them off guard before it can appear.

The charm of Barrie's manner conceals the profundity of his insight. Later, however, he is able to draw on the subtle implications of his images. He observes that "you"—an ambiguous, portmanteau category that could include himself, the reader, and the children of Arthur and Sylvia Llewelyn Davies to whom the play was dedicated—are relieved at bedtime to have Nana's reassurance that the Neverland is "all make-believe." But then he adds: "Of course the Neverland had been make-believe in those days" (i.e., when the child was awake), "but it was real now, and there were no nightlights, and it was getting darker every moment, and where was Nana?" (Novel, p. 61).

But Barrie was an artist, not a scientist. His images of the superego and its interaction with the id, therefore, lack descriptive precision. What he communicates marvelously instead is the *felt experience* of resistance—the pressure exerted by the superego. Just before the children, led by Peter, make their final descent into the seething maelstrom of the unconscious, he suddenly includes a passage so extraordinarily perceptive and yet so plainly intuitive in scope that he himself seems not fully to have grasped its meaning.

The passage in effect describes a final flourish of resistance by the superego, a sort of last-ditch stand before the real dream on the Neverland can commence. Swooping low over "the fearsome island," the children notice that Peter's eyes have begun to sparkle and that his body tingles to the touch. Abruptly Barrie says:

> Nothing horrid was visible in the air, yet their progress had become slow and labored, exactly as if they were pushing their way through hostile forces. Sometimes they hung in the air until Peter had beaten it with his fists.
> "They don't want us to land," he explained.
> "Who are they?" Wendy whispered, shuddering.
> But he could not or would not say. [Novel, pp. 61–62]

This sequence can be read as mere device—a kind of mysterious rumbling of the literary drums to heighten tension and suspense. But I think it also shows how profoundly Barrie understood the fact, if not the theory, of resistance. His implicit point, like Freud's, is that although we may all journey to our idiosyncratic Neverlands at night, the "hostile forces" of the superego make it a thoroughly difficult undertaking. This is why we can usually only "break through" when asleep or when, as in the case of a parapraxis, the superego is momentarily off guard. Incidentally, resistance is also the reason most of us forget our dreams—quite like the way the Darling children and the lost boys soon forget all about the Neverland and Peter after returning to the mainland and reality.

In these remarkable passages and elsewhere Barrie makes explicit his interest in detailing the topography of what he calls the "map of a child's mind." At its core, of course, he locates the Neverland, a poetic version of the Freudian id. It is, Barrie suggests, the child's mind during sleep—a formulation very close to

Freud's. In it are to be found, in a significant series of related images, religion, fathers, murder, hangings, a hook-nosed old lady, caves with subterranean rivers, savages, and lonely lairs (Novel, p. 19). The sequence, "fathers, murder, hangings," reverbates with particular meaning in a post-Freudian era, as may perhaps the hook-nosed old lady and the caves with underground streams. Later Barrie talks of "unexpected patches" in the Neverland that rise and spread threateningly at bedtime. "Black shadows" move about within it and the frightening roar of predatory beasts (familiar Freudian dream-symbols of sexuality) may be heard (Novel, p. 61).

Barrie's Neverland, however, is more than merely dark suggestive hints. In fact he endows it with an ambiguous status quite like Freud's conception of the unconscious, settling on it not only archetypal representatives of physical terror—beasts, savages, murderous pirates—but also fantasies of gratified sexuality.

The chief of these is the marriage between Peter and Wendy, itself replete with Oedipal significance. Although there has been no formal ceremony beyond the exchange of kisses and thimbles in the nursery, their marriage—that is, their symbolic sexual union —is treated as a fact shortly after Wendy's arrival on the island. She repeatedly refers to herself as a wife and mother, as does the narrator, and in the chapter called "The Home under the Ground" behaves exactly as a stereotypical Victorian wife. Peter reciprocates. She calls him "Father" and he responds by referring to her as his "old lady." They both cast the lost boys, together with John and Michael, in the role of their children.

The patriarchal family is recreated down to its most subtle details, including, at one point, even a sly hint of growing sexual rivalry between Peter and John, the eldest "son." Perpetually cleaning, cooking, and darning, Wendy exclaims happily: "Oh, dear, I'm sure spinsters are to be envied" (Novel, p. 102). Later, in the chapter pointedly entitled "The Happy Home," she is directly referred to as a housewife and we see that the children have begun to call her "Mummy." "Father knows best," she is inclined to say loyally when the boys complain to her of Peter.

Beyond this, *Peter Pan* confronts heterosexuality primarily in the figure of Tinker Bell, although there is a noticeable prurience in the way Barrie deals with Tiger Lily and the mermaids. Tink, however, is openly a sexy creature, modest and brazen by turns. She tends to wear seductive *negligées* in her curtained-off *boudoir*, and is "slightly inclined towards *embonpoint*" (Novel, p. 37). (Given the sexual connotations of France in the Victorian mind, it may be significant that these French euphemisms are used almost exclusively in relation to her. The single exception, which we will notice later, tends to support the point.)

When we first encounter her, Tinker Bell is "exquisitely gowned in a skeleton leaf, cut low and square, through which her figure could be seen to the best advantage" (Novel, p. 37). Peter describes her as "an abandoned little creature," and she retorts that she glories in her abandonment (Novel, p. 133). She is subject to raging sexual jealousies and, pushed by Wendy into the uncomfortable role of "other woman" in Peter's life, contrives to have her rival murdered. Like the other "heroic" characters in the story, she can fly (well known in Freudian dream analysis as a symbol of sexual intercourse) and, as a common "street fairy," may have participated in the drunken orgies which occasionally take place in the Neverland. Drunken orgies? Certainly. We gather this from Barrie's suggestive remark that, as Peter sleeps on guard one night, "some unsteady fairies had to climb over him on their way home from an orgy" (Novel, p. 95).

It may be objected, of course, with some justice, that these are rather ponderous reactions to what could have been intended merely as light-hearted satire. But in fact I think something more interesting and complex is involved. Barrie appears to be making use of one of the important but unrecognized conventions of writing for children: the Double Address. On the one hand the author speaks directly to his principal audience, his voice and manner serious and gentle, even conspiratorial. From time to time, however, he glances sidelong at the adults listening in and winks. Naturally, his jokes and references on these occasions are not meant to be understood by the children. And thus he is permitted a privileged discourse, unique to the genre, in which he is able simultaneously to quarry his own unconscious while denying, with a smile, that he is doing so. Most of the humor in *Peter Pan* is of this type.

Barrie completes his portrayal of the Neverland by claiming three more things about it. The first is that each individual possesses his own private island—Wendy's is concerned with this, John's with that, and so forth. This is an insight quite acceptable to the Freudian. At the same time, however, each Neverland participates collectively in the symbolism of its culture, or, as Barrie puts it, "the Neverlands have a family resemblance" (Novel, p. 19). By implication, then, and Barrie goes along with this, waking reality is imaged as "the mainland" (Novel, pp. 102, 105, 107).

These details are important, not only because they indicate the purely literary nature of Barrie's intuitions but also because of their sharply autobiographical character. As we have already seen, he was aware that his creative imagination was drawn compulsively to the idea of an island. To this we need only add that he once acknowledged in a public talk, possibly revealing more than he intended, "I should feel as if I had left off my clothing, if I were to write without an island."[10] In order to create, it seems, he needed to put on the disguises of his unconscious. Without them he felt literally, perhaps even sexually, exposed.

Barrie's Neverland then is an unpredictably predictable universe to which each dreaming child can fly. It is a place where the inhabitants—Wendy and Tinker Bell, specifically—can die and yet survive death; where aging and growth can be transcended; where children may marry, and kill bloodthirsty pirates; where there are wild beasts of prey, and savages dangerous and worshipful by turns, and where half-perceived hints of adult sexuality and licentiousness abound. It is, in other words, an authentic vision of the Freudian id.[11]

At the center of the Neverland stands Captain Hook, at once Peter's greatest foe and the enemy of all small children. When he first bestrode the London stage, according to Daphne du Maurier, children were carried screaming from the stalls. In the story itself, both John and Michael weep in terror when his name is first pronounced because, says Barrie, "they knew Hook's reputation" (Novel, p. 63).

Yet this instant knowledge is a curious thing. After all, Hook is a fictional personality with no existence outside Barrie's imagination—unlike, for example, the Knave of Hearts in *Alice*. Certainly he has a literary ancestor in "Captain Swarthy," a "black man" and a pirate Barrie invented for the Davies children; but the reference is too esoteric to account satisfactorily for the universal recognition Barrie claims for Hook and with which he was received. When his name comes up in *Peter Pan* there has been nothing, including Peter's tone and manner, to justify the terror the boys display.

What is even more puzzling about their behavior is that, as we subsequently learn, "Hook was not his real name" (Novel, p. 167). Who is he, then? Barrie is as evasive about this as he was about the hostile forces of the superego. One possible explanation is that he is the author himself, for Barrie admits in his Preface that Captain Swarthy "is held by those who know to be autobiographical" (Play, p. xxiii). Unfortunately, however, this explanation obscures more than it reveals, for more than six years earlier, as we noted at the outset, he had already identified himself with Peter Pan ("Desperate attempt to grow up but can't"). In fact the apparent contradiction points to its own solution. As we shall see, he was both Pan and Hook, an unconscious condensation.

Barrie himself never understood this. In *Peter Pan* and elsewhere he is as genuinely ignorant of his villain's true identity as are his readers. Hook is simply "a dark and solitary enigma," an "unfathomable" man, the revelation of whose identity would "set the country in a blaze" (Novel, pp. 148, 166, 167).

Hook is also immensely powerful. During the final battle with the boys we are told that "this man alone seemed to be a match for them all" (Novel, p. 185). He is a cold-hearted killer whose menacing hook, as his man Skylights discovers, deals instant death. As the tale progresses his dark shadow looms ever larger until Peter, muttering "Hook or me this time," is forced at last into the final confrontation.

At the same time he is an oddly attractive individual, more an anti-hero than a fiend. "Thou not wholly unheroic figure," as Barrie apostrophizes, he is "not wholly evil" (Novel, pp. 190, 156). Disarmingly handsome, he loves flowers, music, and good clothes. He is also something of a gentleman and of course—one of those winks at the adults—an old Etonian. Finally, he possesses an outstanding brain and a code of honor which he calls "good form." His death is grotesque and almost pathetically triumphant.

The reader will have anticipated my view that Hook represents the Oedipal Father. Daphne du Maurier, who watched her own father play the role many times, describes his impact in terms which ineluctably evoke the Freudian idea:

> He was a tragic and ghastly creation who knew no peace, and whose soul was in torment; a dark shadow; a sinister dream; a bogey of fear who lives perpetually in the grey recesses of every small boy's mind. All boys had their Hooks, as Barrie knew; he was the phantom who came by night and stole his way into their murky dreams.[12]

If Hook is the Oedipal Father, however, then within the structure of the story Peter Pan himself must be his Son. In great part the tale's popularity derives from its dramatization, in symbolic terms, of the Oedipal Son's victory over the Father. When Peter defeats Hook, every son in the audience crows with glee.

If this reading seems a little forced, let us recall that once the children descend into the unconscious Peter and Wendy undergo what is in effect a marriage. They set up house; they have children; Peter goes out to work and Wendy darns socks. At the same time, however, their roles oscillate ambiguously. Wendy is now a mother, now a wife; Peter simultaneously her husband, son, and, as he insists on being called, "The Great White Father" (Barrie's original title for the play). The Oedipal nature of their relationship emerges unmistakably in the following exchange:

> "Ah, old lady," Peter said aside to Wendy, warming himself by the fire and looking down at her as she sat turning a

heel, "there is nothing more pleasant of an evening for you and me when the day's toil is over than to rest by the fire with the little ones near by."

"It is sweet, Peter, isn't it?" Wendy said, frightfully gratified. "Peter, I think Curly has your nose."

"Michael takes after you."

"Dear Peter," she said, "with such a large family, of course, I have now passed my best, but you don't want to change me, do you?"

"No, Wendy."

Certainly he did not want a change, but he looked at her uncomfortably; blinking, you know, like one not sure whether he was awake or asleep.

"Peter, what is it?"

"I was just thinking," he said, a little scared, "It is only make-believe, isn't it, that I'm their father?"

"Oh, yes," Wendy said primly.

"You see," he continued apologetically, "it would make me seem so old to be their real father."

"But they are ours, Peter, yours and mine."

"But not really, Wendy?" he asked anxiously.

"Not if you don't wish it," she replied; and she distinctly heard his sigh of relief. "Peter," she asked, trying to speak firmly, "what are your exact feelings for me?"

"Those of a devoted son, Wendy." [Novel, pp. 132–33]

Sophocles excepted, it would be hard to find a more articulate literary presentation of the confusions and gratifications inherent in the Oedipal situation. It is notable too that at the crux of this exchange Peter is unsure whether he is dreaming or not—in other words, from the Freudian point of view the scene constitutes an almost classic wish-fulfillment. At its conclusion Peter is simultaneously Wendy's son, husband, and father to her children.

Yet this satisfactory arrangement is broken up, and by none other than Hook himself. He does so, furthermore, not only because he is the incarnation of evil but because he is, directly, Peter's sexual rival. He wants Wendy for himself.

Hook is indeed a highly sexual figure. First, he is overwhelmingly seductive. Wendy in particular displays a curious ambivalence towards him, as indeed she should, given the nature of this dream. Certainly she hates him, but at the same time she is not immune to his charm. After he has kidnapped her brothers and the lost boys, she nevertheless politely takes Hook's arm and allows him to escort her away from the "happy home." Barrie says that this was just a "slip" on her part because she is "fascinated" and "entranced" by his gentlemanly manner; he is "so frightfully *distingué*." But of course there are no slips, and in the context of the tale the meaning of this episode is clear. (Other than in the passages describing Tinker Bell, this is the only occasion in the story when French is used. Once again it appears in a scene charged with sexual significance.)

In more oblique but perfectly recognizable ways Hook's figure is replete with graphic phallic symbolism. The most vivid is the mighty iron hook for which he is metonymically named—a dangerous weapon which occasionally twitches or hangs idle of its own volition. He also wears a florid hat—according to *The Interpretation of Dreams* frequently a symbol of masculinity. And finally, in an amusing symbolic emphasis, he is shown smoking simultaneously not one but *two* cigars, in a strange double holder of his own design. These detailed images, as we see, turn out to be important in the story's climax.

My point that Hook is (unconsciously) the Great Black Father in the tale may be clinched by recalling that in the stage version, following a tradition that goes right back to the original production under Barrie's own direction in 1904, the part of Hook is always played by the actor cast as Mr. Darling. He is thus literally Wendy's father in elaborate disguise. When she takes his arm, therefore, and Peter rushes hotly in pursuit vowing vengeance, the archetypal Freudian triad (Oedipal Father–Mother–Oedipal Son) is complete.

But Peter Pan is not Hook's only enemy. His other indefatigable foe is Time itself, emblematically presented in the relentlessly pursuing crocodile. On the Neverland, where "it is quite impossible to say how time does wear on" (Novel, p. 102), the crocodile is chro-

nology personified. "It must have been not less than ten o'clock
by the crocodile," the narrator observes at one point; and, more
explicitly elsewhere. "The way you got the time on the island
was to find the crocodile and then stay near him until the clock
struck" (Novel, pp. 159, 129).

Peter's final victory and the emblematic crocodile are linked in
many ways. First, of course, Hook ultimately perishes in its jaws.
Additionally, it has been imprinted on him by Peter's act—an important detail, for it shows among other things that the boy has
already symbolically castrated the male parent. Peter's final victory is thus implicitly assured. This is indicated by the fact that
at the moment of his amputation Hook's time starts to run out:
the crocodile begins to tick. It will not cease, as we are told on
more than one occasion, until the very hour of his death.

And then, in a stroke of real narrative genius, Barrie brings
these elements dramatically together. His point seems to be that
time itself is on the child's side. Just before the climax of the
action—the final confrontation between the father and his son—
two things happen simultaneously. First, the crocodile's clock
stops running, and we know then that Hook is doomed. Second,
Peter himself begins to imitate the sound—unconsciously, but so
perfectly that when he climbs aboard the *Jolly Roger* the crew
believe the crocodile itself has come at last. "It was Fate," Barrie
has them thinking (Novel, p. 176). In these final startling moments Barrie allows all the deadly temporal meanings associated
with the crocodile to gather around his hero.

Peter thus becomes both Time and Fate. He is also, in a closely
related thought, Youth. Throughout the story Barrie has suggested
that what Hook finds most irritating in Peter is his boyishness,
his "cockiness." Now, in the final battle, Hook realizes that his
opponent is something more than "Peter Pan the avenger," as
he melodramatically calls himself.

> Hitherto [Hook] had thought some fiend was fighting him,
> but darker suspicions assailed him now.
> "Pan, who art thou?" he cried huskily.

"I'm youth, I'm joy," Peter answered at a venture. "I'm a little bird that has broken out of the egg." [Novel, p. 188]

I take this awkward exchange, which the text immediately dismisses as "of course . . . nonsense," to be an indication of Barrie's dim perception that his protagonists stood for issues larger than themselves. Within a page Hook is dead, slain by his own symbolic progeny.

My general argument can be affirmed, I think, by an examination of the way in which Barrie follows up the defeat of Captain Hook. In Freud's analysis of the Oedipal dream, it is necessary that the youthful victor seal his triumph by replacing the father he has overthrown. Thus Oedipus becomes King of Thebes and marries his own mother. In *Peter Pan* Barrie offers us another version of this process, simultaneously completing the transformation of his hero (begun when he assumed the crocodile's emblematic status) and discovering a striking *denouement* for his drama. After bursting from the egg at the moment of his father's death, Peter undergoes a final and decisive transformation. He becomes Captain Hook.

It is doubtful if Barrie fully understood what he was doing. Although he prepares us for this event, showing Peter passing by slow increments into Hook, he also writes, perhaps speaking at the same time for himself, that Peter "did not know in the least who or what he was" (Novel, p. 188). At one point he even admits his own confusion.

The crucial moment occurs in the rescue of Tiger Lily, something Peter accomplishes by imitating Hook's voice so brilliantly that even the pirates are deceived. Superficially the incident is meant to illustrate Peter's limitless resourcefulness and to display his capacity for mimicry. More profoundly, however, the scene touches on the nerve of his identity. Barrie seems to have sensed this, but only vaguely, for in the play he suddenly includes a parenthetical comment—it can hardly be called a stage direction —which is, I believe, an authentic glimpse into his own unconscious mind. For Peter "can imitate the Captain's voice so perfectly," Barrie admits, "that even the author has a dizzy feeling that at times he was really Hook" (Play, p. 80).

Later there is another revealing stage direction, suggesting but oddly not requiring a wordless tableau of overwhelming psychological importance. Barrie's language also merits some attention, for it is like a voyeuristic peep at something he both does and does not want to see. The climax of Act V, Scene I is Hook's quasi-suicidal leap into the crocodile's waiting jaws. The curtain falls immediately. Then Barrie adds:

> The curtain rises to show Peter a very Napoleon on his ship. It must not rise again lest we see him on the poop in Hook's hat and cigars, and with a small iron claw. [Play, p. 143]

End of scene. When the curtain does in fact rise again we are back in the Darlings' nursery. The dream is evidently over.

In the novel, however, Barrie explores this idea in more detail. Chapter 16, "The Return Home," reveals that all the boys have become pirates and Peter, "it need not be said," is their captain. So he has literally replaced Hook as master of the *Jolly Roger*. Like Hook, he treats his crew "as dogs," and they obey him with the same fear and trembling. There is even the appalling suggestion, albeit offered with another of those asides to the adults, that the lash itself is used. "Slightly," he writes, "got a dozen for looking perplexed when told to take soundings" (Novel, p. 192). Finally, having taken on Hook's role and manner, Peter assumes his full identity. He forces Wendy against her will to make a new suit for him "out of some of Hook's wickedest garments" and then drapes himself in the Captain's phallic symbolism:

> It was afterwards whispered among them that on the first night he wore this suit he sat long in the cabin with Hook's cigar-holder in his mouth and one hand clenched, all but the forefinger, which he bent and held threateningly aloft like a hook. [Novel, pp. 192–93]

The wheel has come full circle. Having destroyed the Oedipal father the triumphant son becomes the Oedipal father. He takes his place completely.

These points look back to the whole question, which we touched on earlier, of whether Barrie was his hero or his villain. They suggest that, like the schizoid Mr. Lapraik, he was both.

Notes

1. Bruno Bettelheim, *The Uses of Enchantment* (New York: Knopf, 1976), pp. 5, 155.

2. Andrew Birkin, *J. M. Barrie and the Lost Boys* (New York: Clarkson N. Potter, Inc., 1979).

3. Ibid, p. 297.

4. Cynthia Asquith, *Portrait of Barrie* (New York: E. P. Dutton, 1955), pp. 220–21.

5. J. M. Barrie, *Peter Pan, or the Boy Who Would Not Grow Up* (London: Hodder and Stoughton, 1928), pp. viii–ix. Hereafter cited as "Play," parenthetically within the text.

6. Birkin, p. 253.

7. Asquith, p. 26.

8. Ibid, pp. 45, 66.

9. J. M. Barrie, *Peter Pan* (Puffin Books, 1978), p. 230. Hereafter cited as "Novel," parenthetically within the text.

10. Harry M. Geduld, *Sir James Barrie* (New York: Twayne Publishers, 1971), p. 29.

11. A psychoanalyst has pointed out to me that what I term the "id" is an inclusive definition of the Freudian unconscious, or "mixtures of id and ego that are unacceptable in waking life, censored by conscious ego values and superego attitudes."

12. Birkin, p. 110.

The Story of the Story: The Willow Pattern Plate in Children's Literature

Ben Harris McClary

The first known publication of *the* "willow pattern story" was in a British family magazine, *The Family Friend,* in 1849. The introduction asked:

> Who is there, since the earliest dawn of intelligent perception, who has not inquisitively contemplated the mysterious figures on the willow-pattern plate? Who, in childish curiosity, has not wondered what those three persons in dim blue outline did upon that bridge; whence they came, and whither they were flying? What does the boatman without oars on that white stream? Who people the houses in that charmed island?—or why do those disproportionate doves forever kiss each other, as if intensely joyful over some good deed done? Who is there through whose mind such thoughts as these have not passed, as he found his eye resting upon the willow-pattern plates as they lay upon the dinner-table, or brightly glittered on the cottage plate-rail?

Appealing to the reader's sense of nostalgia, the writer, "J. B. L.," continued:

> The old willow-pattern plate! . . . It has mingled with our earliest recollections; it is like the picture of an old friend and companion, whose portrait we see everywhere, but of whose likeness we never grow weary.

The commentator concluded, declaring the "story" of the willow pattern "is said to be to the Chinese, what our Jack the Giant-Killer or Robinson Crusoe is to us."[1]

Contrary to J. B. L.'s last statement, the willow pattern was not a direct product of the oriental mind; it seems instead to have been a product of western interest in the East. The chinoiserie craze, which had been the province of the aristocracy, crested in

1760, according to Hugh Honour, but, filtering down through the strata of society, in its wane it left the lower classes infatuated by anything tinged with orientalism.[2] This interest prompted Thomas Minton, a Staffordshire potter, in 1780 to devise a crowded oriental-patterned plate which almost immediately captured the imagination of the British public. Known as the willow pattern because of the centrally placed willow tree shown in blossom in spring before its leaves develop, the design soon appeared in imitation among the wares of other western pottery makers and, most historians of the art declare, was carried to China, where it was copied for the British and American export trade, shortly becoming one of the staples of that lucrative market.

The evidence suggests that the story developed out of the plate design—rather than the reverse. Indeed, in nineteenth-century popular literature, one encounters several widely differing stories derived from the willow pattern plate,[3] but *The Family Friend* version, through repetition, has become *the* story.

A child's rhyme of indefinite origin—but apparently predating the first prose version of the episodic adventure—seems to have been the first telling of this story. In part, the rhyme, referring to the willow pattern plate as "she," declared:

> So she tells me a legend centuries old
> Of a Mandarin rich in lands and gold,
> Of Koong-Shee fair and Chang the good,
> Who loved each other as lovers should.
> How they hid in the gardener's hut awhile,
> Then fled away to the beautiful isle
> Though a cruel father pursued them there,
> And would have killed the hopeless pair,
> But a kindly power, by pity stirred,
> Changed each into a beautiful bird.
>
> . . . .
>
> Here is the orange tree where they talked,
> Here they are running away,
> And over all at the top you see
> The birds making love always.[4]

PRACTICAL PUZZLE.—No. 1.

CHINESE MAZE.—THE WILLOW-PATTERN PLATE.*

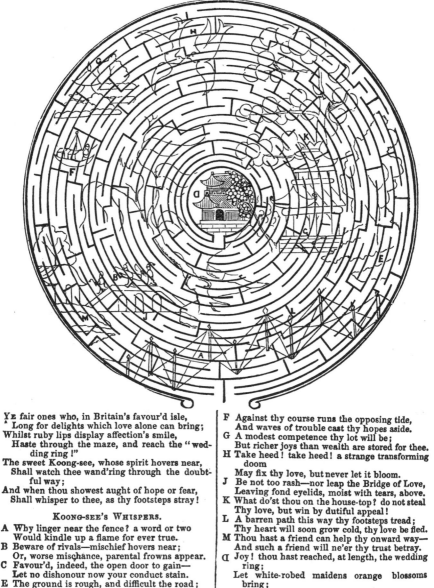

YE fair ones who, in Britain's favour'd isle,
 Long for delights which love alone can bring;
Whilst ruby lips display affection's smile,
 Haste through the maze, and reach the "wed-
  ding ring!"
The sweet Koong-see, whose spirit hovers near,
 Shall watch thee wand'ring through the doubt-
  ful way;
And when thou showest aught of hope or fear,
 Shall whisper to thee, as thy footsteps stray!

KOONG-SEE'S WHISPERS.

A Why linger near the fence? a word or two
 Would kindle up a flame for ever true.
B Beware of rivals—mischief hovers near;
 Or, worse mischance, parental frowns appear.
C Favour'd, indeed, the open door to gain—
 Let no dishonour now your conduct stain.
E The ground is rough, and difficult the road;
 But, faint not, thou shalt reach thy love's
  abode!

F Against thy course runs the opposing tide,
 And waves of trouble cast thy hopes aside.
G A modest competence thy lot will be;
 But richer joys than wealth are stored for thee.
H Take heed! take heed! a strange transforming
  doom
 May fix thy love, but never let it bloom.
J Be not too rash—nor leap the Bridge of Love,
 Leaving fond eyelids, moist with tears, above.
K What do'st thou on the house-top? do not steal
 Thy love, but win by dutiful appeal!
L A barren path this way thy footsteps tread;
 Thy heart will soon grow cold, thy love be fled.
M Thou hast a friend can help thy onward way—
 And such a friend will ne'er thy trust betray.
Œ Joy! thou hast reached, at length, the wedding
  ring;
 Let white-robed maidens orange blossoms
  bring;
 Oh may your years of happy wedlock be
 Bright as your hopes, and from misgivings free!

* See the "Story of the Willow-Pattern Plate," Pp 124, 151, VOL. I.,

By 1849 when *The Family Friend* published "The Story of the Common Willow-Pattern Plate," the design had become the stereotype of China in most western minds. It was a household feature as no other china pattern had—or has—ever been. This careful explanation of the "picture," thus, had a wide appeal and a ready audience among Victorian readers.

The story which J. B. L. wrote and illustrated with parts of the plate design was about Koong-se (notice the slight variation from the rhyme's name for the heroine), who was in love with her mandarin father's former secretary. Determined to keep them apart, her father had a fence built around his estate and a suite of rooms constructed over the water so that he could keep her there, under constant observation from the main house. Nevertheless, the lovers managed to communicate by way of a coconut-shell boat carried by the tide moving in and out under Koong-se's luxurious prison.

Responding to a plea from Koong-se, Chang disguised himself as a beggar and entered the mandarin's house to rescue his love, who had been betrothed to a cruel Ta-jin or duke. Koong-se gave Chang the casket of jewels the Ta-jin had paid as her dowry, and they ran out of the house. Unfortunately, the drunken mandarin, who had been celebrating with the Ta-jin, saw their departure and ran after them. On the willow pattern plate they can be seen on the bridge: Koong-se carrying a distaff, a sign of womanhood; Chang with the box of jewels; and the mandarin brandishing a whip in his rage.

The lovers escaped to the home of Koong-se's former handmaiden and were married in a secret ceremony. When the mandarin's soldiers came to the house in search of them, Koong-se and Chang fled through the back window onto a boat. This little vessel took them to a new life on a small island far away. In the years that followed, they developed the once-barren island into an agricultural paradise. Chang, resuming his early literary interests, wrote an agricultural treatise which made him famous throughout the land, but tragically the treatise revealed their whereabouts to the vengeful Ta-jin. With a large party of soldiers,

British earthenware willow plate, c. 1880. From the collection of the author.

he attacked the island and killed Chang. To avoid capture, Koong-se set their house on fire and perished in the flames. According to J. B. L., the story ends thus:

> The gods— (so runs the tale)—cursed the duke for his cruelty with a foul disease, with which he went down to his grave unfriended and unpitied . . . ; — but in pity to Koong-se and her lover they were transformed into two immortal doves, emblems of the constancy which had rendered them beautiful in life, and in death undivided.[5]

In the United States, this story was printed separately for the juvenile trade in 1888. Taken directly from *The Family Friend* text, *The Story of a China Plate* was "arranged and illustrated" by Clara Winslow Weeks. Printed in blue ink with a circular plate-like format, it was handsomely ornamented with drawings of selected pieces of blue willow.[6] In 1913 this book was issued again, this time by the Trow Press of New York. Earlier, in 1897, *The Family Friend* story had been published as a sales-promotion pamphlet by Tiffany's of New York for its specially commissioned willow pattern dinnerware by Booth's of England. In this publication the text was preceded with the statement: "Messrs. Tiffany & Co. have been unable to ascertain the author's name."[7]

In England *The Family Friend* text, with slight modifications, has been in print continually since 1922, at least when the De La More Press published it with an introduction by Alexander Moring, as no. 8 in the St. George Series. After World War II, London's Richards Press kept it available for both tourist and home trade.[8] In 1977 John Baker, Publisher, 35 Bedford Row, London, was the proprietor of the Moring edition.[9]

Meanwhile, in 1923 the willow plate had provided the motif for a Nancy Drew–type novel entitled *Kitty's Chinese Garden,* by Joan Leslie. Before leaving her Twickenham home to go with her doctor father to live in Pekin, China, Kitty Clavering studied a blue willow plate. After reviewing the *Family Friend* plot, she added: "I'd like to get into a willow-plate garden. We had an operetta of Aladdin at school, and I daubed a willow-pattern back-scene. But that was blue and white. A real garden would have all the colours—real willow, real bridge, real water, and real little house with one, two, three twisty roofs on top. I do hope we shall find a willow-plate garden—somewhere—somewhere."[10]

She found just that. In China, as the jacket copy reads:

> she meets a mysterious old Chinaman, who, on the grounds of gratitude for Dr. Clavering's services, leaves to Kitty a real Chinese house and garden—just like a garden on a willow-pattern plate. Afterwards it turns out that the old gentleman is not a Chinaman at all—he is a Clavering, a great-uncle of Kitty's, who had not been heard of for some thirty years. Before Kitty comes into her property many exciting things happen, among them a fire in which she nearly loses her life.

The story ends happily with Kitty and her boyfriend "in the willow-plate garden . . . sitting on the ascent of the Chinese bridge."[11]

As Kitty's reference indicates, the pattern had made its stage debut. In 1901 it had been used as the backdrop for a comic operetta entitled "The Willow Pattern" produced at the Savoy Theatre in London; this, however, was intended as primarily adult entertainment.[12] In 1931 Samuel French, Inc., in New York, published in its One-Act Plays Series "The Willow Plate" by Florence Ryerson and Colin C. Clements, a play ideal for juveniles. Seventeen years later, Samuel French, Ltd., in London, brought out Eric Willing's "Willow Pattern: A Chinese Legend." The author's note concerning the setting suggested: "It is not necessary to construct a faithful replica of the traditional Willow Pattern Plate, though at the producer's option, the proscenium might carry out the Willow Pattern motif in shades of blue and white." He then gave technical lighting instructions on how to achieve "traditional blue."[13]

In 1940 Leslie Thomas was responsible for *The Story of the Willow Plate, Adapted from the Chinese Legend,* published by William Morrow and Company. The illustrations, done by Thomas, were often enlarged portions of the willow design with details filled in. This adaptation of the story forsook Victorian language

Koong-se and Chang being pursued by her irate father. From *The Story of the Willow Plate,* adapted and illustrated by Leslie Thomas. Copyright 1940 by Leslie Thomas. Used by permission of William Morrow & Company.

and was intended to appeal to children from four years of age.[14]

Also in 1940 appeared Doris Gates's Newbery Honor Book *Blue Willow,* a highly romanticized, *Grapes of Wrath,* young people's story about Janey, a daughter of an Okie family, whose most prized possession—which had belonged to her great-great-grandmother—was "a blue willow plate, and in its pattern of birds and willows and human figures it held a story that for Janey never grew old."[15] The story it told was the *Family Friend* version in simplified form. Like Kitty, Janey found her dream garden and house—though Janey's was in Texas, an adobe house beneath a large willow tree, a location which gave the illustrator, Paul Lantz, some pains to create the design of the willow pattern.

Efforts to deal with the willow pattern in verse exhibit a wide range of quality. There are the rich, related areas of folk balladry and children's rhyme. An example of the former is an "Old Staffordshire Song":

> Two pigeons flying high,
> Chinese vessels sailing by:
> Weeping willows hanging o'er,
> Bridge with three men, if not four:

> Chinese temples, there they stand,
> Seem to take up all the land:
> Apple trees with apples on,
> A pretty fence to end my Song.[16]

Paralleling this is a striking nineteenth-century child's rhyme which Mrs. Alice Calcott Edwards, ninety years of age in 1979, learned in her youth from her English parents:

> Two swallows flying high,
> A little boat a-passing by,
> A little church that looks so fair;
> Twice a week we worship there.
> Wooden bridge, with willows over;
> Three little men a-going to Dover.
> Chinese mansion, this tree's handsome:
> Here dwell King George and his wife,
> Lord and Lady of the mansion.[17]

This is a remarkable anglicanization of the design, the concluding lines referring to George IV's Royal Pavilion in Brighton, the culmination of chinoiserie in England.

There is the inevitable playful doggerel, characterized by A. M. Burgess's *History of the Willow Pattern*, privately printed in 1904. Here the oriental trappings are totally ignored in favor of the gothic romance aspects of the story, including a castle.

> Now in it [the castle] there dwelt an old, gouty lord
> With a beautiful daughter 'twas said he adored.
> There were many who called him a greedy old elf,
> For keeping the maiden all to himself.
>
> There lived in the castle besides the last two,
> A nice, handsome fellow—they called him Andrew,
> Who wrote my lord's letters—his whims understood,
> But made love to the maiden whenever he could.[18]

Finally, a rather distinctive collection of poetry dates from the nineteenth century, such as Andrew Lang's "Ballade of Blue China" and Dorothy Parkin-Bell's "Willow Pattern," written some eighty years apart but each telling the same *Family Friend* story.[19] Included in this category are several anonymous works. One piece, a poem of more than three hundred lines, concludes:

> And though all this happened so long ago
> In the Flowery Land, they still can show
> The willow tree, where Chang used to go
>   To meet the Mandarin's daughter.
>
> And often yet do the poets sing
> How the two to their island home still cling,
> For the doves are forever upon the wing
>   Above the shining water.[20]

The most recent poetry addition to the willow pattern canon is in Veryl Marie Worth's *The Legend of Willow Pattern*, a thirty-six page compendium containing an assortment of illustrations and lore relating to the design. Featured is a twenty-three page anonymous verse rendering of Koong-Shee's story with original art work by June Twitchell McAtree. Beneath drawings of willow ware containing food, the text declares:

> Whatever the food you serve, daughter,
> Romance enters into the feast,
> If you only pay heed to the legend,
> On the old China ware plate from the East.[21]

Of all uses of the willow pattern in children's literature, there is probably none more surprising than its appearance as the subject for a successful coloring book in England in 1942. As one of the titles in the Powell Perry Colour Book Series, it was available in both octavo and quarto sizes. This particular item, illustrated by Guy Rodden, was reissued in 1944. The children were left to determine for themselves whether they would cling to traditional blues and whites or be adventuresome with their colors, as some potters have occasionally been with the pattern through the last two hundred years.

The unique relationship between the design and children's literature is perhaps best epitomized in Hans Christian Anderson's "The Sandman." On Saturday night, instead of telling young

Hjalmar a story as he had done on previous evenings, the Sandman
opened his magic umbrella over Hjalmar's bed and showed him
a story:

> Suddenly the umbrella looked like a Chinese bowl. Inside it
> there was a whole world: blue trees and blue bridges, with

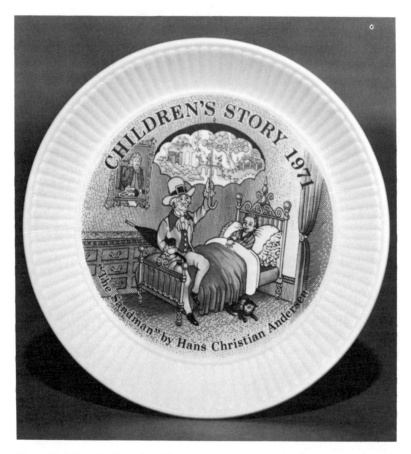

Hans Christian Andersen's "The Sandman," using the pursuit-on-the-bridge
portion of the willow design as the "umbrella story," was the subject of this
1971 Wedgwood plate, now much sought after by collectors. Photograph provided by Wedgwood.

little Chinese men and women standing on them and nodding their heads at Hjalmar.[22]

This scene was the subject of Wedgwood's 1971 plate in its Series of Children's Stories for Young Collectors, using the bridge and the neighboring sections of the blue willow pattern as the umbrella story.

But surely in our time the ultimate test of the impact of a children's story is its adaptation to commercial fantasy—such as we find in the stories developed into life-simulating fantasy by Disneyland and Disney World. In this area the willow pattern scored early: in 1936 in Preston Park, Brighton, England, the willow pattern was created in real life for the pleasure of the public. There, in natural color during the day and under specially designed lights at night, local residents, day-trippers, and tourists are given the opportunity to become a part of the pattern.[23]

Notes

The basic research for this paper was made possible by a grant from the National Endowment for the Humanities.

1. J. B. L., "The Story of the Common Willow-Pattern Plate," *The Family Friend*, 1 (1849), 124. The text is on pp. 124–27, 151–54. No conclusive identification of the author can be given, but initials, style, and other, slighter evidence suggest that he may have been John Baxter Langley, whose *A Literary Sandwich: A Collection of Miscellaneous Writing* was published in London in 1855.

2. *Chinoiserie: The Vision of Cathay* (London: John Murray, 1961), p. 141.

3. In 1838 Mark Lemon in "The Celebrated Wedgwood Hieroglyph, Commonly Called the Willow Pattern," *Bentley's Magazine*, 3 (1838), 61–65, assumed that his readers knew the design by heart or had a plate nearby to follow his original version exploring the "action" of the story.

In 1844 one of the most amusing versions came from *Punch*, which, in a separately published parody of the catalogue of American Nathan Dunn's Chinese Collection then on exhibit in London, explained: "Perhaps, however, the earliest record that we have of Chinese customs is to be found in the willow-pattern plate. From this it would appear that the Celestials are in the habit of fishing from the tops of bridges, with bait something like oranges, by means of lines not long enough to reach the water. It follows, therefore, that the Chinese fishes, if they are ever caught, must be in the habit of springing out of the water, and seizing in their mouths the bait, that is held at a distance of several feet above them." *Punch's Guide to the Chinese Collection* (London, 1844), p. 6.

In the southern United States an oral tradition with an English background says that Chang was a musician and the object he is seen carrying is an enchanted nightingale.

Ralph and Terry Kovel speculated that "one Chinese legend . . . may be the true story of the willow pattern. A political group that tried to overthrow the government circulated the dishes to remind the people of their aims. The three figures represented three Buddhas, past, present, and future. The doves were the souls of those slain in battle, and the pagoda was a symbol of shelter for escaping monks. There are no early Chinese examples of the design with the figures, but the legend claims they were all destroyed by the government." *Know Your Antiques* (New York: Crown Publishers, 1978), p. 21.

4.   Quoted from Ada Walker Camehl, *The Blue-China Book* (New York: E. P. Dutton, 1916), p. 287.

5.   *The Family Friend*, 1, 154.

6.   New York: Albert B. King, 1888. Included in *Wright American Fiction, 1876–1900* [Microfilm] Research Publications, Inc., No. 5846, Reel W-21.

7.   *The Legend of the Willow-Pattern Plate*, p. 1.

8.   My copy is dated 1963. The manager of the Westminster Cathedral Bookshop told me in 1969 that this was one of the shop's most popular items, especially among American tourists.

9.   The fifth printing, dated 1975, by Adam and Charles Black, London, was priced at £1.75.

10.   London: Oxford Univ. Press, 1923, p. 68.

11.   *Kitty's Chinese Garden*, p. 276.

12.   Libretto by Basil Hood, music by Cecil Cook.

13.   "Traditional blue," Willings indicated, would result from a blending of lavender, steel blue, and middle blue. For spots he advised using steel blue, for the bridge and acting area lavender (pp. 26–28).

14.   In 1977 the Thomas version was still available in a 1969 paperback edition from Schocken Books.

15.   New York: Viking Press, 1940, pp. 23, 26–28.

16.   Quoted from *The Story of the Willow Pattern Plate* (London: Richards Press, 1963), p. 5.

17.   Quoted from *The Willow Notebook*, no. 9 (Sept. 1979), p. 2.

18.   [United States]: n.p., n.d., n. pag. The quotation is taken from the New York Public Library copy: P156088.

19.   Lang's poem was written c. 1880 during a resurgence of interest in orientalia, especially things Japanese. Lang's contemporary Max Beerbohm—tongue-in-cheek—wrote in his essay "1880": "Tea grew quite cold while the guests were praising the Willow Pattern of its cup" (*The Works of Max Beerbohm* [New York: Charles Scribner's Sons, 1896], p. 47). "Ballade of Blue China" is included in *XXXII Ballades in Blue China* (London: Kegan Paul, Trench & Co., 1933), pp. 55–56. Dorothy Parkin-Bell's poem is a contemporary work. *Willow Pattern and Other Verses* (Bristol, Eng.: Burleigh Press, 1966), pp. 1–6.

20.   *The Story of the Willow Plate* ([United States]: n.p., n.d.), p. 24. Probably of British origin, this poem has been reprinted by The Mountain Homestead, Hiwassee, GA, from "a very old copy" found by Mrs. Jane K. Head. Letter from Mrs. Head of The Mountain Homestead, 13 December 1978.

21.   Oakridge, OR: Fact Book Co., 1980, pp. 11–12. The syndicated column

"Hints from Heloise" received a request for a reprint of the "delightful story about the design on 'Blue Willow' dishes" which had appeared in the column "a few years ago." The columnist provided the *Family Friend* version in condensed form. My specific reference is from the *Fayetteville* [NC] *Times*, 18 Dec. 1978, p. 13-A.

22. *The Complete Fairy Tales and Stories,* trans. Erik Christian Haugaard (Garden City, NY: Doubleday, 1974), p. 185.

23. See my "England's Willow-Pattern Garden," *The Willow Notebook,* No. 18 (March 1981), p. 4.

Lear, Limericks, and Some Other Verse Forms

William Harmon

The limerick—in its familiar, five-line form with a rhyme scheme of *aabba*—was neither invented by nor perfected by Edward Lear, who wrote, in fact, very few verses that qualify technically as limericks. Lear's "nonsenses" share the limerick's general metric and rhythmic scheme: two lines of anapestic trimeter, two lines of anapestic dimeter, a fifth line of anapestic trimeter; but Lear's usual rhyme scheme and his arrangement of the lines do not meet the standards of the perfect limerick.

It is not that he lacked a model. Perfect limericks existed before Lear's birth in 1812, and he is known to have been familiar with volumes that appeared in the early 1820s: *The History of Sixteen Wonderful Old Women* (1821) and *Ancedotes and Adventures of Fifteen Gentlemen* (c. 1822).[1] To the latter Lear gave credit for his first introduction to the form, and he singled out one verse for particular attention, even drawing three sketches in illustration (the text and drawings in the original volume are anonymous, but the artwork has been attributed to Robert Cruikshank):

> There was a sick man of Tobago
> Liv'd long on rice-gruel and sago;
> But at last, to his bliss,
> The physician said this—
> "To a roast leg of mutton you may go."[2]

The verse was printed as five lines, and it is rhymed perfectly; that is to say, it is a classic limerick in form. Never, to my knowledge, did Lear even attempt this exact format. He did, it is true, keep to the habit of ending his first line with a place-name (customarily a provincial or colonial place), but he seems never to have construed the stanza as one of five lines. Even in his sketches for "There was a sick man of Tobago," Lear combined the third and fourth lines as one, a practice followed quite consistently in his *Nonsense* books. Along with the adherence to the four-line format (sometimes in Lear's sketches reduced to three or two), Lear followed the format of *some* of the verses in the volumes from the 1820s, whereby the last line, instead of rhyming, merely varies the first line and still ends with the same word. All the verses that I have seen from *The History of Sixteen Wonderful Old Women* do this:

> There was an old woman of Leeds
> Who spent all her time in good deeds;
>   She worked for the poor
>   Till her fingers were sore,
> This pious old woman of Leeds.[3]

Of the verses in *Ancedotes and Adventures of Fifteen Gentlemen,* some rhyme perfectly (as we have seen in "There was a sick man of Tobago," which formally resembles "A tailor, who sailed from Quebec"), but others fall back on variation and repetition:

> As a little fat man of Bombay
> Was smoking one very hot day,
>   A bird called a snipe
>   Flew away with his pipe,
> Which vexed the fat man of Bombay.[4]

Lear drew an illustration for a variant of this verse. It shows a very fat little man, but the caption (written as two long lines) calls him simply "an old man of Bombay."[5]

  Lear published about two hundred and ten of his four-line nonsenses, and in the overwhelming majority he keeps to a single rhyming practice and ends his first and fourth (last) line with the same word. In its most characteristic form, the verse begins with a line of anapestic trimeter in which a general type of character (old or young person, man, woman, or lady) is presented, with an indication of place, either general (a garden or a station, say) or specific. The second line, also of anapestic trimeter, rhymes perfectly or comically with the first and, as a rule, sets forth some eccentricity of the person presented in the first line. The third line is anapestic tetrameter with an internal rhyme linking the second and fourth stressed syllable. The fourth line returns to the trimeter and ends with the same word as the first line. Since this format differs so much from the true limerick, and since Lear himself is not known to have used the word *limerick*, I propose that we return to his usage and call these peculiar verses *nonsenses*, as he did. He did not invent the form but he did perfect it.

By my tally, fourteen of Lear's two hundred and ten nonsenses depart from his usual scheme of rhyme and repetition, and all but two of these are in his first *Book of Nonsense* (1846). All are printed as four lines. In ten variants, the last line repeats the end of the *second* line, as here:

> There was a Young Lady of Hull,
> Who was chased by a virulent Bull;
> But she seized on a spade, and called out—"Who's afraid!"
> Which distracted that virulent Bull.[6]

In one of these variations, the line-break is eccentric:

> There was an Old Man who said,
> "How,—shall I flee from this horrible Cow?
> I will sit on this stile, and continue to smile,
> Which may soften the heart of that Cow."[7]

And only four of Lear's nonsenses, all in the volume of 1846, satisfy the rhyme scheme of the perfect limerick. One has to do with a general place ("There was an Old Man of the Coast"); the remaining three stand out as peculiarly unusual and also, I think, peculiarly distinguished:

> There was an Old Man who supposed,
> That the street door was partially closed;
> But some very large rats, ate his coats and his hats,
> While that futile old gentleman dozed.

> There was a Young Lady whose eyes,
> Were unique as to color and size;
> When she opened them wide, people all turned aside,
> And started away in surprise.

> There was an Old Lady whose folly,
> Induced her to sit in a holly;
> Whereon by a thorn, her dress being torn,
> She quickly became melancholy.[8]

On this subject, I must disagree somewhat with the judgment of Herman W. Liebert in two particulars. He says that "Lear made the limerick widely popular,"[9] but it is clear that Lear was dealing in a different form, although the proper limerick was available and possibly popular even before his birth. What remains popular is a form of verse that Lear, with his own utterly eccentric genius, altered beyond easy recognition—a form of verse, moreover, that seems to have survived or escaped Lear's adjustments of its essential nature. "Since Lear," Liebert continues, "the limerick has become a vehicle for wit rather than for nonsense. The *witty* limerick naturally demands a 'punch' in the last line. But Lear was writing nonsense, and rightly preferred, for his last line, an altered repetition of the first."[10] We are all in Liebert's debt for his sensitive and sympathetic annotations of *Lear in the Original,* but I must differ with virtually every idea in the sentence I have just quoted. The distinction between wit and nonsense is by no means prismatic. By "nonsense" Lear seems to have meant "trifle" rather than something illogical, contradictory, or meaningless. And, whatever Lear meant, I do not think that we can get away with aligning wit and punch on one side and nonsense and no-punch on the other. Besides, Lear wrote verses with three kinds of last line, and one seems as nonsensical as another.

Lear's greatness comes from other kinds of verse, especially the longer lyrics and haunting songs: "The Owl and the Pussy-Cat," "The Dong with a Luminous Nose," "The Pelican Chorus," "The Pobble Who Has No Toes," and perhaps a half-dozen others. His nonsenses are much less witty and much less "nonsensical," and they are certainly much less important in the history of children's verse or light verse in general.

His apparent belief that the four-line format is proper remains interesting, however, and I want to conclude by both coming forward into the present and going back into the centuries before

Lear. Since his death in 1888, only two new verse-forms related
to the limerick have enjoyed any celebrity. The earlier of the
two is the clerihew, invented by Edmund Clerihew Bentley (a
distinguished lawyer who also invented *Trent's Last Case*), almost
as though in perpendicular opposition to the general trend of the
limerick. In the limerick, we find an imaginary person put into
a rhyme-word place and more or less chastised by a regular verse
form. In the clerihew, we normally find a real person whose name
forms the rhyme word for some deliberately irregular verses, which
rhyme *aabb* but should not follow a metrical scheme. Here is an
attempt of my own:

> Cesare Borgia
> Would have preferred the situation in Georgia
> Before the Emancipation
> Proclamation.

In their classic forms, both the limerick and the clerihew involve a rhyme with a proper name—a place in the former, a person's name in the latter. I do not know why should this be the
case, except that both verse-forms seem aimed at the exposure of
ridiculous or eccentric behavior, a kind of "singular" conduct
displayed in language by names (the notion of the "singular name"
has been explored by John Stuart Mill in a sober work on logic
and by T. S. Eliot in a frivolous poem about cats). Whatever the
causes of this persistent name-concentration, it is found in yet
another light-verse form, the delightful double dactyl invented
by John Hollander and Anthony Hecht. This form consists of
two four-line stanzas, each made up of four lines of dactyllic
dimeter with a rhyme between the fourth lines of the two stanzas
(these lines are slightly truncated, lacking the two final unstressed
syllables). The first line is usually two dactyllic nonsense words
(as in the title of the definitive collection, *Jiggery Pokery*); the
second line is a name, like "Benjamin Harrison," that scans as two
dactyls. Some later line, normally the second or third of the second stanza, must consist of a single six-syllable word that scans
as two dactyls. In the best double dactyl that I know, George

Starbuck's "Monarch of the Sea," two of these demanding requirements are doubled: the name consists of *four* dactyls, and
there are *two* six-syllable dactyllic words in the second stanza:

> "Jiminy Whillikers,
> Admiral Samuel
> Eliot Morison,
> Where is your ship?"

> "I, sir, am HMS
> Historiography's
> Disciplinarian.
> Button your lip."[11]

Here we have another departure from the limerick model—perpendicular in a dimension other than that of the clerihew, one
might say. Here, as in the clerihew, we rely on a real person's
name, but, as in the limerick, there is strict regularity of rhythm
and meter. The dactyl, we should note, is the opposite of the
limerick's favored anapest. Each in its own way, Lear's nonsense,
Bentley's clerihew, and the double dactyl varies the basic limerick
format.

Despite the different styles of printing, I believe that the fundamental and original form is a matter of four lines. The rhythm
may be anapestic, dactyllic, or anomalous, but, as in virtually all
English poetry since the fourteenth century, the primordial foot
is iambic. Furthermore, as in almost all musical forms, the four
lines each contain space for four stresses, although the inclusion
of a pause or rest can reduce the number of stresses to three. I
speculate that a number of changes have been suffered by the
primal form, but it persists in its original shape in such poems
as Blake's "London," which is four stanzas of four lines each, with
each line containing four stresses. This is the syllabic form called
"8.8.8.8" or "long measure" in hymnals. In the 8.6.8.6 form it is
called "common measure" and is very close to the standard "ballad
measure" and the "fourteeners" of the sixteenth century. In the
6.6.8.6 form ("short measure"), it is the same as the "poulter's

measure" that was the most popular verse-form in English for some years in the sixteenth century; it seems to be the original of certain nursery rhymes ("Hickory Dickory, Dock," for example) and for limericks as well. It may seem treacherous to suggest such a thing, but any nonsense or limerick can be sung to a short-measure tune like that of "Blest Be the Tie that Binds."

> The limerick's story is clear;
> It only begins to seem queer
> If you worry betimes
> About the sad rhymes
> Of that runcible gentleman, Lear.

Notes

1. See Iona and Peter Opie, eds., *The Oxford Dictionary of Nursery Rhymes* (Oxford: Clarendon, 1952), pp. 91, 267, 329, 400, 407–08.

2. Opies, p. 407 and plate XIX. See also Herman W. Liebert, *Lear in the Original: Drawings and Limericks by Edward Lear for his "Book of Nonsense"* (New York: Kraus, 1975), pp. 17, 52–55.

3. Opies, p. 267.

4. Ibid., p. 91.

5. Liebert, pp. 36–37. Liebert does not note that this is very close to a verse in *Anecdotes and Adventures of Fifteen Gentlemen.*

6. *The Complete Nonsense of Edward Lear,* ed. Holbrook Johnson (New York: Dover, 1951), p. 39.

7. Ibid., p. 38.

8. Ibid., pp. 16, 17, 31.

9. Liebert, p. 17.

10. Ibid., p. 18.

11. *The Oxford Book of American Light Verse,* ed. William Harmon (New York: Oxford University Press, 1979), p. 517. A slightly different version may be found in Starbuck's *Desperate Measures* (Boston: Godine, 1978). The poem is copyright © 1978 by George Starbuck, reprinted by permission of David R. Godine, Publisher, Inc.

The Poetry of Halfdan Rasmussen

Marilyn Nelson Waniek and Pamela Lee Espeland

Born in Copenhagen in 1915, Halfdan Rasmussen was educated at the Roskilde vocational high school and the international school in Helsingør. He is the author of one novel and thirty-one volumes of poetry—fifteen of these written for children—and the recipient of many literary prizes. His *Tosserier* (Nonsense), a book of verse for adults, was reprinted seven times in as many years, evidence of the fact that Rasmussen's work is as popular among adults as it is among children. His poems for children have been set to music and recorded; they can be heard on Danish television programs, on the radio, in schools, and in the streets. The more-than-casual tourist in Denmark may notice Halfdan Rasmussen posters on the walls of pubs in Tivoli Gardens and illustrations (by Ib Spang Olsen) from *Halfdan's ABC* (Carlsens illustrationsforlaget, 1967) for sale in Den Permanente, and he may well leave Denmark whistling a merry melody whose lyrics he cannot remember, but which begins, "God morgen, sol!"

Rasmussen's musical lyrics for children capture some of the nonsense English-speaking readers expect in nursery rhymes as well as some of the more serious questions and concerns of young children. Rasmussen's poems are populated by a world of interesting, sensitive, silly, and sometimes very Danish children. All Danes know and love Kasper Himmelspjaet, Nanett, Fraekke Frederik, and Nikolaj. Rasmussen's children value friendship, family unity, and the brotherhood of man; they believe in love and the power of the imagination; they laugh at man's idea that he can achieve mastery over the mystery of nature; they are naively interested in the human body and its functions; and they respond strongly to the old ideals of truth and beauty. Rasmussen is a romantic, but he does not idealize the children about whom he writes. Some of them are naughty, selfish, boasting. Yet there remains in each of

them an air of innocence which allows young readers to smile
at them and shake their heads.

Because his tight formal verse relies to a great extent on sound-
patterns, it is attractive to young children, easy for them to memo-
rize, and fun to sing and recite. The sound-patterns, however, make
Rasmussen's verse difficult—sometimes impossible—to translate. The
assonance of "vaskebjørnens børnebørn" is lost in "the raccoon's
grandchildren"; the alliteration of "Norske nisse nyser ikke" is lost
in "Norwegian elves don't sneeze"; the charming pun of "staa og
tisserpaa en tissemyre" is almost impossible to translate into an
English as innocent as Rasmussen's Danish (our offering is "stand
and wee-wee on some wee, wee ants"). It may be because of this
difficulty that so few of his poems for children are available in
good English translations.

The following translations of poems from *Børnerim* (Det Schoen-
bergske Forlag, 1964) are close to Rasmussen's own original meanings, music and sound patterns, with the exception of the meter
of "way out in the forest" and the name of "Little painter Rasmussen." As translators we wished to capture Rasmussen's wit,
charm, and delicacy and to retain the possibility of singing the
translations to the music which has been composed for the Danish
poems. We find Rasmussen's voice lyrical, his tone not condescending to children, his music delicate and lilting. We are pleased
to introduce him here and to help him make his work better
known in the English-speaking world.

> An inventor named Benton
> from Inventorland
> invents more inventions
> than anyone can.
>
> He's invented fork-mittens,
> invisible pants,
> and blue bedroom slippers
> for house-elephants.

And soon he'll invent
some tree-coats made of leather,
so trees can stay outside
in all sorts of weather!

Good morning, sun! Good morning, morning sun!
You shine on trees and flowers and everyone,
and down on Jens and Karl, those smarty-pants,
who stand and wee-wee on some wee, wee ants.

But wee ants aren't for boys to wee-wee on,
and so I shout, "Hey, stop your naughty fun!
And shame on you for standing over here,
wee-weeing with your wee wee ant-wee-weers!"

Here inside my forehead
lives a little man.
He can eat canned peaches
still inside the can.

He can do a headstand,
somersault and twist.
He can hit big grown-up men—
even with his fist.

He can drive a fire truck.
He can smoke a pipe.
He can walk on water
and stay up late at night.

He can spit long distances,
and say words that are horrid!
But he only does it
here, inside my forehead.

Just inside my auntie's womb
is a little nursery room.
She will soon become the mother
of one twin, and then another.

When I listen with my ear
to her tummy, I can hear
two small babies, very chummy,
there inside my auntie's tummy.

Every mother has a womb
that was once a nursery room.
If you don't become a nun,
maybe yours, too, will be one!

Little painter Rasmussen
surprised a watching crowd
by jumping off a church's spire
and landing on a cloud.

To little painter Rasmussen
the sky was much too gray,
so he took his brushes out
to paint a sunny day.

Little painter Rasmussen
became the sun's best friend:
The sun sets in the west at night
with painter Rasmussen.

My little brown-skinned dolly
sleeps beside my head
My yellow Chinese dolly
also shares my bed.

I have hushed my children
with a lullaby,
kissed their little faces,
told them not to cry.

We are all one people,
all one family.
Sleep, my yellow brother!
Brown sister, sleep with me!

Snowman Frost and Lady Thaw
one bright day in Omaha
found a bench and sat to talk
of love, while resting from their walk.

Said Snowman Frost, a little shy,
"May I kiss you, by and by?"
But, since Lady Thaw was warm,
she melted off his whole right arm!

When he kissed her rosy ear,
he began to disappear.
When he kissed her on the face,
he was gone without a trace!

On a bench in Omaha
sits poor lonely Lady Thaw.
Snowman Frost is melted up—
She can hold him in a cup!

The elf puts on his winter coat,
puts his winter hat on,
finds a muffler for his throat
in his drawer—puts that on,
fills his pockets full of mice,
hears how the cold wind blows,
and then puts on an ice cream cone
to warm his chilly nose!

Way out in the forest
the trolls sat on the ground
counting off the minutes
'til Christmas rolled around.

When December twenty-fifth came
they all jumped to their feet
And yelled, "Hurray! It's Christmas!
Let's hurry up and eat!"

They ran into their barracks,
grabbed bowl and spoon and cup
and gobbled so many goodies
their tummies all blew up!

But then they found the presents
they'd gotten from their mummies—
a lot of king-size packages
of bandages for tummies!

          You can pat
          my dog for a penny,
          and my horse
          for an egg and a half.
          You can pat
          my favorite aunt
          if you give me
          your grandad's moustache.

          You can pat
          my goldfish's hair
          for an apple
          that's ripened just right.
          If you pat
          my lion in there,
          just promise
          you'll pat it *real light!*

Princess Red Wing: Keeper of the Past

John Cech

She bends over the old, upright piano in the corner of the room, slowly finding the chords to "Majestic Sweetness Sits Enthroned" in the hymnal before her. She sings softly to herself. This is the song of the morning, every morning. "I wouldn't think of starting my day without a song of prayer," she says, "like my ancestors did when they opened the door to their wigwam and greeted the day." Her face is creased from many years of those days—84, to be exact —and from their burdens. For it has never been easy for the Indian in America since the coming of the Europeans, and it was not easy for her, growing up proud of her heritage, active and committed to Indian causes in an America where her people were still regarded with contempt as savages. "But the Indian was never in a hurry," she says, her intense, clear eyes sparkling. Now the white man comes to her, for a story. Perhaps because he, unlike her, has lost his past and, through her, hopes to find it.

It happens to be a crisp fall morning, and Princess Red Wing of the Seven Crescents of the Royal House of Pokanoket is at home at Dovecrest. Dovecrest settles in a wooded hollow near a brook in the sparsely populated countryside of southwestern Rhode Island: there is an immaculately tended trading post and restaurant, the Tomaquag Museum of American Indian Artifacts, and living quarters for Red Wing and Ferris (Roaring Bull) and Eleanor (Pretty Flower) Dove and their family. Though Red Wing is not related by blood to the Doves, they have adopted each other. She is a loved, revered member of their community, someone whose age and stature are unquestionably respected. Together she and Roaring Bull preside over many of the ceremonies held at Dovecrest and throughout New England by the New England Council of Chiefs—he as one of its heads, she as its Squaw Sachem.

You can reach Dovecrest by the paved roads that run through Hope Valley or Wyoming, Rhode Island, and veer north to Arcadia State Park. Or else you can take the old Indian trail that cuts south off Route 165, opposite the white country church, and snakes into the woods. "It's quicker," Red Wing advises. "The Indian always knew the best way to go." Deep in the heart of these woods it would not be a surprise to round a bend and find the spirit of one of her ancestors waiting. This is Indian country. Don't be deceived by the gas stations, convenience stores, farms, and villages that you pass. The rights to this land lie deeper than deeded ownership; they remain with those who keep its history and spirit alive. That means the Indian—the Narragansetts, Wampanoags, Nipmunks, Mohawks, and others who have intermarried and settled in southern New England. And that means Princess Red Wing, who preserves the stories and the old ways, carrying them into the present with an eager generosity and passionate, tireless enthusiasm. The lore, legends, ancedotes, and myths are as natural to her as speech itself. After all, she *is* the mythologist: one of the few remaining readers of "the Great Unwritten Book" of her people.

Red Wing will launch into a cycle of stories, hardly pausing for breath, as she offers from the Indian perspective the reasons for the way things are. What better, more poetic, or perhaps more memorable way to explain the flinty, vexing rocks of New England than through the following story, which, though "unscientific," is more powerful than any geology lesson:

> You see all these stones that grow in the field. . . . You know when you are making a garden somewheres, you gotta dig up the stones, everywhere—there's a rock here and a rock there. Well, you see, the Great Spirit, when he was lonesome, He decided to make Himself a man. So He took a piece of stone and carved it into a nice man. When He got it done, it was so cold, He couldn't love it. An' he wouldn't love Him. So He took His great mallet and smashed it, and it scattered all over southern New England. So today, whenever you're trying to make up a garden, you've got to dig up the stones, and every stone's a piece of the man the Great Spirit couldn't

love. So He decided to make His man out of something that grew. Out of a plant, because it has its nourishments from the earth, and its limbs go up this way in praise to his Maker. That's why when the Indian prays, he puts up his arms like that, like the limbs of a tree.[1]

Over tea in the restaurant at Dovecrest, I mention the brilliant leaves which are at their peak that day. Did I know the story of the leaves, she asked, in her pronounced New England accent? My lack of knowledge does not surprise her; few people do, and so she will recall it, patiently and willingly, for the thousandth time:

You know when you were a child, you used to gather the autumn leaves together and jump in the piles and have a good time in them. Well, the Indian children used to play in the autumn leaves also, and they were saddened when they fell to the earth and the snow covered them and they died. 'N' they said to the Great Spirit, "Oh, I wish they could live forever." So the Great Spirit decided, yes, He would make some of them live. Out of the yellow leaves He made the goldfinches. Out of the red ones He made the cardinals, and out of the brown ones the sparrows—and so forth. He made many of them to live. And then the children were happy because they had the birds and some of the leaves were still alive. But those birds were very, very sad because they did not have a song. So the wise old owl called a council, and they sat together in a circle, and he told them that to get a song they must fly up to Heaven to get that song. Now, you know when you start to do something, there's always someone who says, "Me-first! Me-first! Me-first!" That'd be a crow. He went up a little ways and came back with a "Caw! Caw! Caw!" And then there's always someone who pushes up and says "Me-next! Me-next! Me-next!" Old Bluejay who went a little further up came back with a "Chirp! Chirp! Chirp!" But some of those birds were very polite, and they waited for their turn. One by one they went up to heaven and got their songs. By and by, the little meadowlark, sitting back in the circle, went up and came back with a *beautiful* song. And the little woodland thrush said, "I wish I could get a song that sweet but I do not think I can fly that high." Well, she sat right next to the great eagle. So she climbed right on his back, way up under his neck feathers, and when that great eagle started up, up, up on his great wings, there sat the little woodland thrush there at the back of his neck. He flew up as high as he could go and started down. Then she flew up and went further, up and up and up and up until she received the sweetest song from heaven. But it took her so long to get back down to the circle that when she got back, all the birds had been up already. They looked at her. She looked at them. She was so ashamed that she had cheated that she walked right out of that circle, way back into the woods, and to this day she has never come out. And if you want to hear the woodland thrush sing, you've got to go way back in the woods, and you've got to be very quiet, and you will hear the sweetest song from Heaven.[2]

Her legends, what she calls her "Just-Why" stories, form the core of her storytelling performances, whether she is speaking to a group of Girl Scouts or senior citizens or college students. At university classes in children's literature, where she has been making regular presentations for the past fifteen years, she gives perhaps her definitive performances, welcoming the students into the class with the beat of her ceremonial drum and calling out the story of the drum itself. Through this story she tries to capture the essence of the Indians' natural religion. It's the philosophy that she has spent her own lifetime celebrating and seeking to bring to others:

Boom! Boom! Boom! Boom-boom! Boom! The drum speaks. My drum's speaking to you this afternoon. When my brother says, "Whatcher—meetak!" That's how you greet an Indian. This "how" business is some slang that some white people brought in. But we don't ask people "how." When Canonicus

greeted Roger Williams he said, "Whatcher meetak." "Meetak"
means friend. So when you meet an Indian, remember its
"what" not "how."

Now I am reminded this afternoon of a young Indian that
stood on a hilltop . . . with all the glories of nature about
him. And he felt so good that his heart beat and he heard,
"One! (beats drum) One! One!" And then he realized that
everything that his eyes beheld—the high trees, the beautiful lakes, the hard rocks, the rushing waters, the green grass
beneath his feet—was a part of Mother Nature. He slept on
her bosom, he fed from her berries on the bushes, he fished
in her brook. He heard the heartbeat of Mother Nature, and
he heard, "One-two! One-two! One-two!" Then when he realized that everything that his eye beheld, even himself, was
created by a good and a great and an unseen Spirit, he heard
the heartbeat of the Creator of the universe, and he heard,
"One-two-three! One-two-three!" And as soon as he recognized his Creator, he looked inside Him and recognized his
brother, and then he heard the heartbeat of Mankind and
he heard, "One-two-three-four! One-two-three-four!" Then he
made up his drum and he beat out that same rhythm in all
his ceremonies, council meetings, thanksgiving meetings—all
are called together by the beat of the drum. When the drum
speaks the people come, but the drum only speaks when the
people are good.[3]

She plunges ahead, teaching a long-remembered—but for the
audience, new—mythology. Red Wing explains the thirteen moons
of the Indian calendar, represented by the thirteen sections of the
turtle's shell on the rattle that she carries. Then the five thanksgivings her people continue to observe are named anew. Each
has its story, and the last is offered as a corrective footnote on
the first Thanksgiving in American history.

She recounts the Indians' custom of decorating their wigwams
with colored ears of corn, offerings to the Great Spirit in whose
behalf the ears were planted. She tells again the story of the

creation of the earth, the falling from heaven of the Sky Queen, and of how the earth was built on the turtle's back to accommodate the Sky Queen and her two sons, the one who did nothing but good for mankind and the other who brought nothing but evil. Next the story of the fire; then the changing of the seasons; and finally on a lighter note, the "Just-Why" story of the rabbit, how he got his split lip and short front legs from falling out of a tree after a winter's sleep, and how he left his tail behind on a willow bush–giving him a stubby tail and us the pussywillows.

She leaps ahead in time to three "true" stories about the Indian in colonial times and of his often uneasy, frequently humorous coexistence with the white man. The first is a serious, militant allegory about the juniper trees:

You drive through the country, 'specially here in southern New England, and you see an open lot with lots of little green trees growin' up, some this big, some this big, and some this big. They are growing all over the pasture. Some call 'em junipers; some call 'em little fir trees; some call 'em spruce and what not. Well, one day, a farmer over in Rhode Island said, "I want all those trees cut down and out of my lot." Well, this Indian man working for him said, "Those trees tell where an Indian was shot or killed unnecessarily." And the farmer said, "Well, cut 'em down then! I don't want 'em in *my* lot!" So the Indian went out and he cut 'em down. And when the farmer got up the next morning, there were all those trees, all growed up again in his lot—more of 'em. So he called his servant in and said, "I thought I told you to cut down those trees." He says, "I did!" They looked out there and there were the trees. So he sent him out again to cut 'em down. The next morning the farmer got up and he looked again, and there they were, right there and more of 'em in his cow pasture. So he decided to go out and cut 'em down himself. When he got to the last one, when he cut it down, it fell over and killed him. So when you see all those trees growing up in a pasture, that's where an Indian was killed unnecessarily.[4]

The next story reveals a motif in a number of Red Wing's anecdotes in which the supposedly ignorant Indian outsmarts the white man, in a historical updating and redefinition of the Indian trickster figure, which also has parallels with the tricksters of the Uncle Remus tales:

You see, a good many people when they came over here thought that the Indian was some kind of beast or something; they didn't feel they had a mind to think for themselves, you know. And every once in awhile the Indian would work for some of these people, and one day the governor called old Indian John in and said, "If you kill that calf for us, I'll give you two shillings. So, old Indian John went out and killed the calf. Well, by and by the cook was ready to fix dinner, and she said, "I can't cook that calf laying out there in the yard." So the governor called old Indian John back and said, "I'll give you two shillings to dress it and cut it up so the cook can cook it." And he did and took his two shillings and went on. The next day he came back to the governor with two shillings in his hand and said, "No good! Can't spend!" The governor looked at them—two counterfeit shillings, and he wondered how he could have given this Indian two counterfeit shillings. So he took 'em and gave Indian John two good shillings. Well, awhile afterwards John came back with two more and says, "No good! Can't spend!" And the governor's face was red by then and he said, "How could I have given him *four* counterfeit shillings!" So he gave him two more good ones.

Well, the next day, the governor was at the village square, getting a haircut and a shave at the barber shop, and the men were all laughing about how they had warded off on old Indian John these four counterfeit shillings. Then the governor knew that Indian John had brought and warded them off on him! So he called John in and said, "I'll give you two shillings to take this note to the warden at the jail." So John took the note, and before he got to the jail he met a servant of the governor's and said to him, "I'll give you a shilling to

take this note of the governor's to the warden at the jail."
So the other fella took his shilling and went on with the
note. The note said, "Give the bearer of this note a good
flogging." So the governor's servant got the flogging—but
that man did not try to fool that Indian again.[5]

Another story in this same vein is about an Indian who "got
thirsty" during the winter and went to the farmer for whom
he worked to get a drink of cider, which the farmer gladly gave
him since he was such a good worker. After several of these trips,
the farmer thought he'd stop the Indian's unslakable thirst by
telling him that he could have all the cider he could carry away
in a basket. The Indian got the biggest basket he could find and
dipped it in the icy water of a stream until it was coated with
ice, and then he went back to the farmer's, where he filled the
basket with a winter's worth of cider, and didn't lose a drop.
    Red Wing's jokes are well-received and serve as a well-timed
relief from the otherwise serious tone of her presentation. But
they also have their point—that the Indian was no fool; that in
fact, he gave to American civilization much more than it ever
gave him. Red Wing enumerates the ways in which the Indian's
lore has been adapted by the white man—in his food, his herbals,
even in the shape of some of his buildings (Red Wing had con-
sulted years before with the designers of the quonset hut, showing
them the proper way to build that particularly Indian shelter).
She returns to recurring themes: the Indian's natural cleanliness,
expressed in his daily, ritualized bathing; the Indian's health,
recalling how the French, when they first sailed into Narragansett
Bay, were amazed to find a race of tall, strong people, remarkably
free of birth defects, at a time when one European out of five
was crippled, deformed, or retarded; the Indian's natural reverence
for life and the conservationist philosophy which pervaded his
life, demanding of him a dance to thank the spirit of whatever
animal he found it necessary to kill for food. She demonstrates
the bear dance, the deer dance, and she explains their meaning
and power: "Because when he danced this prayer dance, his whole
body and soul became a prayer to the Great Spirit, thanking Him."

And dance she does, with the whole class following her in her ceremonial headdress and elaborately beaded doeskin dress, up and down the aisles of the lecture hall. All the while she beats out the rhythm of the Great Round Dance, which is done whenever various tribes gather together and don't know one another's steps. Depending on the day she may also add her version of the Charleston, which she insists is an Indian dance, or she may teach a game dance in which the performers act out the Four Stages of Life—the hesitant first steps of the infant, the running skips of older children, the strutting of young men and women, and the limping of old people. But Red Wing herself doesn't limp. The spirit of the dance transforms her, enlivening her otherwise

Princess Red Wing leads the Great Round Dance (photograph by Evan Roklen).

stooped frame. She is eternally young again and flying triumphantly, like her name.

II

Red Wing was born on March 21, 1896, in the town of Sprague, Connecticut, near New London. Her mother was Mary Simonds of the Wampanoag Nation, a direct descendant of Simeon Simonds, the young, blue-eyed Indian who accompanied General Washington through his final campaigns and victories and who, it is believed, was the grandson of King Phillip, the Indian Massasoit who adopted the English titles of nobility and made war on the early colonies in defense of his lands, family, and traditions. To this day Red Wing carries the sign of Phillip's house, the Seven Crescents. It makes up part of the title which appears on all of her official documents with the federal government. Her title is not, however, a mere string of words which have lost their meaning, nor is it simply an ornament. Each crescent corresponds to a color, and the colors themselves blend into a cosmic rainbow. Red Wing explains its magic:

> The Seven Crescents are the insignia of the Royal House of Pokanoket. The yellow stands for the Great Spirit. The red stands for the red blood of Mankind. Together you get the orange crescent which is Life. The blue crescent is Earth, and if you add the Great Spirit to Earth, you get the Earth of Life, green with vegetation. If you add Man, which is red, to Earth, which is blue, you get purple, which is the Great Mystery.[6]

Red Wing's father, Walter Glasgo, was born to the line of Mary Sachem of the Narragansetts and was a member of the Glasgo family that established the first iron foundries in Connecticut; their iron was used to make some of the earliest railroad tracks in the state. He was a farmer, a dairyman, a horseman, a gambler, and a drinker. Red Wing insists that the latter two weaknesses never cost him jobs or caused his family undue suffering, although one has the feeling that his penchant for fast horses and strong drink may have stretched their family's resources at times. Red Wing, however, refuses to disturb the memory of what she considers to be an exacting but essentially happy childhood. The strong bonds of love and respect for her parents remain intact. Memories of them are at the tip of her tongue, and they frequently rush back still full of their original emotion. She recalls with wide, youthful eyes the pride she felt as a child of four or five, sitting high atop her father's express wagon when she would join him to make the early morning milk-rounds from the dairy farm he ran in southeastern Connecticut at the turn of the century. She scurried to be on time to go along, pulling on her clothes inside-out in the dark. And he always took her with him, his joyful companion, once he had patiently smoothed out the mistakes of her hurried dressing.

Her mother "never let us forget that we were Indians and different. When we went to school, she made us learn our lessons. There were seven of us, and we had to keep our clothes just so. We'd better not bring any bad marks home for deportment because we'd get punished at home, and we didn't want to get punished twice." Her mother's strictness extended throughout their family life, particularly to table manners. "When we came home," Red Wing remembers, "we sat at the table. There was a white tablecloth and white napkins for each of us. We had to learn to eat and use silver properly. People would say to mother, 'Why do you set all those seven children down to a white tablecloth and napkins and everything? Why don't you put oilcloth on?' My mother'd say to them, 'My children might eat with the President someday, and they have to learn to eat at home.' And college presidents put their feet under my mother's table. She didn't have to say, 'You children go into the kitchen.' Because she knew we were going to sit up there, 'cause we learned our manners at home *every single night.*"[7]

Red Wing's mother's prophecy has nearly come true. Because of Red Wing's long involvement with the United Nations over three decades, she has taken tea with Madame Pandit, talked with

Nehru and Khrushchev, and was on very friendly terms with Eleanor Roosevelt. More recently, she shared the governor of Rhode Island's car when rain dampened the commencement at the University of Rhode Island in 1975, where she and the governor both received honorary degrees (hers was a Doctorate of Human Affairs). She chuckles over the fact that her daughter thought she received a louder and more enthusiastic ovation than the governor when she walked to the podium. Among her many public accolades, she was inducted into the Rhode Island Hall of Fame in 1978, and Governor Joseph Garrahy declared June 23, 1978, Princess Red Wing Day. In 1978 she also received the Iron Eyes Cody Humanitarian Award for National Indian Week. From 1947 until 1970 she was invited to serve as a member of the Speaker's Research Committee of the Under-secretariat of the United Nations. No, she has not dined with the President so far, but, as Red Wing muses, "by now I've got to the point anything could happen."

Throughout her life Red Wing has not fought or rejected her simple, rural beginnings or her traditions. Instead she has embraced both. Her mother's and her people's lessons on obedience (which she names as the Indian's "first law of happiness"), discipline, and the pride of accomplishment, as well as her deeply honored Indian identity, are all qualities that have sustained her.

Since 1945 she has been Squaw Sachem of the New England Council of Chiefs, and this honor permits her to wear the big bonnet and to perform the sacred ceremonies of her closely knit people. Thus she presides at weddings, baptisms, and christenings, and the five festivals of thanksgiving, when the Woodlands Indian sings the song to thank his Maker, as he has done through the generations. But before she achieved such a distinguished rank and special role among her own people, she was offering much the same song for thousands of children of every race as a teacher of Indian crafts and lore and a highly popular teller of Indian legends and myths at summer camps in Connecticut, Rhode Island, Massachusetts, and Vermont.

Over the years and along with her many other commitments, Red Wing has stayed intensely involved with camp work and other contacts with children. For them she always has time. Like all true storytellers and teachers, she gives her gifts away—after all, who can put a price on knowledge or matters of the spirit? Her only payment, and it is a priceless feather in the headdress of her life's accomplishments, is a story she can tell to other children about a boy who, after receiving a magic, courage-inspiring pebble from her one summer, conquered his fear of the water and learned to swim. It is a little, seemingly insignificant miracle which she will keep and share as long as she lives.

Despite a number of serious health problems and major operations, Red Wing remains unflaggingly productive. She has only recently begun to show some signs of slowing down. Still, she can't seem to stay away from Dovecrest or the New England countryside for very long. There she is once more at home showing groups of children around the Tomaquag Museum. Her long-time friend, Eva Butler of Mystic, Connecticut, began the core of the collection that now comprises the museum. Red Wing and she spent eleven years together driving "hundreds of miles to libraries, archives, graveyards, et cetera for data."[8] When Mrs. Butler died in 1969, the museum was left to Red Wing, and she eventually moved it to its present location at Dovecrest, dedicating it in 1972 to the memory of a friend. The museum itself is a fascinating and informal gathering of ancient and recent Indian artifacts, ranging from early stone tools and elaborate nineteenth-century ceremonial costumes and objects to dioramas and drawings made by visiting children. Their gifts are not dismissed or filed away but hung proudly on the walls with Red Wing's other treasures. As one enters the museum, there is even a freeze-dried beaver, a gift from the Smithsonian Institution, so that the children can at least look at what was once a real beaver when she tells about the animal in her tours.[9] "But we've got a toy beaver here that they can pet. See, they've almost worn the ears off the poor creature. We'd better get a new one," she says, with a deep, earthy chuckle.

III

Of the many impressive qualities one could mention about Red Wing, perhaps the one that comes through most strongly is her belief that everything in her world holds significance, and this meaning is almost invariably transformed into a story: it is the one sure path to remembering. She is first and foremost a story-teller, in the most ancient, all-encompassing sense of the word.

Storytelling, we know, holds an indispensable position in American Indian culture—it is a source of history, religion, morals—in short, a whole attitude about life itself. Red Wing does not

Red Wing lecturing on the role of the Indian storyteller for a university audience (photograph by Frances L. Funk).

recall ever having chosen to become a storyteller. It just happened naturally. She learned the tales orally, the old way, from her mother and her mother's mother each day, especially during the winter:

> In the Moon of Storytelling, which is about our February, that's the moon of ice storms and bad weather here in New England. It's about the worst, stormy month of all. January's the Moon of the White Silence. But February, they sat in their wigwams around the fire, the older people, the grandmothers and the grandfathers, and all would tell to the children all the legends, all the stories, all the history of the tribe, which became our Great Unwritten Book. And this came down from mother to daughter, from father to son, and on down through the generations.[10]

As Harry Crews, the Southern novelist, has written, "Nothing is allowed to die in a society of storytelling people."[11] So it was for the Indian and so it is for Red Wing. Nothing is allowed to die, and nothing of importance is overlooked.

There are whole seasons of stories in her, about the plants and animals of the woodlands, about the legends of the tribes and the chiefs of New England, about the Indian tricking the white man. Yet there is no animosity or bitterness in these latter stories. In fact, they are each infused with humor and were doubtless the Indian's way of ventilating the anger and frustration he must have felt, directing it into the healthier channels of laughter and accommodation.

However, Red Wing can bristle over the Indian stereotypes that are perpetuated by the non-Indian world. She is particularly sensitive to the general ignorance concerning Indian culture, and she has spent much of her adult life trying to fill this void with knowledge. When Mount Rushmore was scheduled to be dedicated in the mid-1930s, Red Wing was asked to participate in the pageant. She refused, returning the script because it referred to the "dirty, painted savages of New England." She told the organizers, "You don't know your Indian history. My ancestors jumped into the water every morning to cleanse their bodies, summer and winter. When a new baby was born, they dunked him in that water even though they had to cut a hole in the ice to put him in. 'Course you were fortunate if you were born in June instead of January, 'cause you got dunked just the same."[12]

She addresses with fervor the misconceptions she finds about Indian religion. The thought that officials from Washington believe they have to counsel the West Coast Indians about how to conserve the Columbia River salmon outrages her. The idea runs counter to everything the Indian holds sacred, she maintains.

> All of nature was their great storehouse. Gave 'em everything they needed to eat, to wear, to build their abodes, to build the instruments and weapons—everything. But they never wasted a thing or used anything unnecessarily. They were the greatest conservationists the world ever knew. Now the Indian never worshipped anything he could conquer. But he figured that the sun, the stars, the animals, and all of nature was the Creator's way of speaking to him and maintaining mankind, and *that* was the basis of the Indian's religion. And every single morning they parted the doorway to their abode to go out on a hill and ask for wisdom from their Creator for the day. The Indian's religion went into every phase of his life. That's why ages ago we had a ceremony of thanksgiving for every moon, because the Indian felt he had to stay in favor with his Creator or else the evil spirit somewheres under the earth would come up and destroy him.[13]

For Red Wing this spirit of thanksgiving is the heart and soul of Indian culture, and she will persistently remind the outsider that the Indians of the Northeast still celebrate five thanksgivings. The first is for the maple trees and takes place in March when the sap begins to flow. Following it, in June, comes the Strawberry Thanksgiving, the Thanksgiving of Renewed Friendships, when the Great Spirit gave a girl the gift of strawberries to take back to her brother, with whom she had quarreled. "And since the strawberries were given as a peace offering, we're all at peace when we eat our strawberries. No one gets into the Strawberry Dance with a grudge against anybody else."[14] Then, in late July, there is the Green Bean Thanksgiving, to celebrate the magical gift of this edible bean. And in early October, the Indian commemorates another thanksgiving. According to Red Wing:

> The Great Spirit looked down on His children of the forest, and He knew that some of them weren't as fast as their brothers and sisters, and perhaps a little less ambitious or a little lazier, maybe, but He took pity on them just the same. After the first frost, He turned the warm winds back for a few days so that they could get their harvest in and be safe for the Cold Moon. Now some people call these good, warm days Indian Summer, but the Indian knew just what it was for. He gave them a berry, but He had used up all His sweetness in the strawberries and the raspberries and the currants and the blueberries and the fruit. But they gathered the cranberries He gave them just the same, even though they were a little sour; and they made their cranberry juice and their cranberry sauce and their cranberry bread and all and were thankful for the cranberries.[15]

Finally, there is the story of the first Thanksgiving, with Red Wing's comments on the accuracy of the historical record. Again, as with nearly all her stories, there is a concern to show the spiritual dimension inherent in all Indian life:

> When those Pilgrims came across the water in the little Mayflower, they had used up just about everything they had on the ship, and they would have starved if our Wampanoag mothers hadn't opened up their storehouses and fed them. Then when spring came along, they gave them seed that was strange to them and showed them how to fertilize the virgin soil with dead fish. But that first year, their crops were poor, many of them couldn't stand this wilderness and passed into the land of the hereafter. Another cold winter was ahead of

them, and they didn't feel very festive. Then old Squanto stepped down into Plymouth, and said to Governor Bradford, "When things look dark, when many pass into the land of the hereafter, when the crops are poor, that's the time for the *biggest* feast, for the *biggest* thanksgiving, for the *biggest* dance, to show your Creator that you're not complaining against your hard lot." And Governor Bradford answered him, "That *would* be good for my fainting people. Go call your Massasoit and your people and tell them to come, and we will feast and we will thank God for what blessings we have." And the Wampanoags came with their wild turkey, with their venison, with their bear meat, their potatoes, their corn, their beans, their squash, their pumpkin, their cranberries—enough to feed all Plymouth. They cooked it up and sat down and ate and thanked God. Now history says that it was the first Thanksgiving, and the Pilgrims fed seven hundred Indians, but it was the Indians who brought food enough to feed all of Plymouth and themselves, and for the Indians it was just another thanksgiving, for the harvest of the garden, the forest, the fields, and the meadows. And we still have that thanksgiving today, but we celebrate it in conjunction with the national Thanksgiving.[16]

No matter how many times in the past Red Wing may have recounted these stories, they are still fresh to her, and she never tires of repeating them for new listeners. This is no mere recitation. Her whole being finds its way into the recounting as she moves, barely pausing, from tale to tale. Her voice finds new resonances; her hands dance in the air, like the birds she loves to tell about. In the ceremony to the spirit of giving, or Nikomo (the Indian's Santa Claus), one dances as Red Wing explains, her voice pulsing with ceremonial rhythm, "for the privilege of putting gifts into the circle for less fortunate members of the tribe."[17] It is with that purpose that Red Wing shares her stories, her gift to anyone who listens.

At 84 she continues to bring groups of people, regardless of race or age, to their feet to applaud and join her in the circle dance. Red Wing herself leads the way with her drum and her song, singing out the measure and the message. Like a child she can still play with a joyful, unselfconscious seriousness. Like any great teacher she fuses knowledge and kindness, laughter and humanity. This is her strong, irresistible magic.

Notes

1. Taped interview with Princess Red Wing, Dovecrest, Exeter, RI, 9 October 1980. Portions of this profile appeared in the *Christian Science Monitor*, 24 November 1980.
2. Ibid.
3. Taped performance for children's literature class at the University of Connecticut, Storrs, Connecticut, October 1978.
4. Ibid.
5. Ibid.
6. Interview, 9 October 1980.
7. Ibid.
8. Ibid.
9. Edwards Park, "Around the Mall and Beyond," *Smithsonian*, 11, 5 (August, 1980), 22–23.
10. Interview, 9 October 1980.
11. Harry Crews, *A Childhood: The Biography of a Place* (New York: Harper & Row, 1978), p. 4.
12. Interview, 9 October 1980.
13. Ibid.
14. Ibid.
15. Ibid.
16. Ibid.
17. Ibid.

Childlike Wonder and the Truths of Science Fiction

Madeleine L'Engle

For the last hundred years, the number of people who read fantasy and science fiction has been growing. One of the baffling things about this group—baffling to those who are not hooked on the genres—is that it has no age limits. Afficionados usually start reading as children and continue throughout their lives. I blundered into science fiction when I was a child, with the works of H. G. Wells, Jules Verne, and E. Nesbit. I have read it ever since. In science fiction I found the questions about the meaning of life that all of us ask sooner or later. Children have always been interested in these cosmic questions and riddles which adults often attempt to tame by placing into categories fit only for scientists or adults or theologians. Only recently have fantasy and science fiction been published with age levels in mind, and readers seem to be ignoring such labels. Science fiction and fantasy appeal to a certain kind of mind and not to specific stages of development.

On the surface, science seems to be the most rational of all disciplines, relying solely on intellect without need of the intuitive self. Simple equations—or at least simple in appearance—neatly encapsulate great problems. $E = mc^2$ clearly teaches that "energy equals mass times the speed of light squared." Yet this equation has become so familiar that we forget its wildly imaginative implications. The world of contemporary science, of astrophysics and cellular biology, is itself so fantastic and poetic that it almost seems like fiction. A star that is known as a degenerate white dwarf, or another known as the red giant sitting on the horizontal branch—they sound more as if they come from fairy tales rather than from serious books on astrophysics, such as *White Holes: Cosmic Gushers in the Universe* (Dell, 1977), by John

Gribbin, an astrophysicist who sometimes cites science fiction writers in his studies of astronomy.

Science fiction, we must remind ourselves, often relies upon contemporary science. Space technology and places such as Cape Canaveral, Mount Wilson, or Alamogordo frequently appear in science fiction; and scientists, as well as writers with no particular scientific training, write science fiction. Fred Hoyle, the English astrophysicist, write both science fiction and articles for academic journals. Why does a man such as Hoyle bother with fiction when he is so successful in the "real" world of science? The answer is that science depends as much upon the imagination as upon the intellect. Like a poet, the scientist uses inspiration and intuition. In *The Double Helix,* the book about the discovery of DNA, James D. Watson, who received the Nobel prize for his work in genetics, says several times, "It's so pretty, it's got to be true." Inadvertently he echoes Keats's "Beauty is truth, truth beauty." If a scientific equation is "ugly" the scientist is suspicious; the scientist, like the artist, appreciates aesthetics and balance.

Lay people often envision scientists in white coats, perched on stools in immaculate laboratories, clipboards on their laps, working out problems. Most scientific discoveries, however, come in a flash, often when the scientist is not in the laboratory at all. Einstein's theory of relativity came to him full-blown, and only later did he work out the equations to prove it. Then, because he was a genius but not very good at mathematics, he made several mistakes that other scientists had to point out to him.

Both the scientist and the science fiction writer understand that imagination, improvisation, and intuition are as important as rational thinking. For a good many centuries we have denigrated the subconscious, intuitive self and elevated the conscious, intellectual self. We have forgotten that the conscious self is only that small tip of the iceberg, whereas the subconscious self is the larger part below the surface.

Abraham Joshua Heschel, in *God in Search of Man* (Harper Torchbooks), writes that out of his religious tradition comes "a legacy of wonder." Heschel is talking of "The Religious Man" but he could equally well be talking of the writers and readers of fantasy and science fiction when he says, "One attitude alien to his spirit: taking things for granted, regarding events as a natural cause of things. To find an approximate cause or phenomenon is no answer to his ultimate wonder . . . [which] is not the beginning of knowledge but an act that goes beyond knowledge; it does not come to an end when knowledge is acquired; it is an attitude that never ceases. There is no answer in the world to man's radical amazement" (pp. 45–46).

This sense of wonder constantly prods the imagination of the writer of fantasy or science fiction, and the child, whose sense of wonder has not yet been blunted, goes right along with it: What would life on Saturn, with all its rings, be like? Does a galaxy think? Is it a sentient entity? Do our mitochondria know that they are living with us? There is no end to the questions the sense of wonder prods us to ask, and each question can easily lead to a story.

A young friend of mine told me, with considerable agitation, that her teacher had accused her of "telling a story." This teacher wasn't complimenting the child's imagination; she had accused her of lying. Recently I received a letter from a young mother who wrote that a neighbor had announced she was not going to allow her children to make their minds fuzzy by reading fantasy or science fiction; she intended to give them books of facts about the real world. For these children, I feel, the real world will be lost. They will live in a limited world in which ideas are suspect. The monsters which all children encounter will be more monstrous because the child will not be armed with the only weapon effective against the unknown: a creative and supple imagination.

The lines between science fiction, fantasy, myth, and fairy tale are very fine, and children, unlike many adults, do not need to have their stories pigeonholed. Science fiction usually takes a contemporary scientific idea and then extrapolates: "Yes, but what if . . . ?" In the days before astronauts had landed on the moon, no one was certain just what the surface of the moon would be. We knew that there would be little gravity, but we did not know whether the surface would be hard rock or rock covered with sand and silt. So one science fiction writer described a spaceship landing on the moon. The landing shifted the great layer of fine sand which had built up over the millennia and all the familiar mares and mountains vanished. The speculation of the science fiction writer is not always prophetic, but it always stirs the imagination. We are so accustomed to Jules Verne that we forget that he did, in fact, prophesy many things considered improbable in his day—flying, for example.

Fairy tales usually deal with magic, and magic has power. E. Nesbit used magic to help her protagonists journey into both the past and the future. Although her stories may seem pure fantasy, they touch science fiction, for scientists today conceive of time as nonlinear and suggest that one day it may be possible for us to move along different branches of the tree of time. Ursula Le Guin, in her children's fantasies and in her adult science fiction, touches on myth as well as fantasy and science fiction. In a similar fashion, Susan Cooper's fantasies are deeply rooted in British mythology.

Any story, whether myth, fantasy, fairy tale, or science fiction, explores and moves beyond daily concerns to wonder. A story, instead of taking a child away from real life, prepares him to live in real life with courage and expectancy. A child denied imaginative literature is likely to have more difficulty understanding cellular biology or post-Newtonian physics than the child whose imagination has been stretched by fantasy and science fiction.

The teacher who, with the child, enjoys this stretching (and the stretching of muscles causes healthy growing pains) is aware of human potential. Such a teacher does not neglect the child who does not "fit in" or who cannot come to grips with the curriculum. Thomas Edison was withdrawn from school in the second grade because his teacher considered him uneducable; his mother's faith, her conviction that he was not stupid, led her to tutor him at home. It is not always the bright and well-adjusted child who has the imagination to leap beyond convention to truth, a truth which may upset "grown-ups." Galileo's discoveries did not upset the nature of the universe; they upset only what the established authorities considered to be the nature of the universe.

I remember a science fiction story in which the people of Earth were attempting to colonize a planet with bad weather and hostile inhabitants. The head of colonization picked teams of the brightest and best young men and women available. Team after team went out and then returned, dejected and unsuccessful. Finally a new head of colonization was chosen, who went to the waterfronts, slums, and ghettoes to enlist those who had survived there. These "dregs" succeeded where the others failed. They had the imagination to survive on a hostile earth; this imagination enabled them to survive on the hostile planet. Science fiction appeals to the child with imagination, whether he or she is captain of the sports team, honor student, or the child who lags behind intellectually, athletically, or socially.

A successful story, no matter how soaring the fantasy or how offbeat the science, must be believable. A child must be encouraged to suspend disbelief. Tolkien's hobbits are as realistic to a child as Judy Blume's teenagers, and Anne McCaffrey's dragons are as believable as giraffes. To quote Aristotle, "That which is probable and impossible is better than that which is possible and improbable."

Unfortunately, this "probable impossible" is fraught with risk, and risk implies the possibility of failure and even death. I am worried that we live in a climate where we are not allowed to fail. We are encouraged to take few risks, though "all human endeavor is beset by risk," as Franz König says: "Freedom risks its own abuse, thinking risks error, speech risks misunderstanding, faith risks failure, hope risks despair. The risk of life is death. And man is man only by virtue of his risks of the future."

Perhaps the reason that a mother refuses to give her children fantasy or science fiction is that these genres, like fairy tale and myth, are not only violent, but they involve risk. Why do we shudder at the violence in these tales while the violence of everyday life surrounds us? These stories can help children understand the nature of violence. As for risk—without risk there is no story. The protagonist must always choose, and to choose is to risk. Failure often occurs. In *The Once and Future King* there is death and tragedy as well as heroism and chivalry. In *The Lord of the Rings* Frodo does not always make the right choice. The planet on which a spaceship lands may not support human life. The captain of the spaceship may be bestial and may not care if the indigenous inhabitants are slaughtered. There is risk of failure, of horror, and of death in fantasy and science fiction just as there is in the world of everyday. In John Wyndham's "The Day of the Triffids," most of Earth's inhabitants are struck blind and many are killed, but despite a recognition of darkness and death, there is also an unspoken affirmation of the "all rightness" of things, and I believe that the child—and the adult—needs this affirmation.

Before we can affirm this "all rightness," we must accept "all wrongness," for fantasy and science fiction inhabit dark and unknown regions. Although we often think of fantasies as light, with enchanted mirrors, spaceships winging like sea gulls, and time machines shaped like flower petals, such stories speak to us, at first, of dark things. No one is more aware of the dark aspects of civilization than the storyteller; he knows our insecurities, our loneliness, and our fears. But every storyteller is also aware of the value of the human being.

In a story it is usually an ordinary boy or girl who must confront power, take risks, and stand courageous against fear. Primitive societies had two words for power: benign power was called "mana"; malign power was called "taboo." The great power lines which stretch across our country and make our lights turn on and our refrigerators run contain both mana and taboo. If we turn on a light switch and fill a room with light, then it is mana. If a metal ladder holding two firemen slips and touches a power line, it is taboo. Those who think they can cope with taboo, or can manage it, fall into hubris. They usurp the prerogatives of the gods. This is Edmund's problem in C. S. Lewis's *The Lion, the Witch, and the Wardrobe*. Courage and pride are very different things. Pride masked as fear of failure often keeps us from taking risks, while courage gives us strength to face the unknown.

One of the unknowns which has always fascinated readers and

writers of science fiction is time. The subconscious mind is un-inhibited by linear time: when we dream, time is sometimes fan-tastically altered; in a few moments we may dream hours of ad-venture. As we venture into fantasy and science fiction, we are freed from time. A spaceship may travel at the speed of light, or near it, for short distances, but for trips to distant galaxies or even distant planets in the same galaxy, no speed is fast enough; the spaceship must tesser (go into a time warp). Our nearest star is Alpha Centauri, which is seven light years away. The problem is not only that it would take fourteen years to go there, turn right around, and come back, but that time moves at different rates, and the faster a body moves, the slower time moves. Con-sequently, the people on the spaceship would be caught in Ein-stein's clock paradox: fourteen years would have passed in their own chronologies, but far more time would have passed on Earth, so that a baby left behind when the astronauts departed would have white hair and wrinkled skin when they returned.

These current scientific concepts are more easily understood and accepted by children than by adults. Not only are they new to adults, but they also contradict what was taught only a gen-eration or so ago. Our children and young adults have always lived in a world of increasingly rapid change; they have always known about the power in the atom. They have always known that our Earth is not the center of the universe but an ordi-nary planet on the outskirts of an ordinary galaxy; and that light, swift as it is, is so slow that we are seeing a distant star not as it is today, but as it was billions of years ago when our planet was first being formed. Fresh concepts, which are terrifying to some adults, are casually accepted and understood by children today.

Chronology as we know it began with creation, with the Big Bang. The present "proof" for this theory is the awesome fact that scientists, with their radio telescopes, are picking up echoes of the sound of that primal explosion, which happened so long ago that it is further back in time than most of us can conceive in num-bers. There are also events, tied in with the extraordinary dura-bility of sound waves, which are more like science fiction than actual occurrences. For instance, one of the more delightful mysteries of sound came when the astronauts in one of our early space launches heard a program of nostalgic music over the sound system. They radioed to NASA to thank whoever sent them the program. NASA responded that they knew nothing about it. This phenomenon provoked research: Who sent the astronauts the music? Where had it come from? The radio and television programs for that hour on that day were analysed. None broadcast the music the astronauts heard. Could the astronauts have imagined hearing old popular songs? Was it a kind of mass hallucination? It seemed unlikely. Then it was discovered that that particular program had been broadcast in the 1930s.

How does one explain it? One doesn't. It happened, and from events like this come science fiction stories. There is a story in which scientists from Earth are attempting to communicate with people from another planet but cannot make sense of the sounds they receive. One scientist realizes that the planet with which they are in contact is a large and dense planet, and its period of revolution around its sun is much slower than ours. He tapes the sounds and then speeds up the tape, somewhat like playing a $33\frac{1}{3}$ rpm record at 78 rpm. Soon the scientists begin to make sense of the messages. Time on the other planet moves slower than on Earth.

We do not understand time. We know that time exists only when there is mass in motion. We also know that energy and mass are interchangeable, and that pure energy is freed from the restrictions of time. One of the reasons that *A Wrinkle in Time* took so long to find a publisher is that it was assumed that children would not be able to understand a sophisticated way of looking at time, would not understand Einstein's theories. But no theory is too hard for a child so long as it is part of a story; and although parents had not been taught Einstein's $E = mc^2$ in school, their children had been.

Sylvia Louise Engdahl uses the variability of time in many of her stories, particularly in *The Princess from the Stars*. Time and its vagaries figure in the works of such eminent science fiction

writers as Arthur C. Clarke, William Wyndham, and Theodore
Sturgeon. Lewis Carroll wrote the truth when the Mad Hatter
said, "If you knew Time as well as I do, . . . you wouldn't talk
about wasting *it*. It's *him*. . . . We quarrelled last March. . . . And
ever since that . . . he won't do a thing I ask!"
Most writers of fantasy for children do not write for children;
they write for themselves. "To write for children" is usually synonymous with writing down and is an insult to children. I have
said that children are better believers than grown-ups. They are
aware of what most adults have forgotten: that the daily, time-
bound world of fact is the secondary world, and that literature,
art, and music, though they are not themselves the primary world,
give us glimpses of the wider world of our whole self—the self
which is real enough to accept its darkness as well as its light.

There is something of the fantasy or science fiction monster in
all of us, but mostly we are afraid to admit it. Chewbacca, the
large woolly creature in *Star Wars,* is so appealing because we
are free to recognize ourselves in him as well as in the white-clad
hero and heroine. Rainer Maria Rilke writes, "How should we be
able to forget those ancient myths that are at the beginning of all
peoples, the myths about dragons that at the last moment turn
into princesses; perhaps all the dragons of our lives are princesses
who are only waiting to see us once beautiful and brave. Perhaps
everything terrible is in its deepest being something helpless that
wants help from us."[1] Stories which appeal to our imaginations
enable us to recognize this helplessness and give us the courage
to help.

Notes

1. Rainer Marie Rilke, *Letters to a Young Poet,* trans. M. D. Herter Norton
(New York: W. W. Norton, 1934), pp. 69–70.

Science Fiction for the Young (at Heart)

Frederik Pohl

Over my desk used to hang an adage:

"The person you are writing for knows nothing but can understand *anything*."

I don't know who first said it—it may have been me—but I believe it represents a truth about the readers of science fiction. Science fiction readers come in all ages. Some are seven years old. Some are well past seventy. For the very young, the adage is not entirely satisfactory. Many of them do not have the background to understand much about cosmology or genetics or the "inner space" of the human mind. But it is certain that much of the nominally "adult" science fiction is read by substantial numbers of twelve-year-olds and even younger readers. (I began my own reading when I was ten, with *Amazing Stories* and the works of Jonathan Swift and H. G. Wells—I did not discover that science fiction "juveniles" existed for several years.)

For this reason, there are people who dismiss all science fiction as children's literature. Although a large proportion of science fiction is childishly written and childishly conceived (so is a large proportion of all other kinds of literature), I have little patience with this view. There is no better writing in the world than the best science fiction, and no more exciting, provocative, and insightful examinations of the human condition. My friend Arthur C. Clarke was asked once why he preferred to write science fiction. He replied, "Because it is the only literature that concerns itself with reality." I agree, if I can interpret his "reality" as that single immense reality which confronts all of us, the reality of change. Science fiction is the literature of change.

The single difference between science fiction marketed for an audience of twelve-year-olds and that marketed for a general audience is that the young people's science fiction contains no sex and no four-letter words. This is less for the sake of the readers than for their parents.

Science fiction (I am speaking always of the best science fiction) is not easy reading. It requires almost as much work from the reader as from the writer; it requires an effort to understand realities that do not at present exist, and a willingness to stretch the imagination. Many adults will not make these efforts, and so they avoid science fiction and read best-sellers or watch television. Young people have not been trained out of the willingness to make the effort. It is precisely because science fiction is challenging that it attracts young readers. Courses in science fiction have inspired students to read many books all the way through, some of them for the first time in their lives; this is, in turn, one reason why courses in science fiction have been spreading from colleges to high schools and lower.

When I write a science fiction novel, I keep my adage in mind, and if I am writing about the wonders of relativistic space travel I make sure that I tell the reader what Einstein's relativity implies. I have little doubt that my audience will understand anything I can explain to them. And not much doubt that many readers will need the explanation, whether they are quite young and therefore not yet informed, or, perhaps, grown up, even with a number of degrees, but degrees which happen to be in biochemistry or political science. My contacts with readers assure me that I have substantial proportions of both—and so do most science fiction writers.

The Beginning Place: *Le Guin's Metafantasy*

Brian Attebery

Most writers of fantasy reach a point where they start to defend what they have written against charges of irrelevance or meaninglessness. There are essays by George MacDonald, J. R. R. Tolkien, C. S. Lewis, and many other fantasists that say, "This is real. It matters. My stories are born from and reflect back upon the outside world of perception and action." The impulse is understandable: many readers and, unfortunately, a few writers mistake fantasy's alteration of reality for an evasion of reality. Such readers fail to note how carefully the best fantasists order their creations —how they limit the magical possibilities and bind them to a stringent moral order. Ursula K. Le Guin, in one of these defenses of fantasy, says that "fantasy is true, of course. It isn't factual, but it is true. Children know that. Adults know it too, and that is precisely why many of them are afraid of fantasy. They know that its truth challenges, even threatens, all that is false, all that is phony, unnecessary, and trivial in the life they have let themselves be forced into living."[1]

Le Guin's best known fantasy is the Earthsea trilogy: three tales of wizardry and self-discovery set in a world of islands inhabited by men, dragons, and lesser beings. The high quality of these stories has been recognized in a number of critical essays, in major awards—a *Boston Globe–Horn Book* Award for *A Wizard of Earthsea,* a Newbery Honor Medal for *The Tombs of Atuan,* and a National Book Award for *The Farthest Shore*—and in the response of the children and adults who read them. What kind of response? The same kind that Le Guin, in another essay, tells of having arisen in her upon reading, at age ten, a fairy tale by Hans Christian Andersen: ". . . It was to that, to the unknown depths in me, that the story spoke; and it was the depths which responded to it and, nonverbally, irrationally, understood it, and learned from it."[2]

But having located the truth of fantasy in the unconscious, how can we act consciously in accordance with it: what is the use of a dream upon awaking?[3] That is a question that Le Guin and her predecessors have skirted in their essays. However, Le Guin's most recent fantasy novel, *The Beginning Place,* is largely about the relationship between fantasy and ordinary, daylight reality. It tells, in a sense, what happens when we close the book and drift back from Middle Earth or Narnia or Earthsea. Le Guin explores this relationship by establishing not one but two fictional realms, one fantastic and one modeled on the world we live in. Her protagonists, Irene Pannis and Hugh Rogers, cross from one world to the other, like fictional representatives of the reader as he picks up a work of fantasy and puts it down, adjusting his eyes and his expectations each time to a new order of being. In their actions and reactions Le Guin embodies her notion of the ways fantasy can be used either to evade or to achieve psychological growth.

The Beginning Place opens in a setting that is sharply detailed and yet impossible to locate, for it is set in standardized American suburbia. Its supermarkets, freeways, and apartments, its Kensington Heights, Pine View Place, and Raleigh Drive might encircle virtually any medium-to-large city in America. All is bland, uniform, ersatz. It is a horrible place, but no one in the story seems consciously to recognize the horror, not even the hero, Hugh, a young supermarket checker. Hugh's unconscious, though, is at work. Unruly and fertile, as our unconscious minds tend to be, it protests one evening as Hugh sits at home heating a frozen TV dinner and waiting for his brittle, demanding mother to come home. Choosing as its defense not neurosis but escape, Hugh's unconscious stirs him to panic, drives him out the door, and sets him running:

Right down Oak Valley Road, left onto Pine View Place, right again, he did not know, he could not read the signs. He did not run often or easily. His feet hit the ground hard, in heavy shocks. Cars, carports, houses blurred to a bright pounding blindness which, as he ran on, reddened and darkened. Words behind his eyes said *You are running out of daylight*. Air came acid into his throat and lungs, burning, his breath made the noise of tearing paper. The darkness thickened like blood. The jolt of his gait grew harder yet, he was running down, downhill. He tried to hold back, to slow down, feeling the world slide and crumble under his feet, a multiple lithe touch brush across his face. He saw or smelled leaves, dark leaves, branches, dirt, earth, leafmold, and through the hammer of his heart and breath heard a loud continual music. He took a few shaky, shuffling steps, went forward onto hands and knees, and then down, belly down full length on earth and rock at the edge of running water.[4]

The stream whose music Hugh hears is not in the world of TV dinners and carports. It is across the threshold into the world of dreams, magic, ritual, and renewal. With a careful orchestration of prose rhythms and precise images, Le Guin has deftly drawn us into an altered reality. Just before Hugh begins running he finds himself saying, without willing it, "I can't, I can't." His need takes him to a place where he can—can breathe, can think, can luxuriate in smells and touches of nature, and ultimately, can bring himself to a new order and understanding.

Part of his understanding involves another person, a fugitive like himself. Irene has been coming to this twilight land for several years. It is her sanctuary from an awkward living situation and a threatening family life. Unlike Hugh, she has ventured beyond the stream which is the beginning place of the title, the threshold, and has gone on to explore some of the country beyond. She has met its inhabitants and begun to learn their language. The pastoral town of Tembreabrezi, perched high on a dim mountainside, is her adopted home. The innkeepers Sofir and Palizot keep a set of clothes for her and call her "dear child." Time on this side of the threshold differs from time on the mundane side, so she has been able to spend a day with her friends and yet have been gone only an hour, or spend a week in a single night. She has gone trading in the next town with Sofir and has learned to sew with Palizot. She has met Lord Horn in the manor at the edge of town and has come to know and secretly love the Mayor or Master, Dou Sark.

Because this world has for so long been her own place—she has named it, in her mind, "the ain country," from a Scottish ballad—she resents the intrusion of a stranger. She greets Hugh with a "No Trespassing" sign, hides his camping gear, threatens him with a rock. Hugh retreats, though thereafter he begins exploring the land on his own.

Irene becomes aware that there is a problem in the ain country, a lurking fear that has gradually closed off travel and communication so that only the outsiders Hugh and Irene are free to come and go outside the town boundaries. And Irene discovers, to her frustration, that the townspeople look not to her but to Hugh as their appointed deliverer (or possibly, according to certain hints, scapegoat). She is necessary only to guide him to the confrontation with whatever obscure evil he is supposed to face. Neither Hugh nor Irene can get a clear idea of its nature. Nevertheless, Hugh is willing to go, partly because he has fallen in love with Lord Horn's daughter Allia and partly because it is the first chance in his life to do something of worth. Irene has discovered that her beloved Master Sark is weaker than she had thought, and untrustworthy. She is willing to go with Hugh primarily because she no longer has reason to stay. She has also begun, in spite of herself, to respect Hugh's courage and integrity.

So the two strangers take leave of the village of Tembreabrezi and set out to fight what might as well be called a dragon. Seeing them off are a wise old man, a blonde princess, and a dark traitor. The land of their retreat, the refuge found for them by their unconscious minds, has thrown them into an archetypal conflict, a fairy tale. No refuge is without cost, and the realm of the unconscious is entered only at great peril, because it is the home of dragons, ogres, and the other monsters that lurk in the dim corners of our minds. This particular monster turns out to be a sort of undifferentiated essence of monster. Its weapon is

raw fear and its form, as Lord Horn forewarns, is dependent on the beholder.
Seen through Irene's eyes it is gross, grotesque, humanoid, and female—Grendel's dam. To Hugh, though, it is apparently male:

> "You call it 'her,' " he said.
> "It was." She did not want to speak of the breasts and the thin arms.
> He shook his head, with a sick look, his pallor increasing. "No, it was— The reason I had to kill it—" he said, and then put out his hand groping for support, and staggered as he stood. [pp. 162–63]

The reason hinted at here seems to be that it was obscenely male and threatening to Irene. Each sees in the monster a mirror of his worst, hidden self, the monster self that Le Guin calls, in *A Wizard of Earthsea*, the shadow. ("Shadow" is an important term in Jung's model of the psyche. Le Guin had not read Jung when she wrote *A Wizard*, but she has since found many of his ideas useful in discussing the nature and value of fantasy.[5])

After Irene challenges the monster and Hugh kills it, Irene tends Hugh's wounds and together they make their way back to the threshold. There is no return to the village; Allia and Sark are forgotten. Hugh and Irene are bound together by their experience, their former hostility replaced by a liking growing rapidly into love. Halfway down the mountain, stopping for food, they make love, rather to their own surprise. Home again in the daylight world (only it is night this time, and raining), they remain together and plan to leave the suburb for the city, their lives no longer in stasis, with no more need for this particular escape.

What has Le Guin said about fantasy in this story? First, she reemphasizes her belief that it is valuable, even necessary to human well-being. Hugh, before he finds the threshold, is becoming dangerously dissociated into a robotlike persona and an unacknowledged, unhappy, explosive inner self. Irene is torn between love and resentment for her dead father, her aloof brother, and

her abused mother, and her conflicting feelings leave her perpetually angry, afraid, and unable to make necessary changes in
her own life. By escaping to the other world, both are granted
respite from the demands of others and an opportunity to examine
their lives from a distance. The inner strength that both possess
is allowed to surface. Within the twilight world Irene and Hugh
can be seen to stretch and straighten like newly emerged seedlings.

Le Guin indicates, secondly, that the magic world is potent.
It is not there merely for the convenience of visitors, or for their
amusement. It is full of hidden dangers and rules. Le Guin
represents the danger primarily through her monster, drawing
upon such horror conventions as eerie sounds (a "high gobbling
scream far off in the woods," p. 79) and silences ("The wind
had died. Nothing moved. It was like deafness," p. 132) and the
ambiguous but unquestionably awful physical appearance of the
creature. The rules, and the visitors' problems in learning them,
she shows in several interesting ways. First of all, it is not a
simple matter to get in and out across the threshold. Hugh can
always enter, but Irene cannot, though she could when she was
younger. Irene can always get out, but Hugh twice finds himself simply walking on into more twilight forest where he should
have made the transition into sunlight and the sounds of cars
and airplanes. Only together are they sure of finding both ways
open, just as it takes both of them to defeat the monster.

Language serves as an analog to knowledge of the workings of
the ain country. Irene has learned much of the language of Tembreabrezi, but there are areas where her knowledge fails her. She
knows the words for familiar objects, common activities, and personal relationships, but she is not sure of the significance of more
formidable words. She is not sure whether the word she has translated "king" means that or something quite different. She is un-
familiar with the word that may refer to the monster and might
have been a clue to its nature. She is unable to ask about the
differences between the twilight world and her own: why there
is no sun or moon; why the language includes words for morning
and night.

Hugh and Irene are most in ignorance about the rules governing good and evil, which in this—as in most fantasies—are wound around with magic. There is the monster: it is evil or at least brings evil about. There is the never-seen City with its maybe King: it is almost certainly good. Lord Horn tells Irene that it is because he has been to the City that he is called Lord. There was some sort of compact made with the monster or what it represents a generation ago. A child was sacrificed and the fear driven back temporarily, only to return stronger than before. Irene and Hugh know nothing of how any of this came about or how it relates to the closing of the roads. Irene thinks to herself, "He, and she, and all of them here, were subject to the laws of the place, laws as absolute as the law of gravity, as impossible to disobey and as difficult to explain" (p. 42). And yet they do, they must, reach some kind of understanding in order to act for good and not evil. They begin to understand in the same way Le Guin says a child can understand the deeper significance of a fairy tale: nonverbally, irrationally, below or beyond the level of consciousness. Though the arcane mysteries of the twilight world remain mysteries, it is enough for the moment to know where they must go and what they must do. Irene realizes that it is wrong for her to return to the village; Hugh knows that he must make his stand against the monster. Having learned something about themselves, they understand at least their own roles in the fairy tale they are enacting, even though the history and nature of the fairy tale world elude explanation.

That is not to say that there is no connection between experience in our own world and experience in the other. Le Guin is especially subtle in drawing two kinds of connections—parallels and contrasts—between the two worlds. Physically there are many contrasts: daylight and twilight; pavement and forest; clutter and clarity; and, if time can be considered physical, hurried-up time and deliberate time. All of these make the ain country a kind of commentary on our own lives. We can also see areas in which the two lands are parallel, and that too helps us to see our world from a new perspective. We see in the lives of Hugh's mother,

Irene's brother, and other people in the daylight world the same kind of bargaining with fear that has circumscribed the lives of the people of Mountain Town. Le Guin avoids too-obvious analogs—Hugh's sword equals X, the trail they follow is really Y—because allegorical elements that might just get by in an ordinary fantasy would be obtrusive in this sort of half-and-half tale. Nonetheless, there is enough continuity from world to world to make each a usable mirror of the other. What Hugh and Irene learn, about fear, about love, about themselves, they still know when they return.

One thing they learn, and another of Le Guin's points about fantasy, is that it is, despite parallels, not the same as waking life and should not be experienced in the same way. To do so is to trivialize it. What is rich and mysterious in twilight may seem flimsy in daylight. Both Hugh and Irene are guilty at first of this misunderstanding or misusing of the fantasy experience.

In an essay on style in fantasy, Le Guin proposed that we "consider Elfland as a great national park, a vast and beautiful place where a person goes by himself, on foot, to get in touch with reality in a special, private, profound fashion. But what happens when it is considered merely as a place to 'get away to'?"[6] That is just what happens in *The Beginning Place*; indeed, that question could well have been the seed of the novel. What happens is that the cool, mysterious solidity of the beginning place gives way to the oddly insubstantial, conventionalized, fairy tale world of Tembreabrezi. The name of the place may be a clue. Though it has a respectable etymology, a compound of words for "mountain" and "town," the name sounds like nonsense, especially the kind of nonsense that shows up in cheap, pseudo-Dunsanian fantasy. It is not Le Guin's usual sort of name: "One place I do exert deliberate control in name-inventing is in the area of pronounceability. I try to spell them so they don't look too formidable (unless, like Kurremkarmerruk, they're meant to look formidable) . . ."[7] Names in Earthsea are on the order of *Ged, Pendor, otak, rushwash tea*. The name *Kurremkarmerruk* is different because it belongs to the wizard who is Master Namer—and as such has the only name which means nothing.

In Tembreabrezi, both Hugh and Irene fall in love with people who are merely reflections of themselves: Irene with dark, intense Dou Sark, Hugh with pale, quiet Allia. In Jungian terms these are animus and anima: projections of the masculine component of the female psyche and the feminine component of the male. This is not real love, in Le Guin's universe. Her stories show, over and over, the reaching out to the dissimilar Other which is the beginning of mature love. When Hugh and Irene discover one another, it is a different matter. But Allia and Sark are not even portrayed as real, full characters. We see nothing of their lives unconnected with Hugh and Irene, overhear none of their thoughts. They are daydreams, My Ideal Man/Woman. To underscore the point, Hugh's and Irene's feelings toward them are described in a deflatingly parodic style: "He felt in himself the longing, the yearning to give so greatly to the beloved that nothing was left, to give all, all. To protect and guard her, to serve her, to die for her—the thought was unendurably sweet; again he caught his breath as if a knife had gone into him, when that thought came to him" (p. 101). This is not emotion but the mask of an emotion tried on for size. Love, says Le Guin, can enter into a fantasy world, but it cannot be found there, only representations of it.

J. R. R. Tolkien took his fantasy creation very seriously indeed, devoting much of his life to its development and defending it in the essay "On Fairy-Stories" and the story "Leaf by Niggle." But he never lost sight of its nature, and he began to be disturbed by those who tried to make of it something other than a story. He wrote to a friend, "I am not now at all sure that the tendency to treat the whole thing as a kind of vast game is really good."[8] Those who do so are the people who are reluctant to emerge from the fantasy. Not content with what Tolkien calls Secondary Belief as they read, they attempt to mix the waking world and the dream. They print bumper stickers about hobbits and write stories that are strikingly like Hugh's mawkish musing on Allia. Le Guin, too, disapproves of the alteration of fantasy into a game. A fantasy world, she says in *The Beginning Place*, is not where you live your life, but where you go to begin to comprehend it.

The Beginning Place works better as metafantasy, or commentary on fantasy, than as a fantasy tale. In showing how to emerge from the world of the unconscious, how to, as it were, wake up again, Le Guin is obliged rather to slight the dream. It is a frustrating book to read because Irene and Hugh's story only touches briefly on the story, or history, of the fantasy world. If they truly belonged to the twilight world and were actually, as they seem briefly to be, its culture heroes, its saviors, then we would learn the fate of that world in learning of their adventures. That is the way it is with Frodo and Middle Earth or Ged and Earthsea. In this case, however, the individual drama, the coming of age of Hugh and Irene, is worked out without any corresponding solution of the problems of Tembreabrezi and its countryside. We are left asking questions: What happens to Horn, Sark, Allia? Where is the City and what is it like? Is the twilight a perpetual state or does it mark a long-delayed transition to dawn or utter night? Why are there no birds, no flowers, no songs? Hugh and Irene do not need to know, having reached their goal, but the reader would like to. We are too accustomed to grand finales and happily-ever-afters; like children greedy for more bedtime story we want to know "what happened after that?" We accept Irene and Hugh's return to reality and the implied message about times to dream and times to wake up, but we do so grudgingly, with many a backward glance.

Perhaps Le Guin will return to the beginning place, as she did to Earthsea, and take up the loose threads of its tapestry. Until then, *The Beginning Place* is most satisfyingly read, first, as a tale of two striking characters and their inward growth, and, second, as a fantasy about fantasy, just as *The Lathe of Heaven* is her science fiction novel about science fiction. *The Beginning Place* can tell us much about the richer world of Earthsea and how, like all fully developed fantasy worlds, it may properly be used not as an escape from, but as a means of reimagining, of reseeing the world we live in.

Notes

1. Ursula K. Le Guin, "Why Are Americans Afraid of Dragons?" in *The Language of the Night: Essays on Fantasy and Science Fiction*, by Ursula K. Le Guin, ed. Susan Wood (New York: G. P. Putnam's Sons, 1979), p. 44.

2. Ursula K. Le Guin, "The Child and the Shadow," in *The Language of the Night*, p. 62.

3. After writing this sentence, I recognized it as an echo from Le Guin. The opening section of *The Lathe of Heaven* (New York: Avon Books, 1971), a novel which, like *The Beginning Place,* deals with multiple realities, ends thus: "What will the creature made all of seadrift do on the dry sand of daylight; what will the mind do, each morning, waking?" (p. 7).

4. Ursula K. Le Guin, *The Beginning Place* (New York: Harper & Row, 1980), p. 5. Subsequent quotations from *The Beginning Place* will be indicated parenthetically in the text.

5. Susan Wood, Introduction to Part 2 of *The Language of the Night*, p. 34.

6. Ursula K. Le Guin, "From Elfland to Poughkeepsie," in *The Language of the Night*, p. 83.

7. Ursula K. Le Guin, "Dreams Must Explain Themselves," in *The Language of the Night*, p. 52.

8. Quoted by Christopher Tolkien in his Introduction to *Unfinished Tales,* by J. R. R. Tolkien, ed. Christopher Tolkien (Boston: Houghton Mifflin, 1980), p. 2.

The Spear and the Piccolo: Heroic and Pastoral Dimensions of William Steig's Dominic and Abel's Island

Anita Moss

Author, cartoonist, artist, and sculptor, William Steig has explained why he uses animal characters: "I think using animals emphasizes the fact that the story is symbolical—about human behavior. And kids get the idea right away that this is not just a story, but that it's a way of saying something about life on earth."[1] Readers of Steig's fantasies are not surprised to learn that as a child he was deeply impressed by *Grimms' Fairy Tales,* "Hansel and Gretel," Howard Pyle's *King Arthur* and *Robin Hood,* and especially *Pinocchio.* His two longer novels for children, *Dominic* (1972) and *Abel's Island* (1976), reflect these traditions and have been variously described by critics and reviewers as romances, adventure stories, picaresque journeys, and, in the case of *Abel's Island,* a Robinsonade. Indeed, *Dominic* and *Abel's Island* resemble all of these forms. There is in western literature a long and prestigious tradition of the quest romance which is accented by pastoral interludes; one thinks, for example, of the long pastoral interludes in *Don Quixote* and the world of the shepherds in Book VI of Spenser's *The Faerie Queene.* Blue Calhoun has identified a similar juxtaposition of quest romance and pastoral in William Morris's poem *The Earthly Paradise,* in which the Wanderer's open-ended heroic quest is interrupted by the enclosed structures of idyllic frames, a dialectical balance which Calhoun calls the "mood of energy" and the "mood of idleness."[2] Such a dialectical balance allows the hero to assert his values through the quest and, at the same time, to affirm the value of art and civilization in the garden. True heroes, then, protect community and its values. They are courageous, loyal, resourceful, intelligent, and selfless. Like Virgil's Aeneas, the hero's efforts are devoted to founding and to protecting home and civilization, in contrast to the subversive, antisocial adventurer whose identity is defined wholly in terms of action and whose efforts are in the service of self and in escape from the categories of duty and obligation.[3] Steig's characters, Abel (a mouse) and Dominic (a dog), are both "pastoral" heroes. Their interests are always those of home and community. They enjoy adventures and prove themselves equal to severe tests of their courage and resourcefulness. But the identities of both are finally defined not only by heroic action but also by pastoral contemplation. Both emerge as artists as well as heroes, and both embrace the companionship of women (unlike the adventurer, who usually remains isolated, unmarried, and outside society).

Leo Marx has observed that the pastoral is an elusive, even confusing term, but that it may appropriately be used "to refer to the motive that lies behind the form, and to the images and themes, even the conception of life associated with it."[4] In this sense, certainly, the underlying impulse in Steig's two longer fantasies is pastoral. The innocence of the characters, their affinity with the natural world, their need for the civilized world of art and companionship, the sophisticated detachment of the narrator, and the elegance of Steig's language are all manifestations that the pastoral is a significant dimension of *Dominic* and *Abel's Island*.

When the reader first meets Dominic, he appears to be an adventurer rather than a hero. Without a definite quest, Dominic is merely bored with home. The restless spirit of adventure seizes him abruptly; he packs his various hats, which he wears not for warmth or shelter, "but for their various effects—rakish, dashing, solemn, or martial."[5] From the outset, however, Dominic's adventurous characteristics are tempered by a pastoral dimension; he also takes along his precious piccolo.

Steig gently burlesques the romance by having Dominic receive guidance from an amiable witch-alligator, who advises him to take the high road to adventure and romance, and to avoid the second road. A possible fate of any hero is lotus-eating indolence and idleness; this second road, the witch-alligator warns Dominic, would lead him to excessive introspection, to "daydreaming and tail-twiddling," absent-mindedness and laziness—the mood of idleness without its counterpart in heroic initiative and energy. Thus Dominic receives a cunning spear, not from the Lady-in-the-Lake but from an affable catfish-in-the-pond. The spear and the piccolo help to define the happy balance of pastoral and heroic qualities in Dominic's nature.

Throughout the fantasy Dominic enjoys pastoral interludes, playing his piccolo in the green world, in tune seemingly with the music and harmony in nature. Dominic is infused with sensuous and spiritual enjoyment of nature. Steig stresses repeatedly Dominic's affinity with the natural world in scenes such as this:

"Dominic took out his piccolo and played softly, ever so softly."

The adventure road started out through a shady wood. On both sides the trees stood tall and solemn. The light glowed greenly through their leaves as if through stained-glass windows in a church. Dominic walked along in silence, smelling all the wonderful forest odors, alert to every new one, his nostrils quivering with delight. He smelled damp earth, mushrooms, dried leaves, violets, mint, spruce, rotting wood, animal droppings, forget-me-nots, and mold, and he savored all of it. The odors came as single notes, or percussion shots, or fused together in wonderful harmonies. He invented a melody which he decided should be called "The Psalm of Sweet Smells." [p. 9]

In the pastoral interludes of Steig's fantasy, then, Dominic enjoys *otium,* a condition which Thomas Rosenmeyer has described as "something like the American 'liberty,' a soldier's leave from duty . . . vacation, freedom, escape from pressing business, particularly a business with overtones of death."[6] Rosenmeyer further explains that *otium* "is *not* the abolition of energy, not withdrawal and curtailment, but a fullness in its own right."[7] Schiller describes the pastoral ambience of this kind of literature as "calm— the calm of perfection, not merely the calm of idleness."[8] In his moments of solitary pastoral meditation Dominic acquires one quality essential for the serenity of pastoral calm—a sense of the workings of the universe. Dominic thus needs *otium*—life in the golden noon in the green shade—but he also needs the pastoral of melancholy and self-discovery. As he grieves over the death of Bartholomew Badger, the pig whom he has befriended, Dominic gains at least a temporary insight into the nature of things:

He fell asleep under the vast dome of quivering stars, and just as he was falling asleep, passing over into the phase of dreams, he felt he understood the secret of life. But in the light of morning, when he woke up, his understanding of the secret had disappeared with the stars. The mystery was still there, inspiring his wonder. . . . The moment he stopped being busy, he felt his heart quake. He had to cry. Life was

suddenly too sad. And yet it was beautiful. The beauty was
dimmed when the sadness welled up. . . . So beauty and sadness belonged together somehow. [p. 35]

Dominic senses the need for wholeness, for the unity of being
which all human beings (and maybe dog beings, too) need and
yearn for. Pastoral fulfillment, however, demands not only Romantic solitude in nature, but also the companionship of a company of friends. In his communings with nature and in the homes
of his good friends along the way, Dominic shores up his energies,
assuming and protecting the values of home and community. This
core of value and meaning enables him to struggle victoriously
against the anarchic force which threatens the pastoral serenity
of the community, the evil Doomsday gang.

Heroic initiative is the other important feature in Dominic's
character: "Challenges were his delight. Whatever life offered was
this way or that, a test of one's skills, one's faculties; and he enjoyed proving equal to the tests" (p. 15). When the Doomsday
gang waits for Dominic outside his hole, he tricks them, burrow-
ing away from the hole and surfacing some distance away. Liberated and exultant, Dominic reminds the reader of Odysseus'
boasting to the cyclops, when, as Steig tells us, "Dominic couldn't
resist letting out one short bark to announce his liberation" (p. 17).

Subsequently, Dominic nurses the victim of the Doomsday gang's
terrorist tactics, the sick and dying pig Bartholomew Badger (who
leaves his treasure to Dominic), rescues a yellow jacket in distress,
and finally uses the treasure to make the community safe. When
he learns that Barney Swain, a friendly but helpless wild boar,
has lost all his money to the Doomsday gang and thus cannot wed
his beloved, Dominic unselfishly gives his treasure to the young
couple. He gives the remainder of the treasure to a poverty-stricken,
widowed goose and her gaggle of hungry goslings. Finally, the
Doomsday gang makes a supreme effort to subvert the community
by actually attacking the wedding celebration of Pearl Sweeney
and Barney Swain. Dominic is seriously wounded in the ensuing
battle, but he defeats the Doomsday gang and protects the love

Dominic was always courtly with ladies.

union of the young couple, and hence secures the social values of home and marriage, and the hope for a renewed society.

The fantasy, structured in alternating interludes of pastoral calm on one hand and heroic action on the other, culminates spiritually when Dominic reaches the ideal pastoral garden, in which love, art, and nature blend in perfect harmony. In the prelude to this climax, Dominic has experienced varying moods in nature, including Blakean innocent joy: "The gentle radiance of a rosy sun pervaded the air and little birds sang so lyrically that he took out his golden piccolo and joined them in their music. The world was suffused with peace and warmth" (p. 60). Even Dionysian madness has possessed Dominic. One evening, as Dominic piped for the revels of dancing field mice, he became more and more ecstatic: "the music strove nearer and nearer to the elemental truth of being" (p. 92). In a moment of Romantic agony and ecstasy, Dominic "raised his head, and, straining toward infinity, howled out the burden of his love and longing in sounds more meaningful than words" (p. 92). But Dominic is no solitary Romantic or brooding Byronic hero. Love calls us to the things of this world, and Dominic is called back to a simpler, calmer mood of innocent joy when he finds a worn-out doll lying forgotten in a meadow. His restlessness, his spiritual *angst* vanish when he holds the doll, an emblem of the pastoral pleasure of childhood; the toy inspires an intensely comforting pastoral dream of perfection:

> The little puppy [doll] with the shoe button eyes was quite soiled and damaged from years of handling. It was a run-of-the-mill, worn-with-use doll, and yet it held such magic for him. What was there about this lost plaything that he cared for so intensely? Why did it make him dream of things to come? Sitting with the doll in the rosy light of the setting sun, he knew he would be pleased with his future. He fell into a reverie and was no longer conscious of his surroundings or of passing time. Images of tender April flowers on the soft hillsides, of limpid minty pools in sweet, purling brooks, of hushed, fern-filled, aromatic forests, of benign, embracing breezes, and affectionate skies, of a peaceable world of happy creatures passed before his mind's eye. [pp. 107–08]

Dominic's efforts throughout the fantasy have been on the behalf of community and its institutions. He has cared for the sick and dying, presided over and been a good steward of community wealth and property, made the lives of its children safe, and protected the pastoral oasis, the home and marriage of the wild boars, Barney Swain and Pearl Sweeney. He has celebrated nature in all its moods, enjoyed the present, and glimpsed a visionary future. But throughout these heroic endeavors, Dominic has been alone, with only the beneficent natural world to protect him.

Leaving the home he has made secure for the newlyweds, Dom-

inic surrenders to the forest and seems to undergo a form of death
and rebirth. Too weak from his wounds to struggle against his
enemies, Dominic sleeps, unaware that the Doomsday gang has
surrounded him. Suddenly the woods reverberate with Dominic's
name as the trees express their love for "the brave generous dog
named Dominic." Nature acts in concert against the anarchic
malice of the Doomsday gang, and the members of the gang experience a conversion:

> The terror of this experience, the condemnation from the
> lords of the hitherto silent vegetable kingdom, had penetrated
> their souls. Convinced that Nature itself could no longer
> abide their destructive, criminal ways, they each slunk about
> separately making efforts to reform and get into Nature's
> good graces again, as every wanton one of them had been in
> his original childhood. [p. 136]

Dominic finds himself, finally, in a splendid garden which seems
to blend the best of both art and nature; in the garden Dominic
finds eternal spring, an illustrious peacock, rainbows of flowers
which sound like tinkling bells, and his own sleeping beauty,
whom he awakens because the little dog had belonged to her.
Evelyn, the sleeping beauteous dog, tells Dominic that the little
doll had been hers until she decided one day that she was no
longer a child and had thrown the beloved companion away: "I
remember I was standing in the field thinking about life and about
myself and about growing up. I became eager for the future and
I felt that the doll chained me to the past. So I got rid of it"
(p. 145).

Dominic helps Evelyn to recover her lost childhood and infuses
the present with pastoral joy, which includes art, music, nature,
and ultimately, marriage. Dominic represents, then, an ideal condition, a blend of the innocent, childlike, piping shepherd and
the valiant, heroic warrior. As a rule, the hero is tamed and do-
mesticated; with the embrace of woman and marriage his adventures cease. Steig, however, gives his readers a new kind of adventure—hero and woman equal in innocence and in spirit.

"She was black and shimmered in patterns of luminous purple, yellow, green, blue, and carmine from the windows."

Dominic's adventures will go on, but they will no longer be solitary. Sleeping Beauty no longer has to remain passively waiting in her castle: "Dominic realized he was at the beginning of a great new adventure" (p. 145). Evelyn can embrace her childhood and her womanhood and still go out in the world: "Together they left the little palace" (p. 146).

In *Abel's Island* Steig creates an interesting version of a traditional kind of story, the Robinsonade, in a survival story of an Edwardian mouse, Abelard, who is washed away in a storm while trying to retrieve his wife's kerchief. Once on the island, Abel, previously a mouse who had been at home in drawing rooms, discovers the joys of both the heroic and contemplative moods of the

Abel wished to be in his own home, with his loving wife.

hero. His distinguishing characteristics are chivalry, courage, initiative, resourcefulness, and imagination. On his island he must battle for survival, outwitting an owl who wants to eat him. At the same time he learns the pleasures of communing with nature and the satisfactions of creative work. Abel had left home a pampered mouse with no identity of his own; he returns a wiry-strong artist.

Abelard starts his adventures by accident; like Dominic, he adores his wife and thinks only of home and its domestic comforts. Totally civilized, clinging to his makeshift raft, he thinks:

> When the water subsided, he would descend and go home—and what a story he'd have to tell: Meanwhile, he wished he had something to eat—a mushroom omelet, for example with buttered garlic toast. Being hungry in addition to being marooned like this was really a bit too much. Absent-mindedly, he nibbled at a twig on his branch. Ah, cherry birch: One of his favorite flavors. The familiar taste made him feel a little more at home on his roost in the middle of nowhere.[9]

Indeed, Abel finds that he is able to make a home from his alien environment. As in traditional versions of pastoral, Abel's island bounteously provides his needs: "He munched on the bark of a tender green shoot, his cheek filled with the pulp and juice. He sat there, vaguely smug, convinced that he had the strength, the courage, the intelligence to survive" (p. 16).

Abel reveals his heroic initiative in various attempts to escape the island: he builds a boat, a raft, tries to build a bridge, and finally tries to catapult himself across the stream with his suspenders. Although each attempt fails, he is not discouraged, realizing that the island has indeed become the place where he lives. On the island Abel recovers a lost sense of childhood reciprocity with the natural world:

> He was suddenly thrilled to see his private, personal star arise in the East. This was a particular star his nanny had chosen for him when he was a child. As a child, he would

sometimes talk to this star, but only when he was his most serious, real self, and not being any sort of show-off or clown. As he grew up, the practice had worn off. [p. 32]

Abel's experience on the island, then, helps him to recover this "serious real self." Like a benevolent parent, the island itself provides abundant food in the harvest season: ripe raspberries, groundnuts, mulberries, wild mustard, wild onions, new kinds of mushrooms, spearmint, peppermint, and milkweed, all of which comes to Abel without excessive work. He has ample time for contemplation and meditation. Leo Marx has remarked that nature's abundance without labor is a significant dimension of traditional pastoral. Nature also provides Abel shelter in a hollow log. Asleep in his log, the melancholy rains cause him to reflect on the "poignant parts of life." Abel is sustained by his dreams of home: "The castaway dreamed all night of Amanda. They were together again in their home. But their home was not 89 Bank Street, in Mossville; it was a garden, something like the island, and full of flowers" (p. 48). Thus Abel's experience on his island gives him a new vision of home as a pastoral garden, rather than as the constraints of a house on Bank Street.

As Abel grows in his understanding of nature and as his response to it intensifies, he observes the eternal patterns in the natural world. As he watches the great plan and design of creation at work, he feels "a strong need to participate in the arranging and designing of things" (p. 54). Artistic creation demands the mood of idleness, of leisure, and Steig depicts his animal heroes at work—imaginative work—in their contemplative moments. In these times of leisure Abel transforms the pain of homesickness into statues of his family and friends. Through art he creates the familiar. His world is improved by his artistic efforts, and he searches for other ways to civilize the island and to make a home of an alien environment. Abel maintains a strong connection to the civilized world through art and through two items which he finds on the island—a clock and a book about bears.

Traditional pastoral poems, shepherds' calendars, are organized according to the seasons of the year. Accordingly, in *Abel's Is-*

"Coward!" Abel screamed. "Come down and do battle . . ."

land pastoral pleasance is interrupted by winter and by the terrifying appearance of an owl. The battle with the owl provides a test of Abel's courage, heroic anger, and resourcefulness as he fashions a spear with which to challenge and put to flight the bewildered owl. As winter closes in, Abel retreats into his log. Physically and spiritually ill, Abel survives by remembering the comforts of home. In his cold log, he reflects upon Amanda, the firelight, lentil soup on the stove–domestic pleasures and human companionship. Still he feels isolated, convinced that he is the only living thing in a wintry waste land. Spring, however, brings hope and the renewal of body and spirit. By April, Abel is certain that he and Amanda are no longer isolated from each other; his faith that he will return safely to her grows stronger. At the same time nature has given him much-needed independence: "Abel ate grass and young violet greens, fresh food with the juice of life. . . . At times he felt that he had no need of others" (p. 84).

While Abel still dreams of Amanda and loves her, he has come through an initiation. He has sloughed off the old, spoiled, and pampered self and has been reborn. Renato Poggioli has remarked that European writers of the seventeenth century liberated pastoral from an exclusive concern with sexuality by developing "the pastoral of the self, which in the end transcended all previous traditions of the genre."[10] Abel, the reader is told, had lived on his mother's wealth; apparently his wife has served primarily as a mother surrogate. Secure in his snug urban home, Abel had not really lived. His pastoral sojourn on the island has given him an identity: "He was a wiry-strong mouse after his rugged year in the wilds. The Abel who was leaving was in better fettle, in all ways, than the Abel who had arrived in a hurricane, desperately clinging to a nail. . . . He was imagining ahead to Amanda, and beyond her to his family, his friends, and a renewed life in society, that would include productive work, his art" (p. 106). At last, as a result of his resourceful efforts, Abel's dream of home comes true. Home and Amanda are just the same; only Abel has changed and has found himself embarrassed and uncomfortable in an elegant velvet jacket. While Steig does not resolve Abel's new problem, the reader is left with a sure sense that Abel's abiding love for Amanda, coupled with his newly discovered strength, will insure their future happiness.

In *Dominic* and *Abel's Island*, Steig has created a tension between the pastoral and the heroic interludes, between the spear and the piccolo, a balance which suggests that his heroes, Dominic the Indomitable Dog and Abel the Miraculous Mouse, achieve two characteristics which Rosenmeyer considers essential to the serenity of the pastoral frame of mind: a perspective with the benign universe and fellowship with a goodly company. Their lives are filled with possibility because they know when to play, when to work, when to create, and when to meditate. Their lives are enriched by their affinity with nature, a quality which is blended harmoniously with their love of art and the best of the civilized world. Unlike regressive expressions of the pastoral impulse, such as that of James Barrie's *Peter Pan*, Dominic and Abel willingly face the darker layers of existence—predation, old age, sickness, and death. They infuse the present and the future with the pastoral values of childhood while embracing the pleasures of maturity. Even in maturity they retain their innocence, as well as their imaginations and their sensuous joy in the sights, sounds, and smells of the natural world. Ursula Le Guin has written that fantasy helps to provide the internal exploration necessary to produce a whole, integrated human being—to allow emotional growth and healthy maturity. For Le Guin, "maturity is not an outgrowing, but a growing up: . . . an adult is not a dead child, but a child who survived."[11] So it is with Abel and Dominic.

An important way in which Steig expresses the pastoral in *Abel's Island* and *Dominic* is through his formal, elegant language. Theorists on the nature of pastoral have often remarked upon its civilized and sophisticated qualities, the "double-vision" of a narrator. Blue Calhoun comments on the pastoral narrator's dual perspective: "The pastoral world is a civilized creation. Simple life in a green garden is necessarily the vision of a sophisticated writer, one who is committed by history and temperament to the complexities of city life but who questions its basic assumption."[12] In Steig's fantasies, the elegant language and the gentle burlesque of fairy tale and romance conventions underscore the artifice of the fantasy world. The courtly manners of Dominic and Abel, their serene restraint, suggest not romantic primitivism but a life in nature improved by art, social grace, and civilization. In *Dominic* the image of the ideal garden at the end, replete with gorgeous artifice, combines the best of the pastoral and the urban worlds. In *Abel's Island* the island itself becomes an aesthetic construct which similarly combines attributes of nature and art. Steig draws upon the language of civilization to depict the natural world—the light in the forest is like a stained-glass window; the sounds of nature are like a symphony orchestra. In fact Steig has spoken of his own long-time delight in courtly language. Having grown up in the Bronx, far from green pastoral bowers, Steig and his playmates created their own linguistic make-believe world of romance. They had read *Robinson Crusoe, King Arthur,* and *Robin Hood* and incorporated the language of these stories into their play. Steig explains: "Here were these kids in the Bronx yelling: 'I'll smite thee, thou churlish knave.' And we thought that was marvelous. We spoke Arthurian language."[13] Dominic's language is equally courtly. After rescuing goose-in-distress Matilda Fox from a Doomsday deathtrap, Dominic gallantly declares: "Your life is my reward. . . . With you in the world, the world is a better place, I'm sure. My name is Dominic. I am at your service, madam" (p. 74). This gallant statement is accompanied by a graceful bow, and the amused narrator adds, "Dominic was exceptionally attentive to ladies." Steig, a child of the city, has acquired his own visions of pastoral, romance, and heroic adventure through stories and their linguistic conventions. The pastoral sensibility in his fantasies is expressed, then, through his playful burlesque of conventions, and his witty play with language. He obviously enjoys naming the pastoral lovers in *Dominic* —the two affectionate wild boars—Barney Swain and Pearl Sweeney, just as he whimsically reverses the names of several animals: the pig is "Bartholomew Badger"; the artistic mouse is "Manfred

Lyon"; and the plump, widowed goose is "Matilda Fox." Steig's elegant language and his playful use of conventions help to define the fantasies as artifice, in sharp contrast to the random world of disordered and chaotic experience. His sophisticated tone and detachment, however, convey amused affection, not contempt, for the pastoral world. The knowing, urbane writer is keenly aware that he is not creating the world as it is actually experienced. The green world of pastoral, the ideal garden—its innocence, heroism, beauty, art, joy, its freedom from greed, ignorance, and cupidity—is an emblem of mankind's possibility, of what the poet dreams in his "deep heart's core," of civilized life as it might be lived. It expresses the wish that human beings may someday attain the fullness of experience and yet retain the innocent sense of newness which assures them that they are at the beginning of a great new adventure.

Notes

1. James E. Higgins, interview with William Steig, "William Steig: Champion of Romance," *Children's Literature in Education*, 9, 1 (Spring 1978), 6.

2. Blue Calhoun, *The Pastoral Vision of William Morris: The Earthly Paradise* (Athens: University of Georgia Press, 1975), pp. 30–31.

3. See Paul Zweig, *The Adventurer* (New York: Basic Books, 1974), p. 47, for a discussion of the differences between the true hero (typified by Aeneas) and the adventurer, the prototype of whom Zweig identifies as Odysseus.

4. Leo Marx, "The Two Kingdoms of Force," *Massachusetts Review*, 1 (1959), 90.

5. William Steig, *Dominic* (New York: Farrar, Straus, and Giroux, 1972), p. 1. Subsequent quotations from *Dominic* will be indicated parenthetically in the text.

6. Thomas G. Rosenmeyer, *The Green Cabinet* (Berkeley and Los Angeles: University of California Press, 1969), pp. 67–68.

7. Ibid. p. 71.

8. Friedrich Schiller, *On Naive and Sentimental Poetry* (Oxford: Oxford University Press, 1951), p. 55.

9. William Steig, *Abel's Island* (New York: Farrar, Straus, and Giroux, 1976), p. 16. Subsequent quotations from *Abel's Island* will be indicated parenthetically in the text.

10. Renato Poggioli, "The Pastoral of the Self," *Daedalus*, 88 (1959), 686.

11. Ursula Le Guin, "Why Are Americans Afraid of Dragons?" in *The Language of the Night*, by Ursula Le Guin, ed. Susan Wood (New York: G. P. Putnam's Sons, 1979), p. 44.

12. Calhoun, p. 9.

13. Higgins, interview with Steig, p. 14.

Home and Away in Children's Fiction

Christopher Clausen

The highest compliment a children's book can receive is for critics to say that it isn't for children at all. When adults annex a book like *Alice's Adventures in Wonderland* or *Huckleberry Finn* for themselves, it achieves a higher literary status than even that of being numbered among the "classic" works for children, works such as *Now We Are Six, Treasure Island,* or—a more complicated case, as we shall see—*The Wind in the Willows.*

The criteria by which a book may be placed in one category or the other have been much discussed but never clearly defined, and they are a great deal less obvious than they may seem. To say that a book appeals to people of many different ages is no help here; all the books I have listed do that, as do the *Iliad, Old Possum's Book of Practical Cats, Gulliver's Travels,* and most books about the Civil War. Nor is it enough to identify the primary audience that the writer had in mind, since *Huckleberry Finn* and the Alice books were written, illustrated, and marketed for children. Realism is no criterion; most fiction for adults is no more realistic than most children's fiction. That a book raises issues which are intellectually beyond the comprehension of most children may seem a slightly more promising standard; yet how many adults are equipped to comprehend the linguistic and logical issues in *Through the Looking-Glass,* the moral issues in *Huckleberry Finn,* or indeed the full range of questions raised by any profound work of literature? That many adults understand more of these thing than many children is hardly an adequate basis for confident taxonomizing.

It is improbable that any single standard can be used to tell us which of the books we deeply admire are "really" children's books, which adult books (a phrase with contemporary connotations that imply sexual interest as a criterion), and which genuinely ambiguous. The books we *don't* deeply admire may present fewer problems, but then the question of their status is correspondingly less interesting.

This essay will speculate on why some books fall into one category, some into another. My intrinsic approach will not, admitted-
ly, apply to all works of fiction, but where it does apply it should
almost infallibly distinguish books that are genuinely for children.
It applies strikingly to two of the works cited above, *Huckleberry
Finn* and *The Wind in the Willows,* about which Grahame's biographer had this to say: "It is interesting to compare the double
theme which preoccupies Grahame in *The Wind in the Willows*—
the judgment of Innocence on the World, the deep basic symbolism
of the River—with the somewhat different treatment both receive
in Mark Twain's *Huckleberry Finn.* Twain's classic had appeared
in 1885, and there is little doubt that Grahame knew it well. He
certainly gave a copy to his son."[1] Twain's influence on Grahame's
book is palpable, not so much in the use both make of the River
as in the tall tales and female disguise by which Toad escapes from
a series of captors. Both are stories of escape and return, of naive
innocence ambiguously overcoming the perils of the Wide World,
of civilization making ominous advances into the heartland of natural goodness. Each ends with the protagonist and his friends re-
stored to honor and fortune. Yet nearly everyone will agree that
Grahame has written a genuine children's book and Twain has not.
Why? I believe that a key to what appeals to children in Grahame's
book is this: in *The Wind in the Willows,* the major escape (Toad's)
is from prison to home. Although several of the characters are
tempted by travel, home is clearly where the characters belong and
where, after many vicissitudes, they return. As Mole feels when he
has found again the home he left on a spring morning:

> He saw clearly how plain and simple—how narrow, even—it all
> was; but clearly, too, how much it all meant to him, and the
> special value of some such anchorage in one's existence. He did
> not at all want to abandon the new life and its splendid spaces.
> . . . But it was good to think he had this to come back to, this
> place which was all his own, these things which were so glad
> to see him again and could always be counted upon for the
> same simple welcome.[2]

For the River-bankers, there is no place like home; and while that attitude may not in real life be any more characteristic of children than of adults, it is certainly common in children's books. In *Huckleberry Finn,* on the contrary, the escape is *from* home, and it is never repented of or shown to be mistaken, although it is not altogether successful. Home, for Huck and his author, is the problem, not the solution. Huck says in the beginning: "The Widow Douglas, she took me for her son, and allowed she would sivilize me; but it was rough living in the house all the time, considering how dismal regular and decent the widow was in all her ways; and so when I couldn't stand it no longer, I lit out. I got into my old rags, and my sugar-hogshead again, and was free and satisfied."[3] Returning to the Widow's makes Huck feel "so lonesome I most wished I was dead" (p. 9). At the end of the book, returned home once more, he hasn't changed his mind and is on the brink of another escape: "But I reckon I got to light out for the Territory ahead of the rest, because Aunt Sally she's going to adopt me and sivilize me and I can't stand it. I been there before" (p. 229).

For Huck, home is the place where, when you have to go there, you almost wish you were dead. In contrast to home, there is the raft, symbol of random motion and effortless escape. "We said there warn't no home like a raft, after all. Other places do seem so cramped up and smothery, but a raft don't. You feel mighty free and easy and comfortable on a raft" (p. 96).

When home is a privileged place, exempt from the most serious problems of life and civilization—when home is where we ought, on the whole, to stay—we are probably dealing with a story for children. When home is the chief place from which we must escape, either to grow up or (as in Huck's case) to remain innocent, then we are involved in a story for adolescents or adults. As Geraldine D. Poss says of an earlier Grahame children's story, "The world which [the characters] envision is one which simply ignores death, women, and pressure to achieve,"[4] a statement which might with almost equal justice be made about *The Wind in the Willows.* It is precisely "death, women and pressure to achieve" that Huck Finn tries to escape by leaving home. Grahame's characters, how-

ever, live in a place that gives them few reasons for escape, a fact
which inevitably leads some critics to the suspicion that their author has done their escaping for them. Thus common opinion is
correct: *The Wind in the Willows* is a children's book, and *Huckleberry Finn* is not.[5]

Viewed in this light, the ancestor of all journey books, *The Odyssey*, is an instructive mixture. Ithaca after the Trojan War is in
many ways far from being a privileged place, yet Odysseus' aim
throughout the poem is to return there, and he is clearly right to
do so. In his ten-years' journey home from Troy, he encounters
enough picturesque monsters and boys'–own adventures to furnish
a shelf of children's books. The modesty of his goals and his success
in achieving them make Odysseus unique among epic heroes, and
in modern times *The Odyssey* has almost certainly been read by
more children (and more often adapted for young readers) than
any other epic. Later writers, however, have frequently found its
ending disappointingly tame and have transformed Odysseus into
an emblem of the proto-modern, searching mind by taking him in
late middle age permanently away from Ithaca. Hence the sequels
by Dante, Tennyson, Kazantzakis. The final escape is not from monsters or suitors, but from a safe domesticity.

"Escape" is one of the most thoughtlessly used words in the critical vocabulary, particularly when coupled with the phrase "from
reality," and in analyzing stories that either narrate escapes or are
alleged to be escapist, we need to be careful about what we mean.
In defending fairy stories and other forms of fantasy against the
negative connotations of the word, J. R. R. Tolkien provides us
with the beginnings of a useful distinction:

> In what the misusers are fond of calling Real Life, Escape is
> evidently as a rule very practical, and may even be heroic. In
> real life it is difficult to blame it, unless it fails; in criticism it
> would seem to be worse the better it succeeds. . . . Why should
> a man be scorned if, finding himself in prison, he tries to get
> out and go home? Or if, when he cannot do so, he thinks and
> talks about other topics than jailers and prison-walls? The world
> outside has not become less real because the prisoner cannot

see it. In using Escape in this way, the critics have chosen the wrong word, and, what is more, they are confusing, not always by sincere error, the Escape of the Prisoner with the Flight of the Deserter.[6]

To escape means simply to get away from something unpleasant; both unmerited imprisonment and duty may be unpleasant, but our moral judgment of the escaper will depend largely upon which of these categories of experience he is escaping. In *Huckleberry Finn,* almost no readers will judge Jim unfavorably for escaping from slavery, just as in *The Wind in the Willows* Toad's escape from prison is clearly the right course of action for him to take. Whether Huck is quite so justified in escaping from religion, education, manners, and clothes into what can be only a temporary idyll is more debatable; those moralists who believe in good citizenship, strong neighborhoods, and the work ethic will certainly say no.

It is when we try to decide whether whole books and their authors are escapist, however, that the question becomes really complicated. With what view of reality and the consequences of action is an author required to present his audience of children or adults? If he believes, as both Twain and Grahame did, that full participation in the adult, civilized world is a form of imprisonment, is he required to show his characters accepting such participation as their duty, or may he allow them to attempt whatever forms of escape seem most practicable to them? And if they try the second alternative, must their author show them failing? Twain did so and is regarded as a realist, despite the fact that Huck begins and ends the story independently wealthy and Jim is freed by the providential death of his owner. Grahame chose instead to create an environment which is substantially free from the pressures of adult civilization—although those pressures are certainly felt in the story —and at the end of their adventures, his characters are as safe and happy as they were at the beginning, having learned anew to reject the Wide World of manmade laws, motor-cars, and jails. We are probably safe in assuming that middle-class life along the Fowey River *circa* 1908 was in actuality pleasanter than frontier life on

the banks of the Mississippi in the 1840s; we have no warrant for
concluding that Grahame's book is more escapist, in the negative
sense of the word, than Twain's. If modern civilization is a moral
disaster, then getting away from it (by staying home, in the case of
a children's book) is a duty in both life and literature, so long as
we are clear about our reasons for rejecting it.

Regardless of whether home is benign or terrible, of course, people do like to get away sometimes, and Grahame's characters are
no exception. *The Wind in the Willows* is the story of their varying attempts at adventure and of the lessons they learn about home
and escape. The book begins when Mole, fed up with spring cleaning, ventures out of his hole and discovers the river. "Something
from above was calling him imperiously" (p. 2), and in answering
the call he soon finds himself sharing Rat's broader and more so-
ciable way of life. Indeed, it looks for awhile as though Mole's new
life will represent a genuine break with the past, for he shows
such signs of venturesomeness that Rat, the wisest of all the characters, feels compelled to warn him against the world that lies beyond the horizon:

> "Beyond the Wild Wood comes the Wide World," said the
> Rat. "And that's something that doesn't matter, either to you
> or me. I've never been there, and I'm never going, nor you
> either, if you've got any sense at all. Don't ever refer to it again,
> please." (p. 14)

Leaving home for a while is all right only if one doesn't go too far,
or for too long. Neither Rat nor Mole ever ventures into the Wide
World; that act of folly is left to the most foolish of all the characters, with dire results. When Mole goes even so far as the Wild
Wood, he finds it a place of fear and menace; after his rescue, he
recognizes that he has been taught a lesson he will never again
forget:

> The Mole saw clearly that he was an animal of tilled field and
> hedgerow, linked to the ploughed furrow, the frequented pas-
> ture, the lane of evening lingerings, the cultivated garden-plot.
> . . . He must be wise, must keep to the pleasant places in which

his lines were laid and which held adventure enough, in their way, to last for a lifetime. (p. 101)

It is after the Wild Wood that he begins to miss his hole, to search for it with much difficulty, and to appreciate it more than ever when he has found it again.

The Rat is a much more adventurous animal as well as a more experienced one, and his reluctance to travel widely cannot be due to either ignorance or timidity. As he has warned Mole against the Wide World, so he warns the footloose Toad against wandering about in a gipsy caravan, a warning which events justify when Toad, after nearly a fatal encounter with a motor-car falls in love with a mechanical transport (That the car is the chief symbol—a negative one—of the modern world in Grahame's book is appropriate, since it represents both rapid travel and industrialization.) Rat is so consistently wise throughout the book that it comes as a major surprise when he too is tempted with the wanderlust against which he has all along warned. The agents of temptation are swallows preparing to migrate south. "With closed eyes he dared to dream a moment in full abandonment, and when he looked again the river seemed steely and chill, the green fields grey and lifeless. Then his loyal heart seemed to cry out on his weaker self for its treachery" (p. 211)

The vocabulary makes it clear that for Rat to leave like the birds would be the flight of the deserter, an evasion of responsibility, and a denial of what he knows about life. Having overcome temptation, however, he is almost immediately plunged into a hypnotic state by the yarns of the Sea Rat, a true escapist if ever there was, who has much to say about the glories of Sicily and Constantinople.

Mechanically he returned home, gathered together a few small necessaries and special treasures he was fond of, and put them in a satchel; acting with slow deliberation, moving about the room like a sleep-walker; listening ever with parted lips. He swung the satchel over his shoulder, carefully selected a stout stick for his wayfaring, and with no haste, but with no hesitation at all, he stepped across the threshold just as the Mole appeared in the door. (pp. 229–30)

This time Mole, determined teacher of a lesson he himself had learned only recently, returns the favor and prevents the folly of an escape from home. That roaming the world is such a temptation, even for the less flighty characters, demonstrates beyond doubt that the virtues of home are a lesson of experience, not merely an instinct of the fearful. Huck Finn's preparations before he departs from the "home" where Pap is holding him prisoner are told in quite a different tone:

> I took the sack of corn meal and took it to where the canoe was hid, and shoved the vines and branches apart and put it in; then I done the same with the side of bacon; then the whisky jug; I took all the coffee and sugar there was, and all the ammunition; I took the wadding; I took the bucket and gourd, I took a dipper and a tin cup, and my old saw and two blankets, and the skillet and the coffee-pot. I took fishlines and matches and other things—everything that was worth a cent. I cleaned out the place. . . . I fetched out the gun, and now I was done. (pp. 30–31)

The contrast between two attitudes towards home, and two kinds of escape, could hardly be better illustrated.

Of the major characters in *The Wind in the Willows,* it is only Toad who for any considerable length of time sets home at naught and gives way to the temptations of distance. We should remember that properly speaking, he is Mister Toad of Toad Hall, an Edwardian landed gentleman, and that as a gentleman he naturally possesses a confidence (unwarranted, of course) in his ability to make the inhabitants of the Wide World do his bidding; this confidence is entirely unshared by any other character in the story. Among other things, *The Wind in the Willows* is a satire on Toad's belief that traditional social distinctions count for much in the alien world of twentieth-century human civilization. (In Twain's world he might be a Grangerford.) It is not until Toad finds himself described in the courtroom as an "incorrigible rogue and hardened ruffian" (pp. 149–50)—all he has done, after all, is to "borrow" a motor-car— that he begins to understand the virtues of home. His escape involves the humiliation of dressing up as a washerwoman, and since he has forgotten to remove his wallet from the abandoned garments of his true rank, he undergoes a salutory education in the life of poverty before reaching the sanctuary of Rat's home. He is even tossed into a canal by a woman of plebian habits (p. 243).

Once he reaches the river-bank, a further shock awaits him: Toad Hall is in the hand of invading stoats and weasels. At this point (though not for the first or the last time), Toad is properly repentant of his past and puts himself in the hands of his friends, Rat, Badger, and Mole. By use of an underground passage into Toad Hall that only Badger knows about—Toad's ignorance embraces not only the Wide World but even his own house—the heroes overcome the occupying forces, and Toad Hall is liberated. Henceforth Toad will abide more humbly and wisely at home—or so his friends hope.

The price of Toad's travels, then, is to have to fight for his home when he returns. Appropriately, the last chapter of *The Wind in the Willows* is entitled "The Return of Ulysses." The benign pastoral enclave is not a free gift of the gods; like Ithaca, it needs to be guarded by wisdom, discretion, and sometimes force. Toad's escape from home (the flight of the deserter) makes necessary the far more desperate flight back (the escape of the prisoner), as well as the battle that follows. The second escape is, of course, implausibly easy; merely breaking jail and returning home does not normally guarantee immunity from the law. But the lessons of the adventure are plain—if not to Toad, at least to the reader.

What, by way of epilogue, about J. R. R. Tolkien? In *The Hobbit*, his early children's book, Tolkien created a race of beings who, in the felicity of their surroundings, their preference for living in holes, and their reluctance to seek adventures in the wider world, are recognizably indebted to *The Wind in the Willows*.[7] Bilbo Baggins, whose attachment to home is similar to Rat's, is prevailed upon by the wizard Gandalf to take part in a quest so that he may learn about the dangers of the outside world. (Those who will not inform themselves about evil, Tolkien seems to be saying, are likely to have no defense against it when they find themselves forced to protect their homes.) Bilbo's quest is successful, both in its immediate object and as a device for educating him, but it is significant that the only reward he seeks is to be allowed to return home. This wish is repeated throughout the book as a sort of refrain. Once returned, he finds that his house and effects are in the process of being sold at auction, and his repossession of home, though not as arduous as Toad's, costs him considerable bother. At the end of the book, however, he has returned to a well-earned domesticity, interrupted only by occasional visits to the Elves. There is no indication that he will ever again trade the placid virtues of home for the more speculative benefits of adventure. Even the great ring of power has come to serve the domestic purpose of helping him avoid unwelcome callers. The lessons he has learned do not qualify his attachment to home; rather they equip him to defend his island of peace against an increasingly threatening world outside.

Lord of the Rings, which is generally agreed not to be a children's book, comes to rather different conclusions. Frodo Baggins, his two cousins, and his servant Sam set out with a reluctance equal to Bilbo's on a far longer and more dangerous quest. On their return, they find the Shire occupied by the very forces of evil they have helped to vanquish in the world outside—the hobbits who stayed home not having learned the lessons of defense—and although the invaders are quickly put to flight, Frodo finds it impossible to settle back into domestic life. After the terrible pain and temptations he has experienced, only the wisdom and healing power of the Elves can make him whole. The Shire, for all its virtues, is simply too narrow a place after what he has learned and undergone. Home has been outgrown, and Frodo commits a more elegant equivalent of lighting out for the Territory. Setting out with Bilbo (who is not at all the home-loving character he was in *The Hobbit*) and the lords of the Elves for the Grey Havens, he tries to explain himself to the uncomprehending Sam:

"But," said Sam, and tears started in his eyes, "I thought you were going to enjoy the Shire, too, for years and years after all you have done."

"So I thought too, once. But I have been too deeply hurt, Sam. I tried to save the Shire, and it has been saved, but not for me. It must often be so, Sam, when things are in danger: some one has to give them up, lose them, so that others may keep them. . . . You will be the Mayor, of course, as long as you want to be, and the most famous gardener in history; and you will read things out of the Red Book, and keep alive the memory of the age that is gone, so that people will remember the Great Danger and so love their beloved land all the more. And that will keep you as busy and as happy as anyone can be, as long as your part of the Story goes on.

"Come now, ride with me!"[8]

"Come now, ride with me!"—these are Frodo's last words, and in this context at least, they could not be the last words of the main character in a children's book. The Escape of the Prisoner has taken on a dimension that transcends the distinction between home and the wide world. It is Sam, however, the boy hero who never grows up,[9] protagonist of a thousand stories of adventure for children, who pronounces the book's last sentence when he returns home at nightfall: "Well, I'm back."

Notes

1. Peter Green, *Kenneth Grahame: A Biography* (London: Murray, 1959), p. 202.

2. Kenneth Grahame, *The Wind in the Willows* (1908; rpt. London: Methuen, 1960), p. 127. All quotations hereafter will be identified parenthetically in the text.

3. Samuel L. Clemens, *Adventures of Huckleberry Finn* (1885; rpt. New York: Norton, 1977), p. 7. All quotations hereafter will be identified parenthetically in the text.

4. Geraldine D. Poss, "An Epic in Arcadia: The Pastoral World of *The Wind in the Willows*," *Children's Literature*, 4 (1975), 81. Poss considers interestingly the question of whether *The Wind in the Willows* is really a children's book and arrives at a negative conclusion based on the difficulty of its vocabulary and "the longing for a golden age" which it embodies. But some children do long for golden ages, and the vocabulary was less difficult in the England of 1908.

5. Home, of course, may represent many different values in books for either children or adults, but it is noteworthy that the security of a conventional family is not available to the main characters in any of the books I am discussing. Nor do any of them seem to miss it. Huck, Rat, Toad, Mole, Bilbo, and Frodo are all permanently celibate, and the only surviving parent any of them has is

Pap Finn. For a very different treatment of "homes" in *The Wind in the Willows*, see Lois R. Kuznets, "Toad Hall Revisited," *Children's Literature*, 7 (1978), 115–28.

6. J. R. R. Tolkien, "On Fairy-Stories," in *The Tolkien Reader* (New York: Ballantine Books, 1966), p. 60.

7. Like *The Wind in the Willows*, *The Hobbit* was first told to and then written for children; it also possesses the rarer distinction of having been accepted for publication by a ten-year-old. See Humphrey Carpenter, *Tolkien* (Boston: Houghton Mifflin, 1977), pp. 180–81.

8. J. R. R. Tolkien, *The Return of King* (Boston: Houghton Mifflin, 1965), p. 309.

9. Not in the story itself, at least. The fact that Sam has a wife and child when Frodo departs, and plays an adult role in governing the Shire, merely makes him a more conventional character than Frodo, not a maturer one. As his age and social status increase, Sam evidently comes to share Frodo's outlook. The appendices tell us that after raising his children and serving as Mayor for many years, he too leaves the Shire and passes over the sea (*Return of the King*, p. 378).

There's No Place Like Oz

Margaret Hamilton

I walked quickly along Fifth Avenue and Central Park. Suddenly, I heard at my back, "Excuse me, Miss Hamilton? You *are*—yes, you *are*—gosh! I'm sorry to interrupt your walk; but I've always hoped for this! I'm a great fan of yours—could I ask you a few questions about *The Wizard of Oz*?"

"Yes, but kindly ask them as quickly as possible," I answered. "I have a dentist appointment."

"Oh, yes! Thank you! You don't know—"

"Yes, I do," I thought; "I have heard this before."

"I'm so excited I could die!"

"Please don't."

"No, I won't. Don't worry," he said, "but I'm so excited I've forgotten all the things I wanted to ask."

"Well, calm yourself. I will *not* melt. Let's sit here on this bench."

"Let's see," he began, "I know—did any of you—did you think when you made—"

"No—we never did," I answered, "at least, I didn't . . . ."

And it is true. I didn't consider, or at least I didn't realize at the time, how popular *The Wizard of Oz* would be. The picture has touched thousands of people. People are forever stopping me on the street, making me late for dentist appointments, to ask about the picture.

That afternoon at home, I decided that, while I really did not have all the time I felt I needed to think things through, I must get a hold on the answer to that question which had plagued and fascinated me for years: What is it that makes that picture so special, what is it that captures our attention, our imagination, that appeals to us, that makes us want to share it with others? The picture resembles Christmas. We want to *share* it. And now, thanks to our somewhat bedeviled TV, we can see it at home with people we love and who love us.

The word *home* comes to mind. The picture gives us a warm and lovely feeling and yet an anxiety, and it raises a question. Who among that odd crew in Oz triggers this? Go back to the very beginning. There is a little girl, Dorothy, who is late coming home because she feels trouble is following her. She is full of her trouble and needs to share it and feel safe. But Uncle Henry and Auntie Em have their own trouble—barnyard trouble. Dorothy is suddenly in the way. She is told to find a place where she won't get in the way. Her beautiful eyes cloud. She thinks she is not wanted. The hurt is unexpected. Where, she wonders, can she go? A lovely song soothes and answers her: over the rainbow. She packs her basket and goes away with Toto, her faithful dog.

We watch a marvelous encounter with a traveling magician, with a magic heart. He deftly turns her toward home. He or a tornado carries her far afield—"over the rainbow" to a new land. Now she is not at home in Kansas and she wants to return but does not know how. No one in Munchkinland can tell her how to get home. We go with her and share the "crowd" of three she invites to go with her. All four travelers have pressing needs which only the Wonderful Wizard of Oz can help.

Now, not the good fairy, not the little people, not the companions, not the forest, not the Wicked Witch of the West, not the Emerald City, not anything else occupies Dorothy's mind and heart but only how to get home. We watch her through all the dangers and disappointments, and we wholeheartedly sympathize with her. The sunshine in her eyes, her smile, her faith, her wonder, the heart-breaking moments of despair touch our own feelings and our spirits rise and fall with Dorothy as she struggles to reach home.

In the final moments, which we know so well, when Dorothy is so near to going home, the Wizard leaves without her. But happily the Good Fairy appears. "Just close your eyes, tap your shoes together [the ruby slippers] and say three times, 'There's no place like home.'" A few minutes later she is home—in her own room and her own bed, surrounded by those she loves. And all across the land, people watching sigh and smile. They are, or at least

I am, left with a glow that never quite leaves and a real sense of satisfaction and a renewal of the magic of home: the place where we belong, where we are welcome, where there is love and understanding and acceptance waiting for us when we come. Home, where we can shed our cares and share our troubles and feel safe and protected. "Home, home, sweet, sweet home / No matter where we shall wander, / There's no place like home."

And do you know, we never lose it. The structure may disappear, but its essence is forever with us. Home has as many different expressions as there are people to recognize them, and there is no other word which conveys to us the same emotion: "Never mind—go home," "I'm going home," "Come home with me." We can always return to that which holds our heart—to Home. That is what that picture tells me.

I think it coincides with the wonderful lesson Dorothy says she has learned at last, about feeling she has lost her home. Her answer to the Good Fairy is, "If I have lost something and I look all over for it and can't find it, it means I really never lost it in the first place." That is subtle, but finally I understood. If you can't find it, it is still there somewhere—you still have it. I pondered over that for years. I used to think, "But I never really *had* it!" Then I listened and thought and remembered, and then, one time, I knew. I had been there. And I still am.

Reviews

J. M. Barrie: Peter Pan and the Idealization of Boyhood

Martin Green

J. M. Barrie and the Lost Boys: The Love Story That Gave Birth to Peter Pan, by Andrew Birkin. New York: Clarkson N. Potter, 1979.

This is the story of the five Llewelyn Davies boys adopted by J. M. Barrie, the boys for whom, about whom, and to some degree with whom he wrote *Peter Pan*. Barrie's relationship to the boys is a part of not only theatrical but also children's literature history; and this book shows that it was also a sizable event in the moral-historical history of the century.

Barrie's sexuality and affections were abnormal. He not only ignored his wife, he paid assiduous court to Sylvia Llewelyn Davies and more or less displaced her husband, at least in the role of father to her five children. He never, however, attempted sexually to seduce her or them. Like a courtly love minstrel, he simply celebrated in her the most adorable woman of her time, and in them the most enchanting little boys. He was not deceiving himself. This book is full of evidence that other people came to recognize their quality too, and that they deserved those titles; the evidence comes in the form of written tributes by friends and of innumerable photographs. The evidence is all the more corroborative for being quite unlike *Peter Pan* in its style; some of it, for instance, is couched in the idiom of 1920s dandyism (an idiom alien to Barrie) and comes from other young men of that decade. But Barrie had long before recognized the boys and created public images for them in literature.

One of the most interesting points is that these were images *for* rather than *of* them. Barrie did not describe the Llewelyn Davieses, except insofar as Sylvia is sketched in as Mrs. Darling in the stage directions to *Peter Pan*. But the play's sensibility obliquely indi-

cates—playfully, by allusion, negation, outlines—a frame for which
the only suitable central icon would be Sylvia and her boys. Barrie
showed London the human types it most cherished in 1904: the
sweetly mocking virgin mother and her handsome, precocious,
cocky little boys. In the play, as in real life, the male progenitor
is dismissed (kindly) as crass and ludicrous.

Soon after the play was first produced, Arthur Llewelyn Davies
fell ill and died. This left Barrie as main financial support of the
household. And soon after that, Sylvia too fell ill and died, so
that he became legal guardian of the boys. This was in 1910, when
the boys' ages ranged from 17 (George) to 7 (Nico). They were
not all—all the time—unmixedly glad to belong to Barrie, who was
a very odd little man, generous to them though he was. This book
suggests some unclear and unhappy interactions between them.
But more interesting than those, to my mind, is the later interaction of the boys with the rest of the world.

George became an army officer in 1914, as did most of his friends
at Eton and Cambridge. His brother says, "Few that survive would
recall anyone whose image serves better as the flower and type
of that doomed generation . . . the bloom of youth on them still
. . . too young to have been coarsened" (p. 228). He was one of
those for whose loss the young of the '20s blamed their elders, and
in whose name they refused maturity for themselves. A figure of
gaiety and charm, he was *loved*. When he was killed in Flanders in
1915, a fellow officer wrote to the family that everyone in the
battalion agreed that he was the best loved of them all, and "there
is no one whom I have loved more" (p. 244).

George had been Barrie's first favorite, and the next was Michael,
the fourth brother. Too young to serve in the war, after it he was
a very popular undergraduate; and he drowned in the river at
Oxford in 1922. The drowning was generally suspected to be a
suicide, indeed a double suicide with his best friend, clasped in
whose arms Michael was found. He, like George, had been the
object of very strong feeling, in some cases overtly homosexual.
"He had tremendous charm—a romantic charm, never sentimental,"
said one of his classmates at Eton (p. 250). Robert Boothby said

he was "the most remarkable person I ever met, and the only one of my generation to be touched by genius" (p. 282); Boothby claimed (writing in 1976) that his own "mistakes" in later life, and those of another of Michael's friends, Roger Senhouse, would never have occurred if Michael had lived (p. 295).

The reader may well judge this to be sentimental exaggeration, but the sentiment was general, and strong, and persistent. It was in 1946 that one of the surviving brothers, Peter (who founded the publishing firm Peter Davies, Ltd.), began to collect material about them all; he kept writing in what he called the Morgue till he committed suicide in 1960. This is the same vein of feeling, in 1915, 1922, 1946, and 1976, as it was in *Peter Pan* in 1904. Barrie then looked forward to life and happiness, while the memorists looked backwards towards death; but the emotional energy in all these cases came out of the cult of the male child. This is what Barrie invented; he took the adventure tale's cult of the boy and turned it into something much more playful, affectionate, potentially elegiac, and obliquely erotic. Of course there had been suggestions of that before, especially in the illustrations to children's books, but Barrie made something of the suggestion. In *Peter Pan* the pirates and the Indians are only fantasies; indeed in the early versions they mingled with harlequins and columbines.

Following Barrie, England made a cult of the boy, which implicitly displaced the values of mature manhood; and the link between the boys and Sylvia, from this point of view, was that the adoration of the virgin mother also displaced mature values. (You can see the same thing in *To the Lighthouse,* where the adoration is of Mrs. Ramsay, a figure very similar to Mrs. Darling, and Mr. Ramsay is displaced.) And it is striking how general, in those circles, was the stress on beauty and charm. The du Mauriers (Sylvia's family) "epitomized the gaiety and Bohemian frivolity of the 90s" (p. 47) and classified everyone they knew as either good-looking or amusing or "a bore." When Arthur Davies met his future father-in-law, the latter's comment was "il est joli garçon"; and Peter Davies, looking back on his parents, wrote "I think Arthur's beauty was not less striking than Sylvia's, and, for

my part, I confess that, much as I venerate all their other lovely
qualities, it is the thought of their beauty which, more than anything else, brings the lump to my scrawny throat" (p. 152).

This very English aestheticism was an important constituent of
the dandyism of the 1920s. It is curious to discover how many
and how direct were the links between these boys and central
figures of that period. We have already mentioned Boothby and
Senhouse, but links to Evelyn Waugh are there, too. Sylvia's best
friend, whose letters are quoted throughout this book, was Dolly
Ponsonby, whose daughter Elizabeth was one of the Bright Young
People, and a model for Agatha Runcible in Waugh's *Vile Bodies*.
And Dolly's sister was Gwen Plunket-Greene, whose daughter
Olivia was the girl Waugh was in love with through most of the
1920s. But of course these biographical details are only adventitious
support for the visible and sensible fact that the '20s cult of the
young man was a continuation of the Edwardian cult of the boy.

The cult persists still. Andrew Birkin, before writing this book,
wrote a series of TV scripts about the Lost Boys and is going on
to the Princes in the Tower. The present book is extremely well
done, as an album of memorabilia—snapshots, diaries, theatre programs, holographs. There is no central discourse, no central statement or point of view; it is an anonymous mosaic, like a page
of a newspaper. As such, it may be said to be like Barrie, for he
too had nothing to *say*, though he could suggest moods, fantasies,
nostalgias, velleities, which could take the place of meaning. Of
course Birkin is much more discreet and editorial. He does not
rival Barrie in any sense. This is nostalgia for nostalgia. But if
one asks for the inhabitants of the original Eden at the end of all
the perspectives, it is again little boys, playing at manhood, and
already imperious, demanding, dangerous, but still innocent, still
blooming, still erotic.

Mediating Illusions: Three Studies of Narnia

James Como

Past Watchful Dragons, by Walter Hooper. New York: Macmillan, 1979.

A Guide through Narnia, by Martha C. Sammons. Wheaton, IL: Harold Shaw, 1979.

Reading with the Heart: The Way into Narnia, by Peter Schakel. Grand Rapids: Wm. B. Eerdmans, 1979.

The past few years have seen the publication of a rash of books on C. S. Lewis. But whether favorable to him or not—and often from publishers of religious evangelicalism—the shabby has outweighed the substantial. The popularizer has been popularized (Clyde S. Kilby, *Images of Salvation in the Fiction of C. S. Lewis* [Harold Shaw, 1978]); Lewis's thought sterilely reformulated (Gilbert Meilander, *The Taste for the Other* [Eerdmans, 1978]); or his Christian substance ridden nearly unto death (Leanne Payne, *Real Presence* [Cornerstone Books, 1979]). The complaint, for example, is not that Payne's book, or others like it, lacks a useful stance; one might well "marvel at the Holy Spirit's use of Lewis's talents." Rather, the weakness is in the narrowness of the author's context: the presumption, not only of premises shared across-the-board with the reader, but of a temperament supposedly common to all reasonable people. Note the number of undefended and perhaps unexamined assumptions in this astonishingly broad and categorical (yet casually posited) judgment: "As the Church, principally through St. Thomas Aquinas, came to accept the Aristotelian epistemology and incorporate it into its theology, the Judeo-Christian understanding of the deep heart (the unconscious mind and its way of knowing) simply dropped from sight." In a brief excursion outside of her narrow context, Payne might have come upon the exploration of the deep heart in *Creative Intuition in Art and Poetry* (Meridian Books, The World Publishing Company, 1954) by Jacques Maritain, the great Thomist. In opposing the modern

attempt to combine good and evil, Lewis is joined—according to
Payne—only by Alexander Solzhenitsyn (this in a footnote); she
does not tell us on what grounds, say, Chesterton is excluded
from that company even though Lewis himself certainly includes
him. Similarly, her reductionist dismissals of Blake, Jung, and
B. F. Skinner (all in footnotes) cannot be taken seriously; to paraphrase Lewis, a small company of like-thinking people—in the
absence of disinterested and rational opposition—can sneak by almost anything.

The Chronicles of Narnia have been particularly harassed, for
the "allegorizers"—equivocating, narrow, and not disinterested—
have had the field largely to themselves. When not simply psychologizing (ordinarily as a means of attack on Lewis's Christian
premises), these interpreters have produced little more than enthusiastic cartographies (Kathryn A. Lindskoog, *The Lion of Judah
in Never-Never Land* [Eerdmans, 1973]) and even a "study kit."
In short, much current work on Lewis, posturing as scholarship,
consists of diatribe, pedantic analyses, or cheerleading formulas.

This unhealthy condition is also unnecessary. The stages through
which work on C. S. Lewis has evolved over the past thirty years
are readily discernible, and anyone coming to the field now will
find a rich and fertile soil. From the first book on Lewis's apolo-
getics—Chad Walsh's *C. S. Lewis: Apostle to the Skeptics* (Macmillan, 1949)—to the best book (and one of the shortest) of all—
Paul Holmer's *C. S. Lewis: The Shape of His Faith and Thought*
(Harper & Row, 1976)—sensible responses have provided a fund of
sound judgment. Furthermore, over ten new books by Lewis himself have been published since his death in 1963. Those who have
"received" rather than "used" (to adopt the distinction Lewis makes
in *An Experiment in Criticism*) the primary world of discourse,
who have declined the imposition upon it of some extraneous purpose, methodology, or theory, have enriched the genuine substance
of scholarship. In particular, the following books have recovered
much of the ground; they are serious, at times profoundly insightful, and highly authoritative: most of *Light on C. S. Lewis*, ed.
Jocelyn Gibb (Harcourt, Brace & World, 1965); Green and Hooper's
C. S. Lewis: A Biography (Harcourt Brace Jovanovich, 1974); James

Higgins's *Beyond Words: Mystical Fancy in Children's Literature* (Teachers College Press, Columbia University, 1970); Lionel Adey's difficult and tendentious *C. S. Lewis's 'Great War' with Owen Barfield* (English Literary Studies, No. 14, University of Victoria, 1978); Peter Schakel's *The Longing for Form: Essays on the Fiction of C. S. Lewis* (Kent State University Press, 1977); Dabney Hart's "C. S. Lewis's Defense of Poesie" (Ph.D. dissertation, University of Wisconsin, 1959), which, if widely accessible, would put a halt to much nonsense; *Lewis: An Annotated Checklist of Writings about Him and His Works*, eds. Joe R. Christopher and Joan K. Ostling (The Serif Series, No. 30, Kent State University Press, 1974); Humphrey Carpenter, *The Inklings* (Houghton Mifflin, 1979), opinionated and full of capricious innuendo, yet fascinating and highly novel; Chad Walsh, *The Literary Legacy of C. S. Lewis* (Harcourt Brace Jovanovich, 1979); Thomas Howard, *The Achievement of C. S. Lewis* (Harold Shaw, 1980); and *They Stand Together: The Letters of C. S. Lewis to Arthur Greeves (1914–1963)*, ed. Walter Hooper (Macmillan, 1979), a work of such classic proportion that if Lewis had written nothing else he would nevertheless be known for this collection alone—Hooper's sometimes startling introduction amounts to a second and perhaps superior biography.

The three newest books on *The Chronicles of Narnia* reflect this tension between using and receiving. Sammons's *Guide through Narnia* taxonomizes the obvious, discovers "parallels," and explains and rewrites passages composed by a man whose thought and writing are among the most pellucid in the language. The scope of Sammons's treatment is insubstantial for a book. Her analyses are little more than descriptions, and the descriptions little more than synopses. We learn almost nothing which is not already obvious and explicit in the *Chronicles* themselves. In discussing *The Last Battle,* she observes blandly that "the wonderful world come[s] to an end" and that "the one person who makes Narnia worth visiting is Aslan himself." In unexplained and misguided fashion she argues that "the mouse's small size deceptively hides his abundant, often impulsive courage." In the final chapter we learn much that is *not* explicit: "Christian Concepts in the Narnia Tales" takes us through "Creation," "the Tree and the Garden," "Sacrifice and

Resurrection," and so on, all after a brief introduction in which Sammons reminds us that the tales are not allegorical. Along the way she does provide a new and useful perspective by citing George MacDonald's essay "The Fantastic Imagination" as a provocative rationale for Lewis's work. But the link is quickly dropped, and an opportunity lost.

Sammons tries to compensate for that loss by providing, in two short paragraphs, an inventory of Lewis's "techniques, such as 'supposition,' 'transposition,' 'illustrations,' 'description,' and 'imagery.'" In the appendices we get even less; there we are told, for example, that 'Charn,' the name of a dead world, is "a form of 'churn,' which means to agitate."

The books by Hooper and Schakel are correctives to Sammons's book and ought to be read together. Notwithstanding weaknesses, *Past Watchful Dragons* and *Reading with the Heart* make the Narnian world accessible to the reader and fully redress the allegorizing imbalance that has thus far prevailed. It is likely that *Past Watchful Dragons* will establish a new foundation for interpreting both the *Chronicles* and Lewis's work in general, a foundation that *Reading with the Heart* stands firmly upon to attain a scholarly and critical insight to which other books have thus far only pretended.

Schakel treats each of the seven books, and their particular unities, separately. He focuses on the images, themes, and structural devices which control the story. Law and grace are the main ingredients of *The Lion, the Witch, and the Wardrobe;* "Putting the Clock Back" is the title of the Chapter which treats progress in *The Voyage of the 'Dawn Treader';* and *The Last Battle* is read in light of Lewis's concept of Joy, or longing. Only when writing about *The Silver Chair* does the author make extensive use of Scripture, but that is because the book is about revelation; "You Must Use the Signs" is the suitable title of this chapter. Throughout, Schakel eschews the allegorical approach, which assumes that the tales require a sort of intravenous feeding, and submits to the independent life of the mediating world. He uses two sources outside that world to illuminate it: archetypal theory, especially that of Northrop Frye, and Lewis's *Mere Christianity*. At times the former seems gratuitous and becomes reductionist, as in the *Silver Chair* chapter where Frye's paradigm of the romance mythos obtrudes on the argument, but Schakel always returns to the world of the stories themselves.

This reliance on archetypes and Lewis's Christian beliefs, though, merely guides Schakel's own highly refined—and impressively informed—sensibility. Of course the Witch is not an allegorical tag for Satan; she "is handled in the manner of romance, not theology," keeping her "place in the Circe tradition." And the link between creation and moral choice as depicted in *The Magician's Nephew* echoes but is not overwhelmed by the powerful significance that Lewis argues for it in *Mere Christianity*. Without being badgered by plot-summary, the reader learns all he needs to know. When Schakel notes the heightening of mystery and of excitement and reveals the rhetorical import of magic in *The Lion, the Witch and the Wardrobe*, with the images which embody it, the symbolic subtext comes clear; Caldron Pool will never be the same. Schakel is sometimes heavy-handed, but he is never trivial. And he is never simply wrong. He knows the tales intimately (note 6 for chapter 7 on the proper order of the books is a revelation); if he has not used Lewis's neglected *An Experiment in Criticism* to the fullest, he has nevertheless abided by it.

Schakel evokes the rhetoric of the Narnian world; Hooper describes its grammar. In the tradition of some Lewis books, *Past Watchful Dragons* is a "preface" to the Chronicles. The purposes are to establish a record of composition, to describe the milieu, especially Lewis's own life, interests, and temperament, out of which the Narnian world emerged, to suggest the appropriate *topoi* of criticism, and to locate Narnia in the larger world of Lewisian discourse. Lewis's beliefs on our relationship to animals, on animal pain, and on myth are given appropriate importance, whereas malignant psychologizing about Lewis's attachment to his mother and about other narrow critical tools are not. Hooper achieves his aims with unsurpassed authority, for he is ideally equipped to look *along* the beam instead of merely at it.

Casually—with some sense of intimacy with the reader—Hooper assembles pieces of conversation, memory, reflection, analysis, refferences, and previously unpublished matter. Pauline Baynes, the illustrator, wrote to Hooper about her involvement with the production of the books, and he not only shares with us much of that letter but tells us something of the illustrator herself. We are taken into the mind, as Hooper actually encountered it, of Paxford, the Lewis majordomo and prototype of Pugglegum the marsh-wiggle. By way of Hooper, we learn that Roger Lancelyn Green remembers hearing Lewis read the Lefay Fragment as early as 1949 and that Green was the first to guess that it was an early attempt to get *into* Narnia. Even the Lewis pets—especially the redoubtable Mr. Papworth—are introduced. Of the new Lewisiana, the sizeable Lefay Fragment is accompanied by the first snippet of a start at composing the *Chronicles,* some of the Boxen stories (juvenilia), a chronology of Narnian history by Lewis, a working outline for one of the stories, and the first version of Eustace's diary, in addition to parts from Lewis's notebooks. Hooper is more steeped in the Lewisian temper and in the oeuvre than anyone else. One might recast a sentence or two, or occasionally tamper with his tone, or add to a chapter ("A Defense of the Fairy Tale" is little more than assertion, without seeing Lewis's views in the light of others), but I would not touch his thoughts on the Lefay Fragment, or his response to those who see Christ's resurrection as equivalent to Aslan's, or his telling insight into the end of *The Last Battle.* This book may be the closest we will ever get to what Lewis would have said himself.

Lewis's life was a relentless struggle to derive meaning from experience. This effort leads to a world of discourse which does not so much attempt to prove the tenets of Christianity as to establish its coherence. By inverting our normal perspective and by making supernatural abstractions concrete, Lewis realizes a world qualitatively different from that ordinarily occupied by the reader—an objective other world with a quiddity all its own. Thus taken out of his normal world, the reader discerns meaning; his experience here points to a plausible elsewhere. If the integrity of the mediating illusion is violated, however, then the dragons of self-consciousness reawake. Lately they (with related afflictions) have been up-and-about. Lately, but perhaps not for much longer.

The Emergence of Awe in Recent Children's Literature

Joseph O. Milner

All Together Now, by Sue Ellen Bridgers. New York: Bantam Books, 1980.

A Gathering of Days, by Joan W. Blos. New York: Charles Scribner's Sons, 1980.

How I Hunted the Little Fellows, by Boris Zhitknov. Translated by Djemma Bider. Illustrated by Paul O. Zelinsky. New York: Dodd, Mead & Company, 1979.

Ladder of Angels, by Madeleine L'Engle. Illustrated by "Children of the World." New York: Penguin Books, 1980.

Words by Heart, by Ouida Sebestyen. Boston: Little, Brown and Company, 1979.

I have long supported a dichotomous way of understanding children's literature, one that is simplistic but helpful. Books reflect one of two basic views of the human experience: Awe and Wonder, the religious perspective, or Self-reliance and Rationalism, the humanist perspective. The religious writer believes that man is entrusted as the steward of the sentient world, but that he is ultimately dependent on the power of God. Mystery and a sense of the limits of rationality are solidly at the center of this world-view. The historical foundations of its humanistic counterpart lie in the Age of Enlightenment; its present hope is that obstructions to the good life for all can be set aside by the judicious use of mankind's powerful mental paraphernalia and by a gradual move to higher levels of moral consciousness. In such a world-view we are inching ever closer to the full perfection of a utopian state.

I have earlier suggested that *The Lion, the Witch, and the Wardrobe* and *Charlotte's Web* are near-perfect representatives of these two contending visions of reality. The one sees dependent creatures delivered from an icy death by the awful hand of the Majestic

Aslan; the other explores the beauteous growth of a young shoat
to full pighood under the tutelage of the wise and self-giving men-
tor Charlotte, whose own immortality is achieved in Wilbur's becoming *like* her in his care for her progeny.

Not surprisingly, last year's list of the most admired children's
books is dominated by the humanist perspective. These books ex-
plicate modern life, offer models of growth, and confront a now-
slim list of previously off-limit subjects. Some become so direct
and precise in their problem-solving style that they edge perilously
close to the realm of pamphlet or guidebook. However, five powerful books emerge whose religious tendencies and artistic elegance
make them what Stevens calls "ten-foot poets among inchlings."
Each departs from the humanist commonalities and yet uniquely
differentiates itself from the other four.

This review of these five does not attempt comparisons but
rather brief explications of each book's religious depth. The order-
ing of books is from the most ostensibly to the least self-consciously
religious. Madeleine L'Engle's readers will not be surprised to find
her illustrated account of the Old Testament, *Ladder of Angels,*
the most directly and unequivocally religious. What seems a bit
new is the deftness and clarity with which she sets forth religious
neo-orthodoxy within the bounds of the book's two defining elements: the Old Testament and children's art. She draws on both
familiar and obscure scriptures to establish a clear theology of God's
awfulness and man's fragility. From the beginning she exemplifies
what she must see as modern man's greatest sin, Satan's timeless
temptation: "You shall be as God." The hubris of man is dramatized in her account of the "clever but not wise" erectors of the
tower of Babel. She makes it clear that Noah, the intemperate
imbiber, could only fashion his wonderful ark because of his obedience to God.

Beyond these famous passages L'Engle selects stories full of mystery and miracle, the very elements which Thomas Jefferson struck
from his Bible and which are a scandal to the reasonable, modern
mind: Moses' shining veil which radiates God's presence; Jacob's
wrestle with the visitant angel at the foot of the ladder; Elijah's
fiery ascent in the chariot; Gideon's visit from the Angel of the

Lord; and Daniel's deliverance from the lion's den. She directly affirms the fact that "angels are wholly real as we" and constantly proclaims a "glory that is on the other side of daily life."

Thus, the Old Testament is not translated into an easy humanism; justice and goodness are not given the same prominence as are God's grandeur and man's finitude. Though the passages are not without warnings against polluting God's world and affirmations of love's inextricable connectedness with life, the dramatization of Abraham's preparation to sacrifice his son Isaac confirms, as it did earlier for Kierkegaard, L'Engle's allegiance to the religious world-view rather than to the humanist one.

L'Engle's use of children's art to illustrate her text might seem to be a part of secular modernity's celebration of the child. It is alive with naivete and spontaneity; it glistens with rich splashes of color; it exhibits the flat, timeless, spaceless lack of perspective of that art. But it is representational, putting meaning and story ahead of a fascination with sheer color, line, and space. And children's art is appropriate in that L'Engle seems to be honoring the Biblical injunction: "Ye must become as a child."

In abstract, Ouida Sebestyen's *Words by Heart* seems a religious *Charlotte's Web*. It recounts the growth of Lena from bright, ambitious girlhood to a maturity equal to that of her too-good black Papa who, at the cost of his own life, teaches her to love her white enemies. The book moves quickly. It opens on the drama of Lena Sills in a new, more westward, and apparently more tolerant community than the southern town her family left behind, using her "magic mind" to defeat her clever white opponent in a Bible verse contest. Unpleasantries are foreshadowed and then explode with a poor white sharecropper's family whom Lena and her father have replaced as "hands" for a wealthy and paranoid woman. Finally, Lena makes a long trek into the wastelands to help her wounded Papa, only to be asked by him to help his assailant (the white sharecropper's son), who is himself near death. The bright and aspiring Lena, her father's unforgetting, less optimistic second wife Claudie, the lonely, unlovely, rich Mrs. Chism, the ignorant and defeated sharecropper family, and the less fully developed white townfolk are all appealingly and convincingly portrayed.

Papa, however, is so much a modern Jesus that readers might find it difficult to suspend their disbelief; his perfection is overwhelming.

That the book lies close to L'Engle's neo-orthodoxy in its opposition to rational humanism is seen from the first lines Lena quotes in the Bible verse contest: "God hath chosen the foolish things of the world to confound the wise." Although she has a personal sense of the words and Winslow, her opponent, knows his verses only in a rote, mechanical way, at this point she sees books and learning as the ultimate measure of life. Papa shares this love of learning with her and speaks of "the promise of her books," but he is finally committed to a life of service and love: "That's what we're here for, to serve each other. . . . The greatest people who ever lived served others." She tries to emulate her father on the playground but can't speak up for the taunted Haney boy; she does better in going to see Mrs. Chism after she gets word that her fine party was a flop, but she is misunderstood; and finally, with great misgiving, she does the ultimate good by taking the torn Tater Haney back home and by never telling Claudie who shot Papa. She is not Papa, but she has trodden close to his steps of pure service. The ideals of obedience and sacrifice win Lena's ultimate allegiance.

Boris Zhitkov's *How I Hunted the Little Fellows* does not seem to qualify as a religious book, yet its basic thrust seems counter to all that the humanist world of books affirms. The translated Russian tale, which commences as though it were going to pay homage to curiosity and imagination, tells of young Boriushka's visit to his winsome grandmother, whose house is full of quaint, fascinating objects. She tells him that one treasure must always remain untouched—the perfect miniature steamship which sits alone on a special shelf. Because he is captured by the ship's lifelikeness and can't release his gaze from it, the wise old woman tells him that the ship holds special memories for her and will be put away for the remainder of his stay unless he promises never to touch it. He vows to restrain himself, but his imaginings overwhelm him steadily.

Boriushka begins to conjure up little folk who sail in this tiny craft, and he wants desperately to enter their miniscule world. He begins his downward path by ascending to the special shelf and peering into the ship to see the tiny folk. Not seeing them, he decides that he can gain proof of their being by leaving a crumb of food for them to pilfer during the night. Like a rationalist, he is trying to develop tangible proof for his beliefs, but the evidence he finds is uncertain and his desires continue to mount. Finally, when his grandmother prepares to leave the house, he feigns sickness so that he can remain at home to make one final, secret probe into the hidden world. He lays hands upon the vessel and in a fit of passion begins to dismantle it, seeking the clever little people. He severs the rope ladders, ruptures the doorways, and even pries up the deck. At last, still believing the elusive folk lurk deeper in the hull of the ship, he swiftly, expectantly reaches in below the deck but finds absolutely nothing. Only at this point does he realize the depths of his wrongdoing and in deep frustration tries to restore the perfect world, but without success. Then in deep remorse and guilt he retreats to his bed. The grandmother returns with the druggist's remedies and finds Boriushka hidden under the covers; and the story abruptly closes with no discovery made or punishment meted out.

No religious words are spoken, but the story of the forbidden fruit resounds in this tale. Curiosity and imagination, rather than being celebrated as they are in much of the best of recent children's literature, are shown to have their ugly and destructive face. Guilt is not only left with little Boriushka because he has brought ruin to his grandmother's special treasure, and magnified because she returns to him with care and help, but the effect of guilt is compounded in the unresolved way the story closes. The wrongness of the act seems all the more certain because only the reader and the boy know of the sundering of the ship.

The fine line drawings that dominate the text add to this feeling and make the lesson all the more widely accessible. The elaborate details of the ship make it almost equally alluring to the reader and the close-up portrayals of the boy make his growing passion and his final horror all the more clear. All of the illustrations thus add to the fine balance of pace and depth that Zhitkov achieves. We know when we finish his book that the authority of elders must be considered, that familiar bonds must be kept, and that some kinds of knowledge can lead to destruction. No overt religious language or reference is made; ideas which lie at the heart of religious orthodoxy are implicit.

Joan Blos's award-winning *A Gathering of Days* is a book which is not wholly given to the religious perspective, but rather to a contest between that world-view and the humanist one, as they are reflected in the diary of young Catherine Hall, from a Sunday in October 1830, to a Tuesday in March 1832. We encounter in Catherine's spontaneous entries a nonintrusive narration of the struggle between her father's rougher, rural authority and God-ridden world and her Bostonian stepmother's more sophisticated, reason-centered view of life. We feel the authenticity of this struggle all the more because Blos skillfully approximates early American syntax through phrases such as "so busy were tongues and finger," "also were the jet buttons used," and "he cares for her not"; presents quaint local customs such as syrup gathering; prints rejected readings and arcane spelling; and refers to recognizable historical events. As the days are gathered from that first October Sabbath, Catherine tells of both the daily matter of her life and its signal moments: giving aid to a fugitive slave, adjusting to her father's new wife, and grieving at the death of her dearest friend, Cassie. All of these events and feelings, though set 150 years ago, call up issues which resonate across our age. Racial justice, communal authority, educational styles, women's roles, and other questions are woven into the fabric of the novel. We see the compliant but questioning Catherine scrutinizing all of these issues, wondering about the mores of the hardy back-country people: she decides, like Huck Finn, that kindness toward escaped slaves is better than legal compliance, although her father thinks otherwise; she challenges Teacher Holt's classroom authority in thinking he "believes that very much; and so do I, I think"; and she recognizes that only the boys are allowed to study higher math.

In a sense the religious view of her father and the humanist perspective of her stepmother stand on either side of all these issues. The acceptance of this central dimension of her father's world is complete at first and her distance from her stepmother is clear when the woman first arrives; but, as the days move on, she is more confused and divided. Early on she attends church twice on each Sabbath (even though she says that it is breathtakingly cold on winter days) and prays dutifully (though she recounts her desire to shorten vespers because of her cold floor). And when her new stepmother arrives from Boston, Catherine self-righteously notes the "open v's at Ann's throat and back and well shaped bodices," is conscious of Ann's overly rational approach to life, and refers to Ann only as "her" and "she." But when Catherine ends her petulance over this invasion of her world, she begins to see Ann in a new light, compares Ann's care for the youngest child with that given by her own mother, and begins to call Ann by the child's endearing name "Mammann."

This strong feeling for Ann precipitates a movement toward Ann's Boston world-view which is best expressed in Ann's response to the illness and death of Catherine's friend Cassie. The rural folk commit Cassie unflinchingly to the local doctor's care and to God's grace. Ann, however, clearly believes that a Boston physician can offer better help and when the local doctor's ineffectual work leads to Cassie's death, she writes to Boston to order a book to help in future cases. Out of her grief at the deaths of Cassie and of an entire family in a rock slide, Catherine wonders, "How can what we call *Providence* so oft, so cruelly, deprive." She begins to question Cassie's mother's report that her daughter died with a smile on her lips. Nevertheless, she seems uncertain about Ann's "faith in books" and the ability to "inform ourselves against another occasion," and concludes by brooding over the two world-views as she asks herself, "Whom shall I believe?" She ultimately answers her own question in part when she recognizes that Cassie has been "called on a greater journey, to rest on the opposite shore," that her recollection has been "a gathering of days wherein we learned . . . to accept," and that "for Cassie it is spring forever." Blos does not violate her young character by having her articulate her religious quandary; the final balance, however, seems to be tipped toward the religious perspective.

Sue Ellen Bridgers's *All Together Now* exudes a life and quality which are indisputedly rich, but a world-view which is the least self-consciously religious of the five. It makes no overtly religious comment and centers on human relationships, yet something almost too delicate to articulate or measure suggests its ties with a religious world-view. It seems clearly out-of-step with most of the books of our day. The presence of the family, as it extends itself vertically and horizontally, and of the larger community run deep in the account of Casey's summer with her grandparents. In contrast, much of today's children's fiction reports the family as extinct or, if alive, merely meddling. As a part of this difference, Bridgers pays homage to powerful adults and attends to them sufficiently to allow her reader to feel both their silliness and their wisdom. Although she focuses on Casey and her relationship to the quick-spirited, but slow-minded, Dwayne Pickens, Bridgers's omniscient point of view carries her into the minds of folk who are placed all along the chronological path of life. She deftly slips into the thoughts of most of her characters and renders a less rarified, more complete assessment of life than is found in much of children's literature. Multiple interior responses to Dwayne's threatened institutionalization by his prideful brother Alva, to the misfire honeymoon and subsequent estrangement of the middle-aged Pansy and Hazard, to the quiet solidity of the elder Flanagan's relationship, and to the on-and-off courtship of Uncle Taylor and the candy-counter girl Gwyn, make the book less parochial and more real than the typical single-issue, youth ghetto books of our time. Furthermore, although Casey's summer includes a good bit of pain and foolishness, Bridgers persistently affirms life at its core; without being a Pollyanna she departs from the current norm of despair by championing brotherhood and love. Casey symbolically plays catch with Dwayne rather than have him continue to thump balls off the metal garbage cans. Even though this act and its articulation as love, "unencumbered by questions of degree or worth," can be seen as essentially the humanist goal, something gnaws at this assessment of her world-view. Perhaps it is the stated assumption that Dwayne's freedom is in God's hands, or the unpitying acceptance of his mental limitations or the admissions of Pansy,

Dr. Kemble, and finally Casey herself that an individual ultimately is unable to control his destiny. Such is not the stuff of humanism.

Thus, these five books stand apart from the humanist crowd, although in form and substance they differ from one another. They are all imaginatively and aesthetically rich, but their most salient appeal may just be their orthodoxy which reverberates in varying degrees throughout their pages.

Sendak's Mythic Childhood

John Cech

The Art of Maurice Sendak, by Selma G. Lanes. New York: Harry N. Abrams, 1980.

From the 1960s on, it has become increasingly clear that one person stands out from the crowd as a primary innovator and extender of the form and subject matter of the picture book: Maurice Sendak. Since Max and the Wild Things' astonishing rumpus into our lives in 1963, Sendak's work has challenged conventions, drawn controversy, set new standards, and, quite simply, delighted and dazzled us. But we may tend to forget that, even before the Wild Things broke through, Sendak had given us a number of books that would have secured him a respected, memorable place in the history of children's book illustration: *A Hole Is to Dig* (1953); *Charlotte and the White Horse* (1955); the Little Bear Books (1957, 1959, 1960, 1961); and *The Nutshell Library* (1962). No other illustrator since Caldecott has had such all-pervasive, if sometimes unacknowledged, impact.

As we know from studying Sendak's art and reading his remarks about those figures who have influenced him, he has built his work on sources from the deep and recent past. Like Autolycus, his "borrowings" are famous and often invisible. Dürer, William Blake, Henry Fuseli, Samuel Palmer, George Cruikshank, Winslow Homer, Marc Chagall, Caldecott, Winsor McCay, and Walt Disney, to name just a few, have inspired his work. He openly admits the influence they have had on him throughout his career, and he pays numerous, loving homages in his books to most of these figures. Yet Sendak's genius has lain in his unique creative alchemy, in his ability to transmute the influence of the masters into a substance that is always and profoundly himself. Sendak claims that "if I have an unusual gift, it is not that I draw particularly better or write particularly better than other people—I've never fooled myself about that. Rather, it's that I remember things that other people don't recall: the sounds and feelings and images—the emotional quality —of particular moments in childhood. . . . My most unusual gift is that my child self seems still to be alive and well."

Through Sendak's capacity to remain true to his own childhood, and through what John Keats called negative capability, Sendak labors to give shape and meaning to its fragmented and frightening fantasies. This creative effort has allowed him to chart and thus guide us through the visions that occupy not only his own, personal childhood but all childhoods. Taken as a whole, his work has provided us with a weave of archetypal expressions that constitute a true, living mythology, a body of stories, both verbal and visual, that touch our deepest longings, misgivings, fears, and beliefs. He shapes anew for the modern child and adult (since there is not a generation of adults that has grown up on his works) that primal stuff that we may try to turn away from but that is inescapably there, in the "rag and bone shop of the heart"—ignored, unspoken, repressed, unconscious, but nonetheless there, present. We do not usually speak of Sendak in these terms, preferring to stay on the surface of his art, but it is time we did: he is our childhood's mythologist.

It is no wonder, then, that Selma Lanes's *The Art of Maurice Sendak* has been an eagerly awaited book—for the curious, the fascinated, and the deeply moved admirers of Sendak's accomplishments. Though Sendak has given many interviews and feature stories throughout his career, Lanes's book is the first full-length study of the man. And the book shouldn't disappoint either the newcomer to or the ardent lover of Sendak's work.

First, the volume is full of visual treasures. Most of the key Sendak books—*Where the Wild Things Are, In the Night Kitchen, The Juniper Tree, Higglety-Pigglety-Pop!,* and *Outside Over There* —are well-represented, with excellent reproductions and illuminating discussions. Visual surprises abound: a pop-up version of a Little Red Riding Hood toy; part of the first dummy for *Where the Wild Things Are,* a mere one-inch strip of a book, so fragile and priceless; early paintings and sketches from his apprenticeship years as an F.A.O. Schwartz window-display designer; a rejected illustration for the Grimm volume; preliminary drawings for *Outside Over There;* family photographs—of his grandparents, his mother, his father, himself—that have surfaced in many of his books. All of these seemingly ephemeral objects take on a significance when we realize, through Lanes's examination of the artist, that they are the vital keys to understanding the workings of Sendak's creative process. As a visual and tactile experience that ultimately informs our sense of the artist, the book, to use Sendak's phrase, "does a Rosie." It drives away the ennui or gloom of a long winter's night or an interminable summer vacation day—as the real-life Rosie, one of Sendak's cherished muses, did for all those "hurdy-gurdy, fantasy-plagued Brooklyn kids."

On another level, the book will satisfy the reader's curiosity about the details of Sendak's life—those charmed and enduring moments that have continued to hold Sendak in their spell throughout his artistic development: his father's stories, his grandmother's animation of a window shade, Ida Perles's chicken soup, a book, a toy, or his Sealyham terrier, Jenny. Much of this background has been mentioned by Sendak in previously published statements. But many of the connections between the life and the work are quite fresh (such as the creation of *Higglety-Pigglety-Pop!*) and have had to be wrested from the very soul of the artist's life. For these revelations Lanes is to be complimented, and we are all in her debt.

Yet there are some problems with Lanes's text. Perhaps the most noticeable of these is that she accepts, for the most part, Sendak's own criticism of his work, often using his words or a paraphrase of them to describe the limitations of a given book. Sendak can be remarkably frank about his successes and failures, so Lanes is generally free to explore their weaknesses. At other points, however, she seems to bridle her criticism when she knows that even though Sendak can see the faults of a work, say, like the illustrations for George MacDonald's *The Golden Key,* he still considers his effort to have been a "labor of love" which he has struggled to bring into being. Given the scope of the book, though, these shortcomings are minor, and Lanes is wise in choosing to spend the major amount of her time on discussions of the works that are central to Sendak's career.

The major flaw in her text is her chapter, near the end of the book, on Sendak's "Recurring Themes." Here she merely summarizes, rather superficially at that, the major symbols and images that appear in Sendak's art: windows, babies, food and eating, flying and falling. These summaries lead her to the following generalizations about the theme of Sendak's work: "If one were to try to verbalize Sendak's major theme . . . it would certainly have something to do with his unending exploration of the normal child's burden of rage, confusion, fear of and frustration with the various uncontrollable factors in his own life: adults who don't understand, limitations that restrict and inhibit, situations beyond worth coping with." She has gotten only the first half right, however, because she has failed to observe the manner in which Sendak transforms these experiences, thus enabling his children to triumph over these disturbing circumstances, to master them and return home from the place of the Wild Things. The "theme" is surely not complete without this return; and, as a coda to her exhaustive research, Lanes fails to touch those final, grand chords about Sendak's art.

In his review of *The Art of Maurice Sendak* (in the *New York Times Book Review,* November 9, 1980), Hilton Kramer is correct when he suggests the difficulties of writing a biography of a living person, especially when that figure is a friend of the biographer, as is the case with Sendak and Lanes. It might have been better, and finally liberating for both the writer and the reader, if Lanes had begun the book with her final chapter, her "Portrait of the Artist as a Private Person," thus establishing her personal relationship with Sendak from the outset.

But Kramer is certainly inaccurate in his review when he claims that the book does not reflect the literary or artistic culture that Sendak was responding to as an artist. The shtetl life of his immigrant parents' past; the allure of the pop culture Sendak grew up with in the '30s and '40s; the powerful hold that the masters of art and literature have exerted on Sendak throughout his career—most are admirably accounted for in Lanes's discussions. To be sure, other, more specific analyses of Sendak's place in relation to the artistic currents of his time are to be written; but these studies would not be possible without the basis for research Lanes has established.

Finally, it is sheer ignorance on Kramer's part to point to the paucity of criticism of children's literature, and it is indeed strange and ironic that an establishment art critic hasn't done a major study of Sendak's work prior to Lanes's book. The importance of Sendak's art (as well as the work of a number of contemporary illustrators) has been well known to critics of children's literature for decades. Generally speaking, it is the art world that has not given him and other artists whose work happens to be categorized and marketed as children's books the full attention they warrant. As Lanes observes in her analysis of Sendak's major work on Grimm: "Curiously, for so intense and richly sustained a graphic work, Sendak's illustrations for *The Juniper Tree* have never received any serious criticism as art. There are, today, no publications like the nineteenth-century English magazine *The Studio,* each issue of which was filled with major critical essays on important graphic work."

Rather than issuing a challenge to literary critics of children's literature, *The Art of Maurice Sendak* prods those dozing, fad-swayed doyens of the art world. Certainly Lanes and Abrams, among others, have been awake and clear-eyed to the vitality of graphic art as it appears in children's books and in their most poetic of forms, the picture book. They are to be congratulated on giving this dimension of art and its chief practitioner today the full attention and respect both the form and the man deserve in *The Art of Maurice Sendak.*

Chinese Literature for Children

Nellvena Duncan Eutsler

Chinese Popular Literature and the Child, by Dorothea Haywood Scott. Chicago: American Library Association, 1980.

Dorothea Haywood Scott in her *Chinese Popular Literature and the Child* provides a valuable service for the Westerner recently attracted to Chinese literature. The book provides an articulate overview of Chinese literature, with background material for those who wish to explore further the long traditions of literature for children. Chinese popular literature had its beginnings between 1765 and 1123 B.C. and is thus the longest unbroken literary tradition in the world, with a wider audience than any other. Chinese literature reflects the historical changes within its culture: a diversity of minority peoples and their various dialects, invasion from without and turmoil from within, and everchanging political philosophies. Through various media the literature has been preserved from ancient times, and Scott recognizes their literary process as a "story of change within continuity."

Scott considers Chinese children's literature in the light of the Chinese system of education. She points out that Chinese thought and pedagogy reflect the influence of sages such as Confucius, Mencius, the Buddhist monks, and the Taoists. She notes the impact caused by differences between scholarly classical writing and colloquial language. The Chinese, who have long been aware of the difficulties posed by these differences, have initiated recent language reforms that have revolutionized the style of Chinese writing; their literature now reaches a much wider audience. Their entire educational process had for centuries inhibited learning by its stylistic and classical requirements. At last the words of Feng Meng-lung, the late Ming Dynasty author and scholar quoted by Scott, have been heeded: "In this world literary minds are few but rustic ears are many."

In order to appreciate and understand Chinese children's literature, we must understand the traditions which shaped China's attitudes toward their children. Not until early in the twentieth century did China recognize the special needs of her children, although Chinese children had access to printed stories centuries before the English or American child had access to a book.

Oral traditions have been as influential for Chinese children as for children from other cultures. By 960 A.D. the storytellers had become a highly professional body of public entertainers. Their prompt books served as the basis for later novels.

Although, as Scott points out, there are no traditional collections of Chinese myths and legends, myths are found imbedded in the whole body of early Chinese literature. Chinese classics provide central sources in the Orient as do the Old Testament, Perrault, Grimm, and others in the Western world. As in the tradition of Western children's literature, Chinese children had their primers (the *Thousand Character Classic* and the *Three Character Classic*) and their early picture books (the *Fifteenth Century Illustrated Chinese Primer,* the earliest known extant copy of which is dated 1436). They had these books long before western civilization had *Babes Booke* in manuscript form (1430), or Caxton's *Aesop's Fables* (1484), or a hornbook (1540), or *Orbis Pictus* (1658).

Scott does not discuss the omission of fables, but she explains that older literary collections contain few stories about animals. This evidence seems odd, since animals play an important role in Chinese myths. In her chapter on "Myths, Legends, and Symbols," however, Scott discusses animal legends and the Chinese use of animal symbolism. It is a shame that when she notes the nine resemblances of the dragon, she lists only "the horns of a deer, the neck of a snake, the scales of a carp," and leaves the reader with "and so on" for the others.

Scott calls fifteenth-century Chinese novels "folk epics," in spite of the fact that Ch'ên Shou-Yi in his *Chinese Literature: A Historical Introduction* (1961) points out that China "is the only outstanding nation with a literary attainment completely devoid of an epical tradition." Ch'ên Shou-Yi explains this phenomenon by arguing that China's ideal human type has been the sage and not the hero. Perhaps fifteenth-century novels, in spite of their length, would better be labeled fantasies in the tradition of Hans Christian Andersen, since they are woven around historical events and combined with the colloquial stories found in the prompt books. These stories are epic in scope, but they lack epic heroes.

In her introduction, Scott urges critics to be aware of original Chinese stories so that they may judge the authenticity of stories retold, and to recognize that "a child's first understanding of a people from another country will be gained through stories read or told about them." She reminds us that "it is extremely difficult to eradicate from a child's mind a false stereotype implanted through misleading pictures or unauthentic stories introduced to them when very young." The problem of interpreting Chinese stories for the Westerner is broad, caused primarily by Western ignorance of the Chinese literary tradition, which Scott's volume will do much to correct.

The volume is nicely illustrated with woodcuts, inscriptions, papercuts, calligraphy, charts, pictures, and drawings. Unfortunately the Chinese character for "east" is placed upside down on the page. The bibliography is extensive, and the index most useful. In short, Scott has made a valuable contribution toward greater understanding of both China and Chinese literature. We would do well to follow Lu Hsun's philosophy expressed in the elegant calligraphy Scott reproduces:

> Fierce-browed, I coolly defy a thousand pointing fingers,
> Head bowed, like a willing ox, I serve the children.

A Striking Contrast: Recent British and American Poetry for Children

Agnes Perkins

Blackburn, Thomas. *The Devil's Kitchen*. London: Chatto & Windus, 1975.

Cole, William, ed. *Poetry of Horses*. New York: Charles Scribner's Sons, 1979.

Fisher, Aileen. *Out in the Dark and Daylight*. New York: Harper & Row, 1980.

Foster, John, ed. *A First Poetry Book*. London: Oxford University Press, 1979.

Fuller, John. *Squeaking Crust*. London: Chatto & Windus, 1974.

Hesketh, Phoebe. *A Song of Sunlight*. London: Chatto & Windus, 1974.

Hughes, Ted. *Moon-Bells*. London: Chatto & Windus, 1978.

Janeczko, Paul B., ed. *Postcard Poems: A Collection of Poetry for Sharing*. Scarsdale, N.Y.: Bradbury, 1979.

Jones, Brian. *The Spitfire on the Northern Line*. London: Chatto & Windus, 1975.

Kuskin, Karla. *Dogs & Dragons Trees & Dreams*. New York: Harper & Row, 1980.

Larrick, Nancy, ed. *Bring Me All of Your Dreams*. New York: Evans, 1980.

Livingston, Myra Cohn, ed. *Poems of Christmas*. New York: Atheneum, 1980.

Mayer, Gerda. *The Knockabout Show*. London: Chatto & Windus, 1978.

Moore, Lillian, ed. *Go With the Poem*. New York: McGraw-Hill, 1979.

Sansom, Clive. *An English Year*. London: Chatto & Windus, 1975.

Few poets seem able to refrain from writing about cats. Cat poems, good and bad, abound, and while it may be unfair to pick parts of individual poems as typical of recent poetry for children, a sample from three poems about cats by writers honored with major awards for poetry for children in the United States and England illustrates different attitudes observable from the two sides of the Atlantic. It's a far cry from the descriptions of returning pets by Aileen Fisher and Karla Kuskin to that of Ted Hughes. Take, for example, Fisher's coy verses:

> At break of day
> he's back to stay
> contented with our sunny dwelling.
>
> But nobody knows
> where Tim-cat goes
> at night . . . and Tim-cat isn't telling.

Or take Karla Kuskin's "cutesy" ending to a longer poem:

> I'm sitting on the chair
> And I don't see where he is.
> I don't see one hair of his.
> I just hear the floorboards scarcely squeek.
> This cat comes and goes
> On invisible toes.
> The sneak.

Compare these with Hughes's picture of the "battered master of the house" who comes through the doorway:

> Recovered from his nearly fatal mauling,
> Two probably three pounds heavier
> Since the last time he dragged in for help.
> He deigns to recognize me
> With his criminal eye, his deformed voice,
> Then poises, head lowered, muscle-bound,
> Like a bull for the judges,
> A thick Devon bull,
> Sniffing the celebration of sardines.

Fisher and Kuskin are winners for 1978 and 1979, respectively, of the American National Council of Teachers of English (NCTE)

Poetry Award. Ted Hughes won the British *Signal* Award for
Poetry in 1979 for *Moon-Bells,* published the preceding year. Not
only are the poems in *Moon-Bells* aimed at a more mature audience than are the 1980 collections of verse by Fisher and Kuskin,
but they also represent a different attitude toward children and
their understandings, an attitude apparent in a good many of the
books of poems from England in recent years. Not all of the British
collections, it must be admitted, are as good as *Moon-Bells.* John
Foster's *A First Poetry Book* is only a garishly illustrated anthology
of easy and mostly trivial verse. But at its best, British poetry for
children is not condescending. It reflects an attitude that takes
both children's abilities and children's literature seriously, as much
poetry that is commended in this country does not.

The poetry awards themselves, of course, are not directly comparable. NCTE has been recently honoring writers who have produced a substantial amount of verse for fairly young children, such
as David McCord and Myra Cohn Livingston, both better tech-
nicians than Fisher and Kuskin. *Signal,* on the other hand, looks
for a high-quality book of poems published during a specific year
and judges by adult standards, although considering only books
for children. If a comparable award were set up in this country,
or if the NCTE emphasis were shifted, one wonders if a suitable
recipient could have been found. It seems doubtful. The books
recently published for children in this country have been largely
works of light verse, trivia, and nonsense, some clever but most
with little poetic merit.

In 1980 no *Signal* award was given. Nancy Chambers, the editor
of *Signal,* explained that "1979's publishing did not provide a suitable, possible winner." The same is true for 1981. Had the award
been instituted earlier, however, there might have been eight or
ten distinguished winners now, stimulated in part by Chatto &
Windus and their Chatto Poets for the Young series, initiated in
1972. Nothing quite like the Chatto series exists in the United
States. The books are produced in a 32-page unillustrated format;
all contain short but original and vivid poems that make demands
upon the young reader's intelligence. By 1980 there were fourteen
of the Chatto books, none of which had been republished in the

United States. Under the general editorship of Leonard Clark, the series fills the need for "short books of contemporary poetry written especially for children" which "present an imaginative challenge to all young readers in search of verse that is original, direct, and very much alive." The books are not all of the same quality, but none of the twelve I have read condescends to readers and all offer a variety of subjects and styles. Even John Heath-Stubbs's *A Parliament of Birds,* although all about winged creatures, gives no feeling of sameness in approach or verse form.

Of the two books published in 1978, Hughes's *Moon-Bells* is more challenging and, to me, more satisfying than Gerda Mayer's *The Knockabout Show.* The latter does, however, offer several clever ironies, as in "Hide and Seek," which describes a return to a favorite hiding place forty years later:

> [It] is full of
> old lumber now and
> a better place to hide in.
> I look into the shadows
> and ask and ask
> *where are they?*

In a lighter mood, "Lorelei" portrays the vanities of the temptress:

> And those suicides by water,
> Though of course they gratify,
> Whilst you wait for Captain Right, are
> Mere fringe benefits, Lorelei.

Some children, and perhaps some adults, will not like or understand all of Hughes's poems in *Moon-Bells.* Hughes, however, is a master of rhythm and image and is able to catch an essence in a phrase. Early morning comes when "First thrush splutters and chips at the thick light," whereas the cry of the tigress "rips the top off the air first / Then disembowels it / She lies down, as if she were lowering / A great snake into the ground." Winter deer ride "their legs / Away downhill over a snow-lovely field / Toward tree-dark—finally / Seeming to eddy and glide and fly away up / Into the boil of big flakes." He avoids the sentimental, even in

poems which lend themselves to sentiment. In "Fox Hunt" he
writes that:

> . . . the fox
> Is flying, taking his first lesson
> From the idiot pack-noise, the puppyish whine-yelps
> Curling up like hounds' tails, and the gruff military
>   barkers:
> A machine with only two products:
> Dog-shit and dead foxes.

His fantasies are wild but not absurd. The title poem, *"Moon-Bells,"* relates the wisdom which Earth bells ring out to the "sav-age tribes" of the moon:

> "The head is older than the book,"
> Shrills one with sour tone,
> And "Beauty is only skin deep
> But ugly goes to the bone."

None of the Chatto books avoids real life, with its earthiness
and terror as well as its beauty. Brian Jones, in "You Being Born,"
tells his daughter of witnessing her birth:

> You shot out from between your mother's legs
> like a rugby ball from a scrum
> and the stocky Geordie midwife caught you neatly
> and cried "Whoops! She's come!"

In "The Farmer's Wife" Thomas Blackburn tells a gripping hor-ror tale of a man whose bride is really a werewolf:

> But notice he did the nightgown
> Of his wife by the river bed
> And how two small feet with four claws meet,
> And the hair pricked up on his head;
> For the ravaged sheep lay savaged
> Under the light of the moon
> And a she-wolf skulked in the brushwood
> With a glittering golden ring.

Some depict unforgettable people, like Phoebe Hesketh's "Sally," who was "a dog-rose kind of girl: / elusive, scattery as petals; / scratchy sometimes, tripping you like briars." Sally survives, even though

> Her mother scolded; Dad
> gave her the hazel-switch,
> said her head was stuffed with feathers
> and a starling tongue.
> But they couldn't take the shine out of her.
> Even when it rained
> you felt the sun saved under her skin.
> She'd a way of escape
> laughing at you from the bright end of a tunnel,
> leaving you in the dark.

Clive Sansom's "Truant" resembles Sally, but the tone of the poem is more humorously matter-of-fact. "Two days in five," it starts, "young Jeremy's not at school," for

> Like compass instincts in migrating birds,
> A mole's obsession for the dark and cool,
> Or wasps' impetuous bee-lines to the jampot—
> He's always had this in-built horror of school.

Some poems are vigorously joyous, as is number 4 of John Fuller's "Half a Fortnight," an apparent jump-rope rhyme:

> Skipping to the shop on Thursday, ice-cream for you and me,
>> I skipped right back on the pavement cracks
> For Thursday is a half-day, its afternoon is free.
>> Good as five new pennies,
>> True as a chippy's eye,
>> Followed my father to Leicester
>> And made my mother cry,
>> Stood my brother in a corner
>> With his left shoe on his right,
>> Didn't come back till half past nine
>> And ate ice-cream all night.

Nothing comparable to the Chatto series has been published for
children in this country in the past decade. Some books of poems
of merit by individual authors have appeared, but not on this level
of diversity and difficulty. This is not, I believe, because we don't
have poets of comparable quality who write good poems which
young people can appreciate. It is very difficult to get any poetry
published, and writers simply have not found a market open for
serious work among publishers for juveniles. In the United States
we have to look to anthologists to ferret out the poems published
in collections for adults which will have appeal for a younger
audience.

Unfortunately, the substantial anthologies of modern poems produced for older children in the late 1960s and early 1970s seem
to be no longer publishable. Permission costs have made contemporary poems expensive to reprint. American anthologies of the
last few years have been slimmer and slighter, and they tend to
be thematically confined. The vast majority are small collections
dominated by illustrations—in fact, picture books sprinkled with
poems. Some compilers, like Lee Bennett Hopkins, seem to turn
these out as soon as they can find a dozen verses on a subject. Others
are more selective, but generally in the highly illustrated books
the pictures overshadow and distract from the poems.

Of the larger anthologies that came to my attention in 1979 and
1980, only three have more than 100 poems, and none more than
112. Of these, two are tightly thematic: William Cole's *Poetry of
Horses* and Myra Cohn Livingston's *Poems of Christmas*. Both
anthologists are experienced in compiling strong collections, and
both books have merit. Perhaps two-thirds of Livingston's poets
are from the twentieth century, although a good proportion of
these are early moderns such as Hardy, Yeats, de la Mare, and e.e.
cummings. Some dozen poems are translations and a slightly larger
number are carols. The level is neither difficult nor condescending.
The collection is, however, somewhat pietistic. In contrast, Cole's
book has more variety of tone, even though all the poems concern
horses. There are story poems, horse show, racetrack, and rodeo
poems, and portraits of horses and riders. The poems vary widely
in tone, style, and authorship, with a number of contemporaries:

Maxine Kumin, Donald Hall, May Swenson, and Alden Nowlan. The other large collection, Paul Janeczko's *Postcard Poems,* contains poems that, as the title indicates, would fit on a postcard. The subtitle, *A Collection of Poetry for Sharing,* further indicates the purpose. With few exceptions the poems are from the recent twentieth century, many by such writers as Ruth Whitman, Josephine Miles, Howard Nemerov, Paul Zimmer, and Stanley Moss. This is a perceptive collection and proves that brief does not necessarily mean trivial.

Of the shorter anthologies, the two most interesting ones, Nancy Larrick's *Bring Me All of Your Dreams* and Lillian Moore's *Go With the Poem,* contain both the good and the faulty. Moore's collection is longer, with nearly ninety poems, and generally easier, with its avowed appeal to middle-school youngsters. Perhaps this is why it includes, among some fine poems, a good many flat poems and some plainly silly. It is a general anthology, with a variety of subjects and modern poems. Indeed, the tone is almost aggressively contemporary, a fact which, ironically, may date it faster than an anthology which strives less to be up-to-date. Larrick's attractive collection contains fifty-six mostly strong, modern selections, but the editor strains to fit some of the poems into the theme of dreams and, more disturbingly, some of the biographical information is incorrect—one poem is even credited to the wrong poet with a similar name.

The overwhelming majority of the poems in these better American anthologies were not written originally for children. They are, however, on an intellectual and poetic level equal to those written and published for young people in the British Chatto series. If we had access to all the books of poems published for children in England, the contrast might not be so striking. Of the more substantial poetry the fact remains, however, that the quality poems that British children have been getting first-hand, in books written for them, American children are getting, for the most part, only second-hand in anthologies.

Classics of Children's Literature

Anita Moss

Classics of Children's Literature, edited by Alison Lurie and Justin
G. Schiller. 73 volumes. New York: Garland, 1976–79.

Since 1976, Garland has designed and published an exceedingly
rich and valuable series, *Classics of Children's Literature 1621–1932*
(117 titles in 73 volumes), selected and arranged by Alison Lurie
and Justin G. Schiller. According to the editors, the series was
designed "to provide a permanent working collection of the
most important and least available texts in English and American children's literature." Thus, such classics as *Alice's Adventures
in Wonderland* (1865) and *The Wind in the Willows* (1908) are
not in the series, although the editors have included less well-
known works such as Carroll's *Sylvie and Bruno* (1889) and Grahame's *The Golden Age* (1895). Works included in the series range
from the earliest surviving version of *Tom Thumbe* (1621) to
John Buchan's fanciful adventure story *The Magic Walking Stick*
(1932). It is possible, of course, to quibble with the editors on the
selections. Why leave out, for example, Frances Brown's little-
known but highly engaging *Granny's Wonderful Chair and Its
Tales of Fairy Times* or Francis Edward Paget's *The Hope of the
Katzekopfs,* both early and significant examples of British fantasy?
In general, however, the series successfully represents the best of
almost every type of children's literature which emerged in the
eighteenth and nineteenth centuries.

Reproduced in photographic facsimile from the first or most
important early edition and printed on acid-free and highly
durable paper, each title is accompanied by a short preface, a
bibliography of the author's works for children, and selected references prepared by recognized scholars in the children's literature
field. The prefaces usually attempt to place the selection in its
appropriate historical and cultural context, to present cogent facts
about the author's life and literary career, to assess the place of

the work in the history of children's literature, and to provide critical discussion and evaluation of the literary merit of the work. While most prefaces contain valuable insights and information, the writers have been allotted small space to accomplish these important tasks. Michael Patrick Hearn's preface to *The History of Tom Thumbe* (1621) is a particularly valuable and lengthy introduction, with useful information about the conventions of native British folk tradition, exploration of the sources of the work and its characteristically Tudor qualities, and an analysis of the significance of the author's somewhat amused and skeptical attitude toward his material.

Unfortunately, not all the prefaces are as detailed and as valuable, although in some instances illuminating critical commentary is provided. Ruth Perry remarks that Sarah Trimmer's *Fabulous Histories* (1786) "manifested a sympathetic concern for animals, rarely found in England before Mrs. Trimmer's time," yet the editor goes on to demonstrate the ironic contrast between Trimmer's well-founded concern for the welfare of animals and the deplorable status of children in late eighteenth-century England. Peter Neumeyer's preface to Andrew Lang's *Prince Prigio* (1889) and *Prince Ricardo of Pantouflia* (1893) describes Lang's controversy with the philologist Max Müller over Müller's postulation that solar myths explained the origins of folk tales, and Neumeyer convincingly refutes Tolkien's charge that the *Prince Prigio* fantasy was flawed because Lang "sniggered over the heads of children" and appealed only to the adult audience by humorously burlesquing fairy tale conventions. Neumeyer suggests the *Prince Prigio* is much more than a burlesque of fairy tale trappings; rather it is a treatment of the nature of evil embodied in the figures of Remora and Firedrake. Other prefaces in this series contain additional critical insights, as in Alison Lurie's perceptive remarks on Lucy Clifford's Victorian fantasy "The New Mother," a tale tinged with nightmarish repression and terror.

Most of the prefaces are balanced and knowledgeable, but some are unaccountably weak. Mark Zaitchek's discussion of George MacDonald's *The Wise Woman: A Parable* (1875), reprinted as *The Lost Princess,* seems to mislead rather than inform. Zaitchek points out that the last ten years of MacDonald's life were spent in "relative obscurity and gloom. . . . By the time MacDonald wrote his third fairy tale, *The Wise Woman* (1875), he was, I believe, preparing for the silence of his last years." Yet given MacDonald's prodigiously productive literary career and the esteem he enjoyed from his public, friends, and family, as well as from some of the most important literary figures of his time (including Mark Twain and John Ruskin), it hardly seems fair to place radical emphasis upon his final decade burdened with physical illness, old age, and senility. Zaitchek comments further that "as he grew older, the religious sensibility which had always informed his best work grew increasingly pessimistic." Such a statement, whch suggests a steady decline in the last twenty years of MacDonald's writing career, ignores the profoundly hopeful quality of many works written long after *The Wise Woman*. Indeed, MacDonald considered *Lilith* (1895) his "last urgent message to the world," a theme which was central to many of his works—that death is an awakening into infinite possibility and spiritual growth, a condition in which all human beings will eventually participate, even that most apparently evil of MacDonald's characters, Lilith. On the other hand, it is fair to say that Calvinism tinges MacDonald's Romanticism throughout his career, as Zaitchek suggests. When MacDonald the Preacher holds sway over MacDonald the Writer, his art suffers, as it does in *The Wise Woman*.

John Seelye has written perhaps the wittiest of the Garland prefaces in his introduction to Captain Frederick Marryat's Robinsonade, *Masterman Ready* (1842). Seelye discusses the work's place in the history of the form established by *Robinson Crusoe* and suggests that, while Marryat's book was influential in developing the narrative of the castaway figure, "*Masterman Ready* is one of those unfortunate books which, like Master Tommy himself, are chiefly valuable as a demonstration of the superiority of others."

Classics of Children's Literature 1621–1932 would clearly be an invaluable addition to any children's literature collection, especially since original copies of the titles remain rare. A strong feature of the series is that it includes examples of almost every type of children's literature which emerged during the eighteenth and nineteenth centuries. Students of the history of children's literature will find examples of moral tales in infinite varieties, such as the awful warning story (exemplified in the series by a moralized version of the Faust legend, *The Prodigal Daughter*, 1771), and Maria Edgeworth's gently rational but lively moral tales in *The Parent's Assistant*. The editors have also selected the best examples of matter-of-fact tales (Thomas Day's *Sandford and Merton*, 1783–89, and *Tales of Peter Parley about America*, 1827); conduct books; Robinsonades; adventure stories; domestic fiction; chapbooks; street cries; religious tracts; early whimsical, masque-like fantasies like William Roscoe's *The Butterfly's Ball and the Grasshopper's Feast* (1807); traditional and literary fairy tales, songs, and ballads; fantasy; Bible stories; religious and secular poetry for children (including Ann Taylor's hitherto unpublished *The Taylors of Ongar: An Analytical Bio-Bibliography*); such educational books as *The New England Primer* (1737) and McGuffey's Reader (1836); travel stories; fables; nonsense; and virtually every other subgenre in children's literature.

Even though some of the titles are clearly ephemeral as literature, they mirror telling attitudes towards the major institutions and values of society—marriage, family, church, work, social class, and education. They also reveal shifting notions of childhood, or of what adults conceived as childhood, all the way from Mrs. Barbauld's gently condescending notions that poetry should not be "lowered to the capacities of a child," through Romantic idealizations of childhood in Mrs. Molesworth's *Four Winds Farm* to Kenneth Grahame's view of adults as repressive, authoritarian "Olympians" in contrast to the spirited and imaginative beings who inhabit the unspoiled "Arcadia" of childhood. Students of children's literature will find ample material for psychological, sociological, historical, and literary studies of these books, with particular possibilities for generic studies. The genres of literary fairy tale and fantasy, for example, include such writers as Charles Perrault, Marie Catherine d'Aulnoy, George MacDonald, Charles Kingsley, John Ruskin, Thomas Hood, Mark Lemon, Christina Rossetti, Mrs. Molesworth, and Dinah Mulock. Study of the works of one author in depth would require access to books outside the collection, however, and many titles remain only in such major rare children's book collections as the Kerlan, the Osborne, and the De Grummond. For example, to study Andrew Lang's original fairy tales, one would need to go beyond the Garland reprint of *The Chronicles of Pantouflia* and read *The Princess Nobody* (1884) and the haunting story *The Gold of Fairnilee* (1888), neither of which appears in the series.

Yet the Garland series remains a valuable resource tool, and students of children's literature now have the pleasure of holding, reading, and examining a veritable secret garden of books very nearly as they appeared at the time of original publication.

Varia

A Nutritious Backhand

Connie C. Epstein

Everyone interested in children today—parent, teacher, librarian, and, yes, the children's book editor, too—seems to have the same preoccupation. How is television affecting the child, especially his or her reading? Books, articles, and talks addressing the concern appear in a steady stream. In fact, the question seems to have spawned a modern industry.

But after a recent dispiriting session of reading what are politely known as unsolicited manuscripts, I found myself wondering if publishers shouldn't be asking an entirely different question. Namely, how is television affecting children's book writers and probably writers in general? The particular manuscript that prompted this reflection was a mercifully short piece about two characters playing tennis. The gimmick being offered was the characterization of the two players: one was a slice of white bread, the other a slice of whole wheat. When I say that the writer's background was in the field of nutrition, I'm sure I don't have to identify the winner of the tennis game, and as I remember the manuscript did not offer any further surprises after its original premise.

Still, the vision of those two pieces of bread playing tennis lingered. How could a writer seriously suggest such a topic for a book? But if the idea titillated me so much, did it have a place somewhere? And then the answer came. Of course, what I had read would make a perfect television commercial for Roman Meal. I bet it would bring a fortune to the company. After all, I'm told that once the Dime Savings Bank initiated the "Road to Riches" in their advertising campaign, in which the sweet little rabbit leads the prince and princess to the castle of their dreams, the number of their depositors skyrocketed. What couldn't a nutritious back-hand do for a baking company?

And then I began to recall other manuscripts that would lend themselves to television advertising. There was the dirty sneaker that didn't want to take a bath (the right soap would surely solve *that* problem!), the dancing magnet named Tilly with one positive leg and one negative leg (a character a faltering shoe company might do well to adopt), and all too many others. Clearly writers have registered that children enjoy animation and so think it logical to transfer the technique to their literature as well. (Or perhaps these writers are indulging a personal taste, as I doubt that many children are starting new accounts at the Dime.)

This resurgence of interest in animation is also having an uncomfortable effect on nonfiction writing for children. When Sputnik blasted off in 1957, a new national resolve to interest our children in science was born. More children's science books were written, and they were written straight. If the subject was the moon, a child could learn what scientists thought it was made of and why it shines. Nonfiction writers developed confidence that they could interest readers without tricks. Once again, however, editors are beginning to see the return of the "moon is green cheese" approach. Manuscripts aiming to inform children about the water cycle tell of Danny Droplet who changes from a raindrop to a piece of hail to part of a river. Perhaps this personification has a place in a film strip, but does anyone really think it's progress to see it reappearing in prose?

Animation is not the only television technique one finds in serious writing today, however; it is just the easiest to spot. Lillian Gerhardt, editor-in-chief of *School Library Journal*, thinks that some of the prevalent styles in current teenage books can be attributed to (in some cases blamed on) the influence of television. Her pet peeve is the single-issue novel, narrated in first person so that it is limited to the scope of one, sometimes immature, sensibility. Frequently the cast of characters consists of only three or four people. They are on stage continuously, in close-up, and the distant setting is almost nonexistent. Is it just happenstance that this structure fits comfortably into a small-size television screen and does not tax the reader unduly? How ironic if this visual age of film is responsible for removing the visual element from modern prose. In any event, the novelist's eye seems to be suffering from tunnel vision.

For instance, a popular single issue in novels has been parental divorce. This social epidemic is changing the child's world overnight. Teachers report second-graders coaching each other in the legal steps to be expected, and school systems devise strategies for looking after children until the single parent is home. So no wonder writers are exploring the effects of divorce on the family. All too often, however, the characters in such a novel are defined entirely in terms of their attitude toward the divorce. It is their only topic of conversation and the sole motive for their actions. Here is tunnel vision again to a deadening degree. As Ms. Gerhardt says, "Just when a child's world is expanding, young fiction is contracting."[1] Is it the children who are watching too much television or those who write for them?

Another disquieting trend is what Betsy Hearne, children's book editor of ALA *Booklist*, calls "pervasive impatience." She says in the September 1980 issue of *Signal* that American writers seem impatient "with development, with time-consuming techniques," that they are anxious "to tell everything at once."[2] Our experience does indeed bear this observation out, especially as it applies to characterization. For example, a writer may tell the reader that a character is greedy instead of taking the time to describe a whole scene in which the person is eating a meal with others and consuming twice his share. Show us, don't tell us, we ask, but the concept is amazingly hard to drive home. The distinction is the difference, however, between a believable character and one who seems manipulated.

Sometimes a writer is too rushed to find out the realistic detail that will add the final authoritative touch to a dramatic scene. I once read a very powerful scene in which a mother was not permitted to see her critically ill infant because doing so would break hospital rules. The mother went into hysterics that disrupted the whole hosptial until she made her point and was finally reunited with her child. The writing engaged the emotions of the reader

completely and had only one flaw: the author had not taken the
trouble to find out what malady the baby could have been suffering from. As a result, the scene never realized its full potential;
the reader knew the writer was just making it up.

And writers rush in another way, too. Frequently they can't wait
to grow up. Each year we see more and more stories from ten-,
eleven-, and twelve-year-olds, sometimes submitted directly, sometimes through the good offices of a teacher or a parent. Long-lost
friends turn up for lunch. Surprise! Out comes their child's picture
book to be considered for publication. The manuscript of a famous novelist's young son reaches the office, having collected a
number of serious professional recommendations along the way.
Why is everyone in such a rush?

Well, for one thing, schools seem anxious to stress creativity
these days. Frequently I hear from writers that they have been
invited to conduct workshops in creative writing for elementary-
age children, and usually they are eager to do so. I guess this is a
good thing, but as the carelessly written manuscripts pile up in
the office, I wonder. I wonder if we are encouraging children to
be writers rather than readers. The volume of our submissions has
probably quadrupled in the last several years, and I gather this
is so for most publishing companies. To us, it seems that more
people want to be writers and fewer want to be readers, or at
least fewer want to buy books.

I agree that schools should be careful about telling a child what
is "good" and "bad" in his reading. Children should learn to evalu-
ate for themselves, and sometimes it can take years to learn to
respond to writing spontaneously and to relax about the precepts
one has acquired in school. But letting a child reach independent
conclusions is different from teaching creativity. I suspect creativity
can't be taught, and when a child does produce work that is original and shows unusual talent, it seems a disservice and even destructive to suggest that such work has commercial potential. There
is little likelihood of that, and it would be unfortunate if the young
writer lost interest in developing his skills because of impatience.

Many adult editorial departments have had to set a policy of
returning unsolicited manuscripts unopened because the volume

has outstripped the capacity of the office to deal with them. Everyone regrets this change, and thank goodness most children's departments have not yet reached this point. But the possibility is there. More awareness of the writer's apprenticeship, more care and thought in the submissions will help to keep editorial offices open to all that much longer.

What we *do* want to see more of are stories that a child can relate to his or her life, written by people who have invested time in mastering the tools of their craft. Let's not allow the sentimental vision of the animators and the copywriters to become synonymous with children's writing. Rabbits have better things to do than start a savings account, and the drought in the northeast will not be broken by Danny Droplet, no matter how kind we are to him. This kind of writing does not belong to the proud tradition that exists in children's books. We must read the books that represent this tradition, however, if we are going to preserve it. So let's celebrate good readers along with good writers.

Notes

1. Private conversation, February 1981.
2. Betsy Hearne, *Signal,* 8 Sept. 1980, p. 151.

Market Trends Don't Write Books, People Do

Jean Karl

As is true for all editors, I suppose, scarcely a day passes when I do not receive a letter from some hopeful author asking: "What kind of books are you looking for now?" or "In what style do you prefer to have books written?" or even "What are the main things you look for in the manuscripts you read?" Others want me to assign them a topic. And still others seem to want a whole course in writing before they will be confident enough to send me their manuscripts.

With many of these people I feel a deep sympathy. It must be hard to look at the variety of books published and read the many books that are written about writing and about children's literature and know what to do. There are so many options open, so many things one might try. And of all those who write, so few succeed even in getting published, let alone achieve some degree of recognition. So what does make a good book, a publishable book?

To those who ask, I often wish I could answer, "I wish I knew." Because no one can ever really give a definitive answer. To some extent, this is because public tastes change from year to year. What once might have been frowned upon suddenly is the darling of the critical elite, and of the children who lie beyond. Just as suddenly, the beloved of the past is scorned and no longer read.

Yet change of this sort—a predilection of popular taste or critical taste that moves from romance to realism to how-to-play-baseball —is illusion, I think, when one defines what a book should be. Surface changes—subjects and styles that move like ripples on a pond—have little to do with deep underlying assessments of what is good. And in some ways these underlying assessments may not change rapidly enough. Though, for reasons still to come, this does not make definition of the good any easier. And this is not to say that all change is necessarily good; there are values that should remain constant. But sometimes it seems, especially in children's books, there is a constancy of outlook that keeps the really new from even well-considered recognition, let alone acceptance.

There are those who will say that the good—the great—has an eternal theme; it explores an idea that belongs to truth and beauty and love, the basics of life as we know it. The surface may be none of these: the story or the information conveyed may be brutal, ugly, or full of lies, yet underneath is the essence of the eternal—the strength of that which has proved true in the long history of the human race and the depths of the human soul. All right. I'll accept that. That does make a great book. At least it makes a core around which a great book can be written.

Others will say that a good book—a great book—must display good writing style. It must take its undying subject matter and deal with it in language that flows with the movement of a story or explanations of the world or the people in it; the two, essence and expression, must blend, must be as one. In addition, especially in a children's book, the words and sentences and paragraphs must convey meaning easily. They must not call attention to themselves but instead be the servants of the author's vision, so that it is the vision that catches the mind and not the cleverness of the language. This, too, I can accept. Style is important to a book.

And finally there are those who will demand that the particulars of the book—the vehicle, whether it be story, essay, biography, treatise, poetry or whatever—be so engaging that the message, that deep underlying truth, is conveyed almost subliminally; it is there but never quite breaks the surface. In other words, the book does not preach. Or if it does, the preaching is so beautifully couched in style that no one notices. The book becomes a whole that captures the root of an idea and builds a tree on it that becomes that idea grown to its most elegant possibilities. It is the only possible expression of the whole of that idea. This, too, makes sense to me. I can accept this.

And no one, I think, can disagree that if all these things are captured perfectly in a book, one has a masterpiece. Or does one? That, I think, is where the problem lies. One can set up ideals for almost any human situation, and especially for books that describe these situations. But too many times when the ideal is realized it no longer seems so ideal. The flawless is beyond human touch.

The essence of a good book is actually a human being. That human being is one who knows something of the world and its people, who knows how people act and love and live and see—and not see—each other. That person also knows something about human striving toward the ideal, toward the perfect, or perhaps toward the not-so-perfect. That person knows despair and rapture, success and failure, love and hate, concern and coldness, frustration and the joy of achievement. In other words, it is the person next door, the person each one of us is. But with a difference—with an urge to express in words the experience of living and the insights that living brings. And those words, if well handled, ultimately help other people see for a moment, through eyes that are not their own, the way life is for someone else.

How does that human being who must write, who must put his or her understanding in words, best approach the task? How does that person choose the medium—the story or whatever—that will carry some part of his or her life to others? Most do not choose. At least that has been my experience. The medium chooses the writer. The idea comes from the great archetypal winds that blow through us all, perhaps, or maybe from the hidden resources of the id, buried since the age of six. Whatever, it comes, perhaps in some fullness, perhaps only in tantalizing hints. In any case it does not come complete in all details, certainly it does not come dressed in style. And at first the deep, deep root of truth that feeds the work may not be all that apparent to the author—only the story is there, demanding to be told. Or the impulse has arisen to tell somone about something: about penguins or peas or pleasant valleys or Pushkin. The author is driven; the idea is all-encompassing; the work is hard and the physical desire to do it sometimes not very great; but the writer has nothing to say about it—the idea must out.

This is the soul of the true author, even when the author writes for money, as most authors do. Whether that idea makes it to the annals of the great depends on craft. And on determination. And on sheer stubbornness sometimes. Sometimes it is the author who is stubborn. Sometimes it is the idea that just will not go away.

It takes all of this to make a book: a human being with an idea that springs from the vast understandings the human race has acquired and who can express that idea with style, inventiveness, and even uniqueness, persisting in what is a most difficult exercise until something has been accomplished.

Then one day it is finished. The above criteria have been met—to some degree at least. Again, nothing is perfect, and no human being is ever going to create a perfect book. But here it is, the product of vision, sensibility, craft, and determination. Surely easy to recognize! No, not at all. Anyone who has ever sat down to read the hundreds of manuscripts that pour into a publisher's office during a year, at least anyone who has sat down to read with care and caring, will know that the masterpiece does not rise like fat on water. In truth, a lot of the water is only too easy to see—and return. But many of these are books that have no essence of a person in them and sometimes have no style or even inventiveness. They are dead works created for unknown reasons.

But there are a number, more than we in the publishing business like to recognize sometimes, that have in them some of the elements of the good and even the great. And how does one choose among these? To choose the best is the obvious answer. And the very best are, I suppose, fairly easy to see. But even there, sometimes, one must wonder and question. Because when one reads manuscripts by unknown authors one is looking for the soul of a human being. One is looking for a person whose vision is broad enough to see the world many times in many different ways—to create many different books. One is looking for a style that will bend and change and adapt to a hundred different demands placed upon it by the needs of inner visions to escape. One is looking for an individual who can probe deeply into his or her inner resources and come up with story or information that cloaks both individual and collective understanding in ways that the young can read and enjoy and slowly come to understand, too. At the same time, that person must be responsive to the views of others—able to clarify and restate and rethink where necessary at the demands of editors and of readers. Even a thousand-page manuscript is not likely to tell anyone all of this, though, to the more-than-casual reader, the person who lives under any piece of writing does become more and more apparent.

It is always a gamble—choosing a book by a new author. Some first books are very, very good indeed. But the first may turn out to be the best. The roots of understanding did not go very deep. Sometimes what seemed to be depth and insight proves to be only a great cleverness that cannot sustain itself beyond an initial idea. The author can write the same book again and again in different guises, but never another. Yet sometimes the book that didn't really work very well, even after a good deal of editorial guidance, does come from someone who will do fine things—but who needs time and help to grow into the writer he or she can become. There are all kinds of problems, for authors, for editors, and for readers, on the way to the very best that is produced. And none of us is, in the end, a truly competent judge of what is good and what is not good in all areas of human thought. Judges and critics are as imperfect as writers.

Why then do I say that the new is often not recognized as effectively in children's books as it might be, if I think that people are looking for all of these good things that we all know make a part of the best? Because, I think, we are all conditioned by our own childhoods in ways that we can never wholly grasp. Whether we realize it or not, our own inner standards, unless we are very careful, are dictated by things we recognize all too well from the past.

Although this is evident in all areas of writing for children, from the earliest of picture books through literature for the adolescent, it is perhaps easiest to explore in fantasy, especially what is called high fantasy. These books, when they are good, do encompass both the richness of human wisdom and the inventiveness of the great storyteller. Yet think: fantasy is free to reach out in a full circle of directions. Yet what is fantasy to most readers—heroes riding out to conquer evil, very blatantly most of the time. And generally the nature of the hero, the shape of the story, the outcome of the adventure must fall into given patterns—the patterns we see in folk and fairy tales and in heroic folk epics, as well as in fantasies of the past—the things we read as a child. Think about the style in which these books are told. The patterns of sentences, even, sometimes seem prescribed. The language must fall only into certain areas of beauty. Style must set the story apart as belonging to a very narrow world of stories. This is not to decry what is done in the name of high fantasy, but it is to say that we sometimes do not allow creative minds to roam as freely as we should.

Recently we have prided ourselves on the things we can say in realistic children's novels—on language and patterns of action that show life as it really is. But they, too, have developed a conventional mold that separates the classic from the questionable. Readers, here, too, seem to need approaches that they recognize. These may not come from quite so distant a past as the heroic folk epic, but may come from *The Catcher in the Rye,* for example, which is a classic of its own sort, and other early books of teenage realism that startled and appealed to adults and then moved on to children.

We put books into bins. We sort them into categories, as we would never really sort people. And if some books don't quite fit the categories, we don't quite know what to do with them. We can't be sure they are good. Because so much is possible, because there are so many manuscripts, so many books, so many ideas, so many ways of writing—and because we fear, in the smaller and smaller time known as childhood, to waste the time of the young reader with less than the best—we look for the patterns we recognize, for the kinds of books that we believe must contain truth because the style and presentation are those that have always carried depth and insight before. And so maybe we miss the truly innovative, the stubborn idea and writer that insist on going in a new direction where we do not feel altogether comfortable. And because children, though conservative, do not have our preconceived ideas, we may be robbing them of books that would clothe the world in a new kind of sense.

What makes a good book? I wish I knew. If I could be sure, my life would be a great deal easier. But it wouldn't be nearly as interesting. And I think I really don't want to be that sure. I hope I can instead be open to life and to change. To the good in whatever form it takes.

Mary Poppins: *Two Points of View*

A number of articles have appeared in the press in which writers quote librarians and specialists in race relations who feel that the book *Mary Poppins* depicts minorities in a way that might be damaging to the psyches of young readers.

For this reason, the editors of this annual thought it would be helpful to present the views on the subject both from a spokesman for the Council on Interracial Books for Children, Dr. Robert B. Moore, Director of the Racism/Sexism Resource Center for Education in New York City, and from the author, P. L. Travers.

The two points of view are expressed in the letters that follow.

A Letter from a Critic

Robert B. Moore

Most children's literature in this country—whether created in the past or the present—has been written, published, and selected by white people. This literature projects a white view of the world, often including the biases and stereotypes used to justify the domination by whites of people of color.

The image of smiling, contented "darkies" has been much more comforting to whites than images of blacks struggling for freedom and dignity—and the former images predominated in children's books for decades. Images of wild, savage "injuns" were rarely challenged by authentic representations of the diverse native peoples and cultures. Asians, Chicanos, and Puerto Ricans were rarely visible and then primarily in stereotypic form. And what better imperialist primer extolling the white man's burden than the adventurous tales of *Dr. Doolittle?* From all of these, and many more, generations of children learned some basic lessons of white supremacy.

Mary Poppins (the book, not the movie) offers a case in point. In a 1974 interview in the *Interracial Books for Children Bulletin* (vol. 5, no. 3), the author, P. L. Travers, said, "Literature and imagination are my world. . . . Imagination is a pure thing . . . goes whither it will." But imagination is shaped by real-life experience and cultural background. Pure imagination surely would have produced passages relying less on such well-worn stereotypes as do the following two examples from the book:

> Beneath the palm-tree sat a man and a woman, both quite black all over and with very few clothes on. . . . On the knee of the negro lady sat a tiny black piccaninny with nothing on at all. . . .
> "Ah bin 'specting you a long time, Mar' Poppins," she said, smiling. "You bring dem chillun dere to ma li'l house for a slice of watermelon right now. My, but dem's very white babies.

You wan' use a li'l bit black boot polish on dem. Come 'long, now. You'se mighty welcome."

. . . There were four gigantic figures bearing down towards him—the Eskimo with a spear, the Negro Lady with her husband's huge club, the Mandarin with a great curved sword, and the Red Indian with a tomahawk. They were rushing upon him from all four quarters of the room with the weapons raised above their heads. . . . Threatening and full of revenge. They were almost on top of him, their huge, terrible, angry faces looming nearer and nearer. He felt their hot breath on his face and saw their weapons tremble in their hands. . . . "Mary Poppins, Mary Poppins—help me, help me!"

Although the above caricatures were already clichés in 1934, when the book was published, Travers claims: "I have no racism in me. . . . I was brought up in a family and in a world where there was no hint of racism of any kind." That is an incredibly naive and ahistorical depiction of Britain at a time when the sun still shone brightly on its colonial empire. By denying the impact of social conditioning, Travers—like so many of us—unfortunately ignores the potential of raising one's consciousness beyond those socially created bounds.

Most of us born on the privileged side of the color line tend to resist the awful truth—that, through no fault or choice of our own, we've been brainwashed with the myths, attitudes, and beliefs of white supremacy. To recognize that, to accept it without guilt, to acknowledge the need and responsibility to change ourselves, is to begin to liberate our imagination, our attitudes, and our behaviors from the culturally imposed blinders of bias and stereotypes.

World events during the last thirty-five years have caused many white writers to become much more sensitive to issues of race and sex than authors who wrote in earlier times. However, as late as 1971, Travers was still using her literary talents to produce a book like *Friend Monkey,* in which onlookers at the London zoo are unable to tell the difference between an African child and an escaped monkey.

This supposedly hilarious scene brings to mind a story recounted by Charlemae Rollins in the *Negro American Literature Forum* (vol. 2, no. 4, Winter 1968). Rollins reports that—after some soul-searching—she had included *Little Black Sambo* in a recommended book list in 1941. Some years later, on a class outing to the zoo, a little white girl called both a monkey and a black classmate "Little Black Sambo," a taunt soon echoed by other classmates. "I can never forget the way that little boy looked. His day was ruined and so was mine. So, I thought, this book *is* harmful. If a book hurts a child, there must be harm in it." Rollins suggests that such books are "wholly unsuited for today's children who are struggling and striving so hard now for unity and for understanding."

Books are only one of many sources transmitting such negative messages to children. However, they provide a significant contribution to the socializing process (see "How Books Influence Children: What the Research Shows," *Interracial Books for Children Bulletin,* vol. 11, no. 6, 1980). It is because of this influence that the Council on Interracial Books for Children has, for sixteen years, worked to promote children's literature free of race, sex, class, handicap, or age bias. The Council seeks to raise the consciousness of teachers, librarians, and parents, encouraging them to select bias-free materials. The Council's Resource Center offers many print and audio-visual materials designed to help librarians and teachers use biased books constructively, by teaching children to recognize stereotypes and counteract their harmful impact.

Those who select children's books should consider more than literary merit. What will be the impact of the book on a child's self-image, personality, and image of others? Will it contribute to liberating or restricting a child's imagination and striving? Will it enhance or inhibit a child's ability to relate humanely with other human beings? Will it encourage the development of human or anti-human values in the next generation?

A Letter from the Author

P. L. Travers

Ah, my grief! That is an Irishism for "the pity of things," *sunt lachrymae rerum.*

To think that any child, black, red, yellow, or white, could not safely come under Mary Poppins's umbrella! Why did not my friends, Mrs. Augusta Baker and, later, Miss Barbara Rollock, both of them pillars of the New York Public Library, tell me that there were things in the first book that could be called racist? Why, when the book made its initial appearance, did a group of black teachers and librarians ask me to meet them in that same library in order that they could tell me how much the book had helped them in their work with children?

I was reminded of this when, at the request of Francelia Butler, of the English Department of the University of Connecticut, I lectured to her students. The theme was "The World of the Hero" and was wholly related to mythological ideas. At the end of it, a black student came up to me and said, "That was great stuff—great! But," he added, "not relevant to me."

"Why not?" I asked. "Aren't you a human being?"

He looked surprised. "You mean that *I* could be one of the Argonauts, or Lancelot, or Prometheus?"

"Why not? Aren't you, too, metaphorically, looking for the Golden Fleece and Fire from Heaven?"

He admitted that he was. "Well, then!" And he went away thinking it over, without, I was sure, a "racist" bee in his bonnet.

Then, some years ago, while staying with friends in Trinidad, I was asked by the library in Port of Spain to talk to the librarians and children. It was a lovely party, and we were all enjoying one another, when I noticed that the smallest child, the one who was *not* breathing down my neck—a boy of about six or seven—was gazing at me steadily, unsmiling, solemn, intent. This interested me. The other children had enthusiastically mobbed me. Why was *he* far from the madding crowd?

So I said to him, "And you? What do *you* like about Mary Poppins?"

"I don't like her!" he said sternly.

I was enchanted. Praise is all very well, but mostly useless. An ego trip. Criticism is where you learn your lessons.

"Why?" I asked him. "Tell me why. Where did I go wrong?"

The somber gaze transfixed me. He was making sure that he had my whole attention.

Then the serious face cracked from ear to ear in a grin of devilish triumph.

"I don't like her. I *love* her!"

The wretch! He had prepared his trick, played it on me, and it had grandly succeeded. He hugged himself with delight at the joke and I hugged him with equal fervour. So young to know the difference between liking and loving!

Within myself I bowed down to him, remembering what I already know—that from children you can only learn. There is nothing of value you can teach them—merely the three R's.

Well, now I am on the Index, it seems. And I have come to know that the pith and core of the attack is in the chapter "Bad Tuesday." Some years ago, a white teacher friend of mine, who makes lavish use of the book in her classes, told me that she was always shy, reading that story to black children, of the piccaninny language that is spoken by the people whom Mary Poppins meets when she and her crew go South. (South as regards the compass, I meant, not the Southern states of the U.S.A.) "And are the black children affronted?" I asked. Not at all. It appeared that they loved it.

Still, rather than that *she* be embarrassed, I changed the language for the next edition, making it elaborately formal. (Remember that the first *Mary Poppins* came out in 1934.) But even that wasn't enough. I was visited by what one might call a "Minority Manipulator" and given a thorough dressing-down for writing the *original* version. "And," he added, accusingly, "there is one place where you speak of a baby as "it." I told him that this was common parlance, that I could not be expected to upend every baby I met in order to discover its gender and that while he was at liberty (it's a free country) to attack me on the piccaninny theme, I could not allow him to instruct me on what to do with a pronoun.

Then, a year or so later, my publisher received a letter from a very nice librarian in New York asking that the *whole* chapter be deleted. Naturally, he was unwilling to do this and asked me to reply.

I said no, for it seemed to me ludicrous to think that any "minority" could possibly feel hurt by it—"minority" is not a word in my vocabulary—and that it would be a pity to prevent children from experiencing in a book what they already know in themselves, that having been naughty they can, in a flash, be made anew, and feel so very good. Grown-ups, more soberly, go through the same experience.

Even reading the chapter again, and very carefully, I was amazed that anyone could take exception to it. For instance, having myself spent two summers with the Navaho Indians and been given an Indian name not so very different from that of "Fleet-as-the-Wind," and having also been shown how to use a tomahawk effectively, I could not see where the offense lay. And I had thought of the people of the South as, roughly, coming from Australia, where I was born, or from the South Sea Islands. How could I have harmed *them*? I had not, of course, met an Eskimo from the North but had been assured by an anthropologist friend that they do (or did then) rub noses—to my mind quite a pleasant form of greeting—and also eat whale meat and blubber. Was this offensive? I had eaten whale meat myself during the war and been glad of it.

And then the mandarin in the East. Had *he* taken umbrage? Somehow, I didn't think so. And, anyway, Confucius having been made a non-Person, mandarins nowadays are thin on the ground and hardly comprise a minority. And was ever mandarin more respectfully addressed than the courtly old gentleman in "Bad Tuesday"?

So I pondered. And it came to me that these affronted champions of the people in the Compass were distressed at seeing them—in a child's imagination only, remember—in a vindictive aspect. But surely everybody knows that at night and at bedtime, any daylight thing or person can turn into something threatening. Michael—how unwisely!—had taken Mary Poppins's compass and used it without permission. Was it any wonder, then—wasn't it, even, in-evitable?—that those from North, South, East, and West would come to avenge their friend? It would seem to me a pity to defraud children of the idea—not deliberately put there by me but arising naturally from the story—of the difference between day and night, cause and effect, the contentment that comes when danger is past, the goodness of the bad!

The book is translated into all languages—the Russians, pre-dictably, stole it—and I am told that it sells well in Swahili. Can it be that, unlike our protesting librarians, all these foreign read-ers understand that the bear is not under the bed in the daytime? It is night that puts him there.

Well, what more can I say? I would not like to think that by not having the first book, children are defrauded of the rest of the canon which nowhere touches upon "minorities." Indeed, it is fair to ask whether that word "minorities," so bravely defended nowadays, is not in itself a pejorative label. It could even be that those for whom it has been invented would prefer not to have it thrust upon them.

Even so, without at all apologizing to anybody for anything—what I have written I have written—I have, for a reason of my own, remade the essential part of the chapter "Bad Tuesday," and now await, with some interest, outcries from such "minorities" as Polar Bears, Macaws, Dolphins, Pandas.

I will tell you what that reason is. Oddly enough, it is a gesture of gratitude, wry but valid, to the valiant protestors. For, because of them, I found it necessary to reread the complete book, a thing I had never wholly done, for I was not given the opportunity at the outset of correcting the proofs. Had I done so I would have found, in another story, an ethical mistake, now altered—one word only, no one will find it—a mistake that to me immeasurably out-weighs any imagined slight to a minority. It is my good fortune that the protestors either did not see it or, what is more probable, passed it by as a thing of naught. In a word, one may in error tell any lie—or half-truth, which perhaps is worse—as long as one takes care not to step on anyone's corn.

Poor children! Sometimes we do too little for them. Sometimes we do too much.

Perrault and Aesop's Fables

Dorothea Hayward Scott

The Palace of Versailles was approaching completion in 1668, although work continued on the grandiose structure until well into the next century. A contemporary description saw it as a magnificent allegory of the idea of the king, with the "Sun-King," Louis XIV, as the reality. Apollo, the king's favourite symbol, presided over that enchanted world as the god of light and the inspirer of muses.

Among the many magnificent features of the gardens designed by the master landscape designer, André le Nôtre, was a labyrinth. A book about it was published by the Imprimerie royale, in 1679, *Labyrinte de Versailles*. In 1682 another guide was published in Amsterdam, *'t Doolhof te Versailles*. This was in French, English, and "Hoog-en Nederduits' "so it might appeare in four languages in print to be serviceable unto these Nations."[1] In it we may read:

Description of the Labyrinth of Versailles

Among all the Groves in the Park at Versailles, that called the Labyrinth is the most eminent, as well for the Novelty of the Design as the Number and Diversity of its Fountains. It is called the Labyrinth by reason of the many intricate Windings and Turnings that run thrô each other, in such sort, as it is impossible not to err in them: now to the end that those who should so deviate, or loose the right Path might be entertained with something delectable, there is not one Turning which doth not affoard the sight of divers Fountains: insomuch that upon every step one is surprised with a new Object.

For the subject of these Water-works were some of the Fables of Aesop made choice of which are so lively expressed, as that nothing can be found of a more ingenious contrivance. The Animals which are of Brass and all in their natural colours are so fitly designed, that they seem to be in the very action which they represent; the more for that they cast out water alluding to the form of speech which the Fable renders them in.

The different Order of every Fountain also makes a most acceptable variety, and the glittering colours of rare shells and fine pieces of Rocks, with which all the Cisterns are adorned and laid in, are so intermixed with the verdure of the Pallisades that one can never be sufficiently satisfied with the number of the Fountains, as to the singular Invention of the same, in the clear expression of what they represent, the beauty of the distinct Animals whereof they are composed, and the prodigious emission of water which they cast up.

'T was held both necessary and much to the purpose to make an exact Description of every Fountain in particular, to concomitate the Plates. And to manifest the faithfull Representation of each Fable we have annexed a brief Description of the Fable it self, with another of the frame and order of the Fountain.

At the Entrance you find two fair brass Statues, painted with proper Colours, the one representing Aesop, the famous Mythologist of Phrygia, the other Cupid; each mounted upon a Pedestal made of pieces of Rocks. Aesop holds in one hand a Roll of Paper, and with the clue of other points at Cupid, who has a thred in his hand, to signify that that [the] God who in such manner ingages in the troubles om [of the] Labyrinth of Love, has not that mysterious faculty of reducing them out, unless he take Wisdom for his Companion, whose ways are manifestly demonstrated by Aesop in his Fables.

Afterwards you find the several Fountains in order being 39 in number. Upon each Fountain is a Plate of Brass, laid ore with a Black Ground, and thereupon a Tetrastich, or Verse of four Lines, made by Monsieur de Benserade: Showing first the Fable and afterwards the Moral.[2]

The Labyrinth itself was begun in 1666 and the fountains in 1672. There are extensive records preserved concerning the whole project, which took more than seven years to complete. The records also show that the idea of decorating the Labyrinth with fountains and sculptures illustrating the *Fables of Aesop* was the inspiration of Charles Perrault.[3] At that time, Perrault was not only the Contrôleur Général de la Surintendance des Bâtiments, an office he had held since 1654 through the good offices of his brother with the powerful finance minister of Louis XIV, Jean-Baptiste Colbert, but by 1665 was also "conseiller honoraire amateur" of the Académie de Peinture et de Sculture. This appointment allowed him to influence the choice of paintings and sculptures used to adorn the royal buildings and parks.

La Fontaine published his first six books of *Fables choisies* in 1668 and dedicated them to the little seven-year-old dauphin, son of Louis XIV and Maria Theresa. It was said at the time that he was angling for the appointment of tutor to the dauphin.[4] The same was said about Perrault with his scheme for the embellishment of the Labyrinth to amuse the young Prince, but in any event, neither was appointed.

By 1673 the Labyrinth was nearing completion, artists had been commissioned to work on the sculptures, and a poet, Isaac de Benserade, received the official commission[5] "to make an exact description of every fountain in particular,"[6] which he did in the four-line verses which were engraved on plates attached to the basin of each fountain. Perrault himself also composed versions of the fables in prose with some verse insertions, and these he gathered together in a sumptuously bound manuscript book entitled *Le Labyrinthe de Versailles,* which he presented to the Royal Library there. This book he published in 1675 but with the title *Recueil de divers ouvrages en prose et en vers.* The official publication celebrating the completion of the Labyrinth was not published until 1679, by the Imprimerie royale with the simple title *Labyrinte de Versailles.* This contained both Perrault's prose versions of the fables and the verse summaries of de Benserade, with full-page engravings of the thirty-nine sculpture-fountains by Sebastien Leclerc. A London publication of 1768, *Ethic Amusements* by Daniel Bellamy, reprinted the quatrains of de Benserade with English verse translations and a prose description of the sculptures and fountains, with the subtitle, *Aesop at Court; or the Labyrinth of Versailles Delineated in French and English, the Plates Engraved by G. Bickham.* From the Paris Edition.

The thirty-nine fables "illustrated" in lead (more reliable records say lead, although the Amsterdam *Guide* says the sculptures were of brass)[7] are as follows, according to the translation of the list:

1. The Owl and Birds
2. The Cocks and Partridge
3. The Cock and Gray-hound
4. The Cock and Diamond
5. The hanging Cat and Ratts
6. The Eagle and Fox
7. The Peacocks and Jay
8. The Cock and Turky-Cock
9. The Peacock and Mag-py
10. The Serpent Anvil and File
11. The Ape and his young
12. The Combat of Animals
13. The Fox and Crane
14. The Crane and Fox
15. The Hen and Chickens
16. The Peacock and Nightingale
17. The Parret and Ape
18. The Ape a Judge
19. The Rat and Frog
20. The Hare and Tortoise
21. The Wolf and Crane
22. The Kite and Birds
23. The Ape a King
24. The Fox and Goat
25. The Council of Ratts
26. The Froggs and Jupiter
27. The Ape and Cat
28. The Fox and Grapes
29. The Eagle Coney and Beetle
30. The Wolf and Porcupine
31. The Serpent with many Heads
32. The Mouse, Cat and litle Cock
33. The Kite and Doves
34. The Dolphin and Ape
35. The Fox and Raven
36. The Swan and Crane
37. The Wolf and the Head
38. The Serpent and Porcupine
39. The little Dog and Ducks[8]

The moral of Aesop's stories rather than the story itself is emphasized in the brief four-line verse summaries, and the stories must have needed further explanation to be fully appreciated by the dauphin. The titles of some of the fables vary from more commonly accepted English forms but I have been able to identify twenty-three of them in the first collection of La Fontaine. Twelve are to be found in one of the standard collections in English for children, *The Fables of Aesop selected, told anew and their history*

"The Hare and the Tortoise," from *Labyrinte de Versailles* (Paris, 1679).

"The Fox and the Grapes," from *Labyrinte de Versailles* (Paris, 1679).

traced by Joseph Jacobs, (first published in 1894), and sixteen are included in the Dover edition of Sir Roger L'Estrange's version (first published in 1692). Two perennial favorites, "The Hare and the Tortoise," no. 20, and "The Fox and the Grapes," no. 28, are illustrated to give the reader an idea of the elaborate design of the sculptures and fountains. Alas, the Labyrinth was destroyed just over one hundred years later, and only a few of the animal statues are preserved in museums.

It is difficult to discern any significant order or meaning in the arrangement of the statues and fountains illustrating the fables, but at the grand entrance to the Labyrinth there stood two figures giving a clue to the allegory of the maze. One was Aesop himself, portrayed as he is traditionally imagined, a hunchback Greek slave holding a scroll in his hand. Opposite him was a statue of Cupid drawing out a thread from a ball held in the other hand. The lesson to be learned from this imagery, according to Bellamy, is:

> "That tho' the God of Love is too apt to involve mankind into a thousand petty broils and perplexities, yet he has the secret art of extricating them out of the maze they are thus led into, when he is accompanied by *Prudence*, to the practice whereof he is here directed by the sage *Fables of Aesop*."[9]

Notes

1. Anthoni Jansz van der Goes, *'t Doolhof te Versailles* (Amsterdam: Hendrik Bosch, 1722), unpaged, sig. **1, verso.
2. Ibid., sig. ***1, recto and verso.
3. Marc Soriano, *Le Dossier Perrault* (Paris: Hachette, 1972), pp. 166–67.
4. Ibid., p. 156.
5. Ibid., p. 167.
6. Van der Goes, sig. ***1, verso.
7. Soriano, p. 167.
8. Van der Goes, sig. L1, recto and verso.
9. Daniel Bellamy, Jr., *Ethic Amusements* (London: G. Bickham, 1768), p. 210.

Bibliography

On Versailles

Alleau, René. *Guide de Versailles Mystérieux*. Paris, Tchou, 1966 (Les Guides Noirs).
Bellamy, Daniel, Jr. *Ethic Amusements*. London, G. Bickham, 1768. Contains

"Aesop at Court or The Labyrinth of Versailles. Delineated in French and English. The plates engraved by G. Bickham." From the Paris edition. London, Printed for ye Editor MDCCLXVIII."

Champigneulle, Bernard. *Versailles.* Paris, Librarie Larousse, 1954. (Arts Styles et Techniques) ch.III Les jardins pendant la règne de Louis XIV.

Labyrinte de Versailles. A Paris, De l'Imprimerie royale, 1679. (Engravings by Sebastien Le Clerc).

Marie, Alfred. *Naissance de Versailles*: Le Chateau-les jardins. Vol. 1. Ouvrage publié avec le concours du Centre National de la Recherche Scientifique. Paris, Editions Vincent, Fréal et cie. 1968.

Matthews, W. H. *Mazes and Labyrinths: Their History and Development.* London: Longmans Green, 1922. Reprinted, Dover, 1970.

Payne, Francis Loring. *The Story of Versailles.* New York, Moffat, Yard and Co. 1919. ch.IV The Gardens, the Fountains and the Grand Trianon.

Van der Goes, Anthoni Jansz. *'t Doolhof te Versailles* . . . Amsterdam, Hendrik Bosch, 1722 (first published 1682).

On Aesop's Fables

Benserade, Isaac de. *Les fables d'Esope, Mises en françois, Avec le sens moral en quatre vers,* et des Figures à chaque Fable . . . les quatrains de Benserade. A Rouen, de l'Imprimerie Priviligiée, 1777.

Jacobs, Joseph. *The Fables of Aesop. Selected, told anew and their history traced* by Joseph Jacobs. Done into pictures by Richard Heighway. New York, Schocken Books, 1966. (first published 1894).

La Fontaine, Jean de. *Fables choisies. Mises en vers* par M. de la Fontaine. A Paris, Chez Claude Barbin, 1668.

L'Estrange, Sir Roger. *Fables of Aesop.* With fifty drawings by Alexander Calder. New York, Dover Publications, 1967 (text first published 1692).

Metropolitan Museum of Art. *Aesop. Five centuries of illustrated fables.* Selected by John J. McKendry. New York, The Metropolitan Museum of Art, 1964.

United States Government. Library of Congress. General Reference and Bibliography Division. Reference Department. *Fables from incunabula to modern picture books, a selective bibliography* compiled by Barbara Quinnam, Children's Book Section. Washington, DC, Library of Congress, 1966.

On Charles Perrault (1628–1703)

Barchilon, Jacques. *Perrault's Tales of Mother Goose. The dedication manuscript of 1695* . . . with introduction and critical text by Jacques Barchilon. New York, The Pierpont Morgan Library, 1956.

Perrault, Charles. *Mémoires de ma vie.* Ed. Paul Bonnefon. Paris, H. Laurens, 1909.

Perrault, Charles. *Recueil de divers ouvrages en prose et en vers.* Paris, Jean Guignard, 1676.

Soriano, Marc. *Les Contes de Perrault, culture savante et traditions populaires.* Paris, Gallimard [1968].

Soriano, Marc. *Le Dossier Perrault.* Paris, Hachette [1972].

Dissertations of Note

Rachel Fordyce

Attebery, Brian L. "America and the Materials of Fantasy." Ph.D. diss. Brown University, 1979. 339 pp. DAI 40:5862A.

Attebery is interested in making critical and historical distinctions between British and American fantasy, while acknowledging both the imitative and unique characteristics of American fantasy. He covers a wide range of thematic approaches and authors, specifically Ruskin, Tolkien, Joseph Rodman Drake, Whittier, Irving, Hawthorne, Vladimir Propp, Baum, Cabell, Burroughs, H. P. Lovelace, Bradbury, Thurber, Le Guin, and Edward Eager. With the exception of the Earthsea trilogy, Attebery believes that American fantasy has not fully absorbed the influence of Tolkien "and a good deal of current fantasy writing results only in lifeless imitation."

Birx, Charles Robert. "Concepts of Death Presented in Contemporary Realistic Children's Literature: A Content Analysis." Ed.D. diss. Northern Arizona University, 1979. 189 pp. DAI 40:1235A.

From a sample of forty-two contemporary, realistic, and critically approved books, Birx draws conclusions about the suitability of the treatment of death in works for preschoolers through eighth grade. He is concerned with who or what dies in each book, the cause of death, and basic concepts related to death: "separation, impermanence, permanence, personification, avoidance, inevitability, universality, magical thinking, guilt, punishment, grief, ritual-funeral, and life after death." He concludes that these thirteen concepts are not treated fully or in sufficient number in the books he explores, and that the treatment of death is rarely appropriate to the age level for which the book is intended.

Burns, Marjorie Jean. "Victorian Fantasists from Ruskin to Lang: A Study in Ambivalence." Ph.D. diss. University of California, Berkeley, 1978. 335 pp. DAI 40:265A.

Burns analyzes both the antiquarian and Romantic interest in fantasy in the nineteenth century, but she is more concerned with the fantasy writers who on one hand apologized for or were reticent about their work, and on the other hand frequently became essayists and critics for the genre. The thesis focuses on Ruskin, Thackeray, MacDonald, Morris, and Lang; and in her conclusion, Burns acknowledges the debt of C. S. Lewis, J. R. R. Tolkien, and Charles Williams to these Victorian writers.

Degraff, Amy Vanderlyn. "The Tower and the Well: A Study of Form and Meaning in Mme. d'Aulnoy's Fairy Tales." Ph.D. diss. University of Virginia, 1979. 242 pp. DAI 40:888A.

Degraff focuses on the psychological aspects of Mme. d'Aulnoy's tales rather than the philological backgrounds, using Bettelheim's *Uses of Enchantment* to clarify her approach. She contends that the tales "reflect important aspects of our inner world including essential phases of psychological development." By tracing the concept of "instinctual domination" in *La Princesse Printanière,*

Le Prince Marcassin, and *Le Bonne Petite Souris* and by showing that "the search for autonomy and identity, both sexual and other, are crucial to a protagonist's psychological development" in such works as *Le Rameau d'or* and *Belle-Belle ou Le Chevalier Fortuné,* she explores the strengths of personality and the processes of maturation. Chapter 3, the climactic chapter, explores the richness of the theme of love in some of Mme. d'Aulnoy's most famous tales: *Marcassin, Le Rameau d'or,* and *Gracieuse et Percènet.*

Griswold, Jerome Joseph. "Mother and Child in the Poetry and Children's Books of Randall Jarrell." Ph.D. diss. University of Connecticut, 1979. 194 pp. DAI 40:5442A.

Griswold shows through the central figures of mother and child in Jarrell's work that the major theme of "separation anxiety and its resolution" is the basis for characterization of the two. His study focuses on *Blood for a Stranger; Little Friend, Little Friend; Losses; The Seven-Year Crutches; The Women at the Washington Zoo; The Lost World;* and *Fly by Night,* and he shows how themes in these works relate to *The Gingerbread Rabbit, The Bat-Poet,* and *The Animal Family.* In an appendix Griswold includes a discussion with Maurice Sendak on the illustration of Jarrell's children's books.

Jones, Steven Swann. "The Construction of the Folktale: 'Snow White.'" Ph.D. diss. University of California, Davis, 1979. 231 pp. DAI 40:5538A.

Using twenty-four versions of "Snow White," Jones explains how a traditional folktale is constructed and identifies "the principles, patterns, and processes by which a folktale is put together." Specifically, he analyzes the sexual, philosophical, and intellectual development of the main character of this tale. Generally, he argues that "the construction of folktales . . . explains the narrative stability of folktales" as well as their consistency and longevity, despite variations of style and motif.

Locke, Duncan Allan. "Teachers as Characterized in Contemporary Juvenile Fiction." Ph.D. diss. University of Oregon, 1979. 111 pp. DAI 40:3001–02A.

Teachers looking for an image of themselves as productive, imaginative, reasonable, nonpunitive, and well-rounded in children's literature will be sorely disappointed if Locke's conclusions are correct. Using a sample of fifty-one high-quality works of fiction for children, drawn from 333 contemporary books with teachers as characters, Locke demonstrates that most teachers are stereotyped and negatively characterized. They are portrayed as eccentric, with little life of their own outside the classroom, and unworthy as models. Appended to this study is an annotated bibliography of significant works that have teachers as major characters.

Loder, Reed Elizabeth. "Personal Identity Concepts in the Context of Children's Fantasy Literature." Ph.D. diss. Boston University Graduate School, 1979. 254 pp. DAI 40:2734A.

This thesis, in philosophy, deals with fantasy rather than realism because of the novel and highly diversified nature of characters in fantasy. It demonstrates, through various philosophical methods of evaluation, that whereas "literary imagination is capricious, . . . 'philosophical imagination' operates in harmony with legitimate philosophical purposes and methods. It is reasoned imagination." Loder is primarily concerned with personal identity theories, memory theories, and their limits as applied to literature. She also proposes aesthetic criteria and standards for evaluating a "good story."

McBroom, Geraldine Lynn. "Young Adult Realistic Fiction, 1967–1977: Images of Adolescent Male Protagonists." Ph.D. diss. Ohio State University, 1979. 196 pp. DAI 40:4575A.

McBroom makes the point that one outcome of the criticism of new realism in novels for young adults has been extensive evaluation of the stereotyped images of females in the literature, particularly since 1960. Her purpose is to analyze the role of males in contemporary fiction for young adults. Focusing on major works published after 1967 which have male protagonists, she scrutinizes "publishing divisions, authors, numbers and relationships of characters, color and economic categories represented, family structures, time spans, settings, narrative styles, topics, and themes of the novels." While these novels may treat atypical subject matter, they appear to be as didactic as earlier works, although the male characters are well-rounded and developing. The conclusion of the thesis gives suggestions for further research and ways to treat the novels in a classroom.

MacDonald, Margaret Read. "An Analysis of Children's Folktale Collections with an Accompanying Motif-Index of Juvenile Folktale Collections (Volumes I and II)." Ph.D. diss. Indiana University, 1979. 1257 pp. DAI 40:1000A.

MacDonald is concerned with setting standards for distinguishing authentic folklore from the "fakelore" frequently predigested for children's consumption. She attributes the confusion to "library misclassification, publisher's misrepresentation, textbook and encyclopedia misinformation, inadequate reviewing, poor teacher and librarian training, and lack of interest in children's materials." The motif index, based on Stith Thompson's *Motif-Index of Folk-Literature* and cross-listed to Aarne-Thompson, includes 510 folklore collections and 188 picture books.

Mahoney, Ellen Wilcox. "A Content Analysis of Children's Book Reviews from *Horn Book Magazine*, 1975." Ph.D. diss. University of Illinois at Urbana-Champaign, 1975. 96 pp. DAI 40:140A.

To negate the "demeaning and unjustified criticism" of children's literature, Mahoney turns to essays and reviews in *Horn Book*. Using standards for literary criticism established in *Elements of Writing about a Literary Work: A Study of Response to Literature* (Purves and Rippere) she concludes that *Horn Book* reviewers are concerned primarily with content and appropriateness, giving secondary attention to tone, mood, and point of view. Other, more subtle aspects of the literature are rarely analyzed. She notes that most *Horn Book* reviews are positive because "reviewing of negatively criticized books involves greater attention to discussion of author's method . . . the structure of the work—the relation of form and content."

Moss, Anita West. "Children and Fairy Tales: A Study in Nineteenth-Century British Fantasy." Ph.D. diss. Indiana University, 1979. 387 pp. DAI 40:4056A.

Moss thoroughly analyzes both the detractors and defenders of fairy tales, fantasy, and children's literature in general during the nineteenth century. The work centers on the contributions of Catherine Sinclair, Mark Lemon, Francis Edward Poget, Carlyle, Wordsworth, Ruskin, Kingsley, MacDonald, Wilde, Carroll, Barrie, and Grahame. The study is balanced between the romantic concept of the child's "higher innocence" and the sophisticated "burlesque of fairy tale conventions, and an anti-romantic vision of childhood" inspired by the French court tales. She concludes that the "functions of the imagination, childhood, and fantasy as agents of discovery, redemption, escape, reconciliation, and enlargement which evolved in nineteenth-century England are still current and powerful in contemporary children's literature."

Riehl, Joseph Earl. "Charles Lamb's Children's Literature." Ph.D. diss. University of Denver, 1979. 226 pp. DAI 40:276A.

Riehl examines Charles Lamb's contribution to children's literature as well as the influence that writing for children had on Lamb's criticism and essays for adults. He shows that Lamb's writing for children was frequently a precursor of aesthetic standards for adult literature. He also places Lamb within the context of works by Hannah More, Anna Barbauld, Sarah Trimmer, Mary Wollstonecraft, Wordsworth, and Coleridge.

Rupert, Pamela Rae. "An Analysis of the Need Fulfillment Imagery in Fantasy Literature for Children." Ph.D. diss. University of Akron, 1979. 295 pp. DAI 40:664A.

This dissertation in elementary education analyzes forty works of fantasy for children, published between 1945 and 1977, in terms of psychological needs and fantasy's ability to promote growth and maturity in its child readers. She concludes that the books do "suggest resolutions to problems," and that "fantasy structures were effectively used to portray concretely and dramatically concerns universal in nature."

Schwebel, Carol Rose. "Teacher's Versus Student's Perception of a Children's Book." Ph.D. diss. Ohio State University, 1979. 177 pp. DAI 40:1865A.

Schwebel's thesis in elementary education, directed by Charlotte Huck, analyzes the degree of understanding that kindergarten students, third-graders, and sixth-graders bring to a children's story book, and compares these results to a teacher's ability to perceive a child's level of understanding. She concludes that teachers assume far too much about a child's ability to grasp meaning and nuance in literature and that they should be more careful in selecting books appropriate to the level of a child's understanding.

Sgroi, Carol Thompson. "The Louisville Children's Theatre: A History." Ph.D. diss. Southern Illinois University at Carbondale, 1979. 189 pp. DAI 40:2993A.

Sgroi narrates the colorful and productive history of the Louisville Children's Theatre under the tutelage of Sara Spencer and Ming Dick. She analyzes both the period of child actors (pre-1975) and the current professional status of the theatre based on playbills, newspaper accounts, interviews, publicity, and the financial records of the theatre.

Smith, Rona. "Sex-Role Stereotyping in Selected American Children's Fiction from 1950 to 1974." Ph.D. diss. New York University, 1979. 239 pp. DAI 40:2964–65A.

Smith's thesis in mass communications is predicated on the belief that children learn to model their own roles on "symbolic models." Presumably, a sex role that is highly stereotypical, but strong, has the ability "to function as a shaper of future perceptions; to cause expectation to take over from reality." While there are differences in the treatment of males and females between 1950 and 1974, the degree of change is not very significant; hence any expectations about a change in role-modeling are almost negligible.

Sutton, Wendy Kathleen. "A Study of Selected Alternate Literary Conventions in Fiction for Children and Young Adults and an Examination of the Responses of Professionals Influential in Juvenile Literature to the Presence of These Conventions." Ph.D. diss. Michigan State University, 1978. 425 pp. DAI 40:513–14A.

Sutton concludes that neither educators, reviewers, or writers of textbooks on children's literature are fully aware of the richness, diversity, and innovation in current literature for children and that none of these "could be regarded as a useful source of information as to changes in juvenile literature," nor do they show to what extent innovation in contemporary adult literature is reflected in children's literature. Essentially, she advocates new, more complex, and more flexible analysis and criticism of juvenile literature.

Thorsen-Collins, Karen Holly. "Color Terms in British Folk Tales and Legends: A Computerized Analysis of Their Grammatical Functions and Symbolic Attributions." Ph.D. diss. University of Pennsylvania, 1979. 258 pp. DAI 40:1624A.

"This study [in folklore] offers possibilities for a model of metaphoric evaluation in the generic definition of narrative styles." It attempts to define grammatical relationships of the color terms used in British folklore and identifies the uses of color "through descriptive associations." Thorsen-Collins bases her thesis on the work of Katherine Briggs in *A Dictionary of British Folk-Tales in the English Language, Incorporating the F. J. Norton Collection.* 2607 color terms are identified in 722 legends and tales.

Tibbets, Sylvia-Lee. "Sexism in Children's Magazines." Ed.D. diss. University of Pennsylvania, 1979. 240 pp. DAI 40:5415A.

Tibbetts explores gender discrimination in eleven popular children's magazines with large circulations to show a ponderousness of male characters in highly typical roles. Men are consistently described as independent, employed, active in social roles outside the home, self-sufficient, and as rule-makers and protectors. Women are depicted as married or widowed, tied to family affairs, caretakers, and generally more friendly than males. She views this limitation of roles in children's periodicals as defeating and limiting to characters of both sexes who cannot reach their full potential as developing, rounded characters.

Tullos, Tanya. "The Role of Women in Children's Literature: What Do Books Recommended by Public Elementary School Librarians Reflect?" Ph.D. diss. Texas A&M University, 1979. 142 pp. DAI 40:6146A.

This elementary-education thesis draws on twenty-seven randomly selected books from 1975 compared with thirty-six titles recommended by school librarians in Texas. Tullos analyzes sex roles in four content areas: "pictorial presence, narrative presence, role options, and descriptive expressions." She finds that there is very little difference in stereotyping between the recommended and nonrecommended books and suggests that librarians, authors, illustrators, and the buying public scrutinize children's books more carefully for bias. The conclusion of the work is an exploration of further research and investigation that might shed light on the problem of sex role stereotyping.

Also of Note

Barta, Patricia Ann Brock. "A Study of Children's Reactions to the Assertive Behavior of Female Characters in Books." Ph.D. diss. University of Minnesota, 1979. 161 pp. DAI 40:3105-06A.

Berman, Ruth Amelia. "Suspending Disbelief: The Development of Fantasy as a Literary Genre in Nineteenth-Century British Fiction as Represented by Four Leading Periodicals: *Edinburgh Review, Blackwood's, Fraser's and Cornhill.*" Ph.D. diss. University of Minnesota, 1979. 358 pp. DAI 40:865A.

Billeter, Anne Margaret. "Selection of Children's Books for Public and School Libraries: Examination of the Books by the Local Librarian as a Method of Selection." Ph.D. diss. University of Illinois at Urbana-Champaign, 1979. DAI 40:11–12A.

Bottoms, Laurie Shaffer. "A Study of Childhood in the Poetry of Theodore Roethke." Ph.D. diss. Fordham University, 1979. 181 pp. DAI 40:848–49A.

Clark, Beverly Lyon. "The Mirror Worlds of Carroll, Nabokov, and Pynchon: Fantasy in the 1860's and 1960's." Ph.D. diss. Brown University, 1979. 429 pp. DAI 40:5847A.

Cook, John T. "Student Attitude: A Comparison of Science Fiction Literature and Reading Values." Ph.D. diss. Brigham Young University, 1979. 167 pp. DAI 40:3931A.

Fauvre, Mary. "The Development of Empathy through Children's Literature." Ph.D. diss. University of California, Los Angeles, 1979. 175 pp. DAI 40:3887–88A.

Foley, Mary Kathleen. "The Sundanese *Wayang Golek*: The Red Puppet Theatre of West Java." Ph.D. diss. University of Hawaii, 1979. 322 pp. DAI 40:6072A.

Gupton, Sandra Lee. "Moral Education as a Part of the Study of Children's Literature: An Inservice Model and Case-Study." Ed.D. diss. The University of North Carolina at Greensboro, 1979. 237 pp. DAI 40:2011–12A.

Hathaway, Joyce Alley Toothman. "The Use of Appalachian Cultures and Oral Tradition in the Teaching of Children's Literature to Adolescents." Ph.D. diss. Ohio State University, 1979. 182 pp. DAI 40:3933A.

Herrin, Barbara Ruth. "A History and Analysis of the William Allen White Children's Book Award." Ph.D. diss. Kansas State University, 1979. 417 pp. DAI 40:4286A.

Heckman, Janet Gephart. "Responses to Literature in a School Environment, Grades K–5." Ph.D. diss. Ohio State University, 1979. 256 pp. DAI 40:3764A.

Isbell, Rebecca Gail Temple. "A Study of the Effects of Two Modes of Literature Presentation on the Oral Language Development of Four- and Five-Year Old Children." Ed.D. diss. University of Tennessee, 1979. 127 pp. DAI 40:3167A.

Koss, Helen Gueble. "A Comparison of Sexism in Trade Books for Primary Children, 1950–1953 and 1970–1973." Ph.D. diss. University of Connecticut, 1979. 176 pp. DAI 40:647–48A.

Kovalcik, Alfred L. "The Effect of Using Children's Literature to Change Fifth Grade Students' Attitudes toward Social Studies as an Area of Instruction." Ed.D. diss. University of Northern Colorado, 1979. 126 pp. DAI 40:2585–86A.

Kutzer, Marybeth Daphne. "Poor Jo: Middle-Class Ideas of Working-Class and Poor Children in England, 1837–1859." Ph.D. diss. Indiana University, 1979. 311 pp. DAI 40:4054A.

Leung, Esther Kau-To. "Evaluation of a Children's Literature Program Designed to Facilitate the Social Integration of Handicapped Children into Regular Elementary Classrooms." Ph.D. diss. Ohio State University, 1979. 299 pp. DAI 40:4528A.

Long, Roger Alan. "The Movement System in Javanese *Wayang Kulit* in Relation to Puppet Character Type: A Study of Ngayogyakarta Shadow Theatre." Ph.D. diss. University of Hawaii, 1979. 278 pp. DAI 40:3401A.

Longman, Dorothy Isreal. "Literary Preference and Gender: A Study of the Poetry Preferences of Selected Seventh and Twelfth Grade Boys and Girls and the Relationship of These Preferences to Knowledge of the Authors' Gender." Ph.D. diss. University of Connecticut, 1979. 91 pp. DAI 40:4516A.

McCall, Carolyn Josephine Hein. "A Determination of Children's Interest in Poetry Resulting from Specific Experiences." Ph.D. diss. The University of Nebraska-Lincoln, 1979. 142 pp. DAI 40:4401-02A.

McGovern, Kevin Joseph. "The Influence of Irish Fairy Lore on the Thought of W. B. Yeats." Ph.D. diss. The University of North Carolina at Chapel Hill, 1978. 336 pp. DAI 40:272-73A.

Motaref, Kianoosh. "From the Land of Roses and Nightingales: A Collection and Study of Persian Folktales (Volumes I and II)." Ph.D. diss. Florida State University, 1979. 652 pp. DAI 40:5539A.

Passow, Emilie Scherz. "Orphans and Aliens: Changing Images of Childhood in Works of Four Victorian Novelists." Ph.D. diss. Columbia University, 1979. 231 pp. DAI 40:2698A.

    Specific treatment of *Wuthering Heights, The Mill on the Floss, What Maisie Knew,* and *The Turn of the Screw.*

Rengel, Faye Joyce. "Patterns of the Hero and the Quest: Epic Romance, Fantasy." Ph.D. diss. Brown University, 1979. 248 pp. DAI 40:5854A.

    See for a treatment of Tolkien and William Morris.

Schwartz, Philip Jay. "A Historical Analysis of Creative Dramatics in American Schools." Ph.D. diss. Rutgers University, 1979. 145 pp. DAI 40:3830A.

Wharton, Linda F. "Black American Children's Singing Games: A Structural Analysis." Ph.D. diss. University of Pittsburgh, 1979. 513 pp. DAI 40:2356A.

White, Diane Virginia. "Child Tragedies in German Literature, 1776-1902." Ph.D. diss. Yale University, 1979. 250 pp. DAI 40:3332A.

Williams, LilliAnne Burwell. "Black Traditions in Children's Literature: A Content Analysis of the Text and Illustration of Picture Story Books about Black People in the United States to Determine How Selected Black Traditions Have Been Portrayed and to Determine What Import These Portrayals Have on the Self-Concept of Children Who are Exposed to These Books." Ph.D. diss. Michigan State University, 1979. 267 pp. DAI 40:4888A.

Contributors and Editors

BRIAN ATTEBERY teaches English and music at the College of Idaho and is the author of *The Fantasy Tradition in American Literature.*

BENNETT A. BROCKMAN teaches English at the University of Connecticut. He has published studies of medieval, Renaissance, and children's literature and has edited several children's literature classics.

FRANCELIA BUTLER teaches children's literature at the University of Connecticut and recently organized the Children's Literature Division of the Modern Language Association.

JOHN CECH teaches English at the University of Florida and is currently the editor of *The Dictionary of Literary Biography*'s three-volume series on American writers for children.

CHRISTOPHER CLAUSEN teaaches at Virginia Polytechnic Institute and State University and is the author of *The Place of Poetry,* a study of poetry and culture since Wordsworth's time.

JAMES COMO is head of Speech Communication and Theatre Arts, York College, City University of New York. He is editor of *C. S. Lewis at the Breakfast Table and Other Reminiscences.*

MICHAEL EGAN is a professor of English at the University of Massachussetts at Amherst.

CONNIE C. EPSTEIN is editor-in-chief of Morrow Junior Books at William Morrow and Company.

PAMELA LEE ESPELAND is a freelance editor and has written several children's books.

NELLVENA DUNCAN EUTSLER teaches English at East Carolina University and has recently traveled extensively in China.

RACHEL FORDYCE is assistant dean at Virginia Polytechnic Institute and State University.

MARTIN GREEN teaches English at Tufts University. His latest book is *Dreams of Adventure, Deeds of Empire.*

DAVID L. GREENE is chairman of the English Department at Piedmont College in Georgia.

MARGARET HAMILTON has been a character actress in about seventy films, including *The Wizard of Oz, My Little Chickadee, The Invisible Woman,* and *The State of the Union.*

WILLIAM HARMON teaches at the University of North Carolina at Chapel Hill. His most recent book is *The Oxford Book of American Light Verse. One Long Poem* is forthcoming from the Louisiana State University Press.

JEAN KARL is editor of children's books at Atheneum Publishers and has published several books for and about children.

MADELEINE L'ENGLE, whose most recent book is *A Ring of Endless Light,* has written more than twenty books and has won international awards.

BEN H. McCLARY is chairman of the English Department at Middle Georgia College and has published books on American literature.

JOSEPH MILNER is chairman of the Department of Education at Wake Forest University and has published extensively on the relationship between religion and literature.

ROBERT B. MOORE is director of the Racism/Sexism Resource Center for Educators, which is part of the Council on Interracial Books for Children.

ANITA MOSS teaches English at the University of North Carolina at Charlotte and has published widely in such journals as *The Children's Literature Association Quarterly, Phaedrus,* and *Mythlore.*

IRA BRUCE NADEL teaches English at the University of British Columbia. He is coeditor of *Victorian Artists and the City* (1980) and author of various essays on the Victorian period.

AGNES PERKINS is a professor of English at Eastern Michigan University and has coedited three anthologies of poems for children.

SAMUEL PICKERING, JR., teaches English at the University of Connecticut. His latest book is *John Locke and Children's Books in Eighteenth-Century England.*

FREDERIK POHL has written more than thirty books, mostly in the field of science fiction. He has won both the Hugo and the Nebula awards.

HALFDAN RASMUSSEN has published poetry since 1941 and is the winner of the Haedersgave Prize awarded by the Danish government.

COMPTON REES teaches English at the University of Connecticut and has written on mythology in children's literature.

GLENN EDWARD SADLER teaches at San Diego State University and is an authority on George MacDonald.

DOROTHEA SCOTT teaches in the library school at the University of Wisconsin and is the author of *Chinese Popular Literature and the Child.*

P. L. TRAVERS is the author of the *Mary Poppins* books.

MARILYN WANIEK is the author of a book of verse, *For the Body,* published by the Louisiana State University Press. Her translation of Halfdan Rasmussen's poems is forthcoming from Black Willow Press.